AFTER THE WORLD BROKE IN TWO
The Later Novels of Willa Cather

Willa Sibert Cather
New York,
September 20
1922

Photographed in the
Cliff Dweller ruins in

After the World Broke in Two

THE
Later Novels
OF
Willa Cather

BY

Merrill Maguire Skaggs

University Press of Virginia

CHARLOTTESVILLE AND LONDON

THE UNIVERSITY PRESS OF VIRGINIA
Copyright © 1990 by the Rector and Visitors
of the University of Virginia

First published 1990

Library of Congress Cataloging-in-Publication Data

Skaggs, Merrill Maguire.
    After the world broke in two : the later novels of Willa Cather /
by Merrill Maguire Skaggs.
        p.   cm.
    Includes bibliographical references and index.
    ISBN 0-8139-1300-4
    1. Cather, Willa, 1873–1947—Criticism and interpretation.
I. Title.
PS3505.A87Z85   1900
813'.52—dc20   90-12486
                                                                  CIP

Frontispiece courtesy of Marilyn Berg Callander
Printed in the United States of America

This book is fondly dedicated
to the Cather scholars of the
Drew University Graduate School
who have taught me so much:
    Jacqueline Berke
    Beverly Busch
    Marilyn Callander
    Barbara Caspersen
    Betty Marsh
    David Massey
    Joyce McDonald
    Jo Ann Middleton
    Laura Winters

Contents

The whole secret of talking to artists, whether it be a professional interview or otherwise, is to enter completely into their mood, not to ask them to come to yours; for the moment to make their gods your gods, and to make their life the most important thing on earth to you.

———— WILLA CATHER, *The World and the Parish* ————

Preface

Willa Cather made extraordinary efforts to keep public attention focused exclusively on her polished and published work. She forbade publishing her letters, asked that all private papers be destroyed, and grew increasingly inaccessible to all but her trusted friends. As the predictable consequence, public interest in the facts of her life remained high, and the result is a body of biographical information one can rely on. As I began this book, I thanked the skies many times for those scholars whose work preceded mine. To a number of them I would like to pay special tribute.

First and foremost, I thank James Woodress, whose literary biographies I rely on for the crucial facts on which my readings are based. My debt for his dedicated lifetime of work on Willa Cather, as my admiration for his careful research practices, is immeasurable. Another important influence on me has been the audacious psychobiography of Sharon O'Brien, whose insights in *Willa Cather: The Emerging Voice* (1987) led readers to the point at which Cather came into her artistic maturity. At about that point, this study begins. What I offer here is not a competing biography or psychobiography but rather an intellectual history, primarily derived from Cather's published work. I agree that this author is one of the country's most autobiographical. I also believe that her emotions affected and created her ideas, and that the record of both can be traced through her novels. Thus, a careful reading of what's put into, as well as left out of, the novelistic texts renders a record of their creator.

Most interesting to me has been the growing realization that Cather's ideas often gestated—or mutated—over years and decades. She kept returning to earlier insights and images to reexamine both her suspicions and her conclusions. There's a sense in which all Cather's convictions remained tentative. Like Emerson, whom she read, she protected the right to change her mind. Perhaps for that reason, images she first described in her youth frequently resurfaced years later, though not necessarily to produce the same effect. Her intellectual history conveys a traceable paradox: she often restlessly returned to the same starting point in order to set off in a new direction after an opposite conclusion. I trust the epigraphs and discussions that follow will illustrate these points. And because Cather published much at an exceptionally early age, we can trace recurrent patterns and ideas, as well as the changes she rang on them.

ix

Before beginning, I would like to applaud not only the biographers but also the fine critics who have preceded me. With many of these scholars of all ages, I have carried on in my head the conversations that produced my own conclusions. I have especially valued the mentoring voices of Susan Rosowski, John J. Murphy, David Stouck, Bruce Baker, Richard Giannone, William Curtin, L. Brent Bohlke, Patricia Lee Yongue, Jean Schwind, Judith Fryer, Larry Berkove, and those teachers who were my students. One of the most instructive has been the voice of Bernice Slote, whose shrewd texts I have learned to observe with an attention I normally save for fiction.

In the year following her death, I would also like to pay special tribute to Mildred Bennett, who wrote the first book on Willa Cather in 1951. Bennett's intense identification with the Willa she found for herself through the pages of Cather's novels has never been surpassed. Because Mildred Bennett spent a half-century working to preserve the artifacts from which Cather's fiction derived, the rest of us received a clearer sense of that fiction's grounding in tangible fact. Through Bennett's work we grasped what Cather tried to tell us—that imagination importantly expresses itself through arrangement, as well as invention.

I would like to thank my colleagues Edwina Lawler, for generously locating and translating two Heine poems; James Hala, for instructing me in basic facts about medieval drama; and Marilyn Callander, for reading this book chapter by chapter and for donating the photograph that provides our frontispiece. I am deeply grateful to James Woodress and John Murphy for reading substantial parts of this manuscript and for making suggestions I found invaluable.

For permission to reprint here portions of essays I first published in journals, I warmly thank the editors of *American Literature, Mississippi Quarterly, Renascence,* and *The Willa Cather Pioneer Memorial Newsletter.* Portions of chapter 8 appeared in *Religion and Literature* 17, no. 3 (Autumn 1985); reprint permission granted by *Religion and Literature,* University of Notre Dame, Notre Dame, Ind. Portions of chapter 9 first appeared in *Literature and Belief* 8 (1988), published by Brigham Young University, Provo, Utah.

Especially I thank my office staff—Yasuko Grosjean, Linda Blank, and Leslie Riordan—who tactfully guarded my door and thus made this work possible.

AFTER THE WORLD BROKE IN TWO:
The Later Novels of Willa Cather

CHAPTER ONE

Never Been Said Before: Introduction

*That is what it means to write poetry; to be able
to say the oldest thing in the world as though it
had never been said before.*

——————— WILLA CATHER, *The World and the Parish* ———————
from the *Courier*, March 10, 1900.

By New Year's Day of 1922, forty-eight year old Willa Cather had reached a professional high point and was resting after the climb. She had just finished the manuscript of her fifth novel, visited Nebraska for two months, and returned to New York for Christmas. She was recognized both abroad and at home—in her several homes—as an illustrious, some even thought heroic, personage. Most recently, she had completed an arduous four-year struggle with the intractable material of *One of Ours,* and had earned a vacation.

Having lifted eyebrows about as high as they would go in Red Cloud, Nebraska, during her unconventional adolescence, Cather was now considered the hometown lass who had made good in the big world beyond Red Cloud's borders. She had traveled widely, for business and pleasure, and had earned "success according to the rules American society laid out for men."[1] She had begun her first newspaper column in her nineteenth year and had been hailed as the best as well as the bloodthirstiest theater critic of the West before she graduated from college. She had become a

professional editor at the age of twenty-two, and before she re-
tired from business, Samuel McClure had declared her "the best
magazine executive I know."[2] Her poetry had been noticed, her
short stories praised, and her novels hailed widely. H. L.
Mencken, of all unlikely critics, had declared in *Smart Set,* after
reading her most recently published novel of 1918,

> *My Ántonia* is not only the best done by Miss Cather,
> but also one of the best that any American has ever
> done, east or west, early or late. It is simple; it is
> honest; it is intelligent; it is moving. The means
> that appear in it are means perfectly adapted to its
> end. Its people are unquestionably real. Its back-
> ground is brilliantly vivid. It has form, grace, good
> literary manners. In a word, it is a capital piece of
> writing. . . . The whole enchantment is achieved by
> the simplest of all possible devices. . . . Here a
> glimpse, there a turn of phrase, and suddenly the
> thing stands out, suddenly it is as real as real can
> be—and withal moving, arresting, beautiful, with
> a strange and charming beauty. . . . I commend the
> book to your attention, and the author no less.[3]

Mencken's ecstatic praise of *My Ántonia* was especially important because the spokesman himself was widely recognized as a
hatchet wielder. His views of this novel, however, were not dramatically different from other critics.[4] With *My Ántonia,* published in 1918 and already in French[5] and Czech[6] translations,
Cather had secured her position as one of America's foremost
writers. She had every reason to be proud of her accomplishment.
A kibitzer might easily announce that she had bid a grand slam,
professionally, and had made it in spades.

In such a situation as followed the appearance of *My Ántonia,*
any artist must choose whether to repeat the work that has earned
fame and glory or to try something new. In fact, Cather's choice
was predictable, for her pattern was already well established. She
had always tried a new experiment with every book she wrote.
Alexander's Bridge, her first published novel, established her ability
to engineer a tightly balanced fictional projection, in the manner

of James or Poe, which would *not* collapse under the stresses of critical scrutiny, as her hero's bridge collapses. In *O Pioneers!* she had demonstrated the opposite talent by opening up her new novel to the prairie air, proving by her looser construction that her novels could follow nature and naturally display its predictable irregularities. Pursuing the possibilities of realistic fiction further in her third novel, Cather fashioned *The Song of the Lark* simultaneously as a female success story, a depiction of the world of music, a female's bildungsroman, and a "full-blooded" treatment of her heroine's character and psychology. That bel canto performance had in turn been succeeded by *My Ántonia*, about which she later said, "If one is going to do new business the patterns cannot help, though one does not deliberately go out to do that. *My Ántonia*, for instance, is just the other side of the rug, the pattern that is supposed not to count in a story. In it there is no love affair, no courtship, no marriage, no broken heart, no struggle for success. I knew I'd ruin my material if I put it in the usual fictional pattern. I just used it the way I thought absolutely true."[7]

Always involving "new business," Cather's novels had steadily advanced her critical standing and her number of devoted readers and admirers. In spite of minor setbacks or occasional protests,[8] everything Cather tried seemed more or less successful at the time of its appearance. She had repeatedly experimented in every volume, and had always brought off her experiments to critical acclaim.

Pursuing this superficial outline of Cather's life, we guess that after *My Ántonia*, Cather was psychologically ready to try her most audacious literary experiment, and that turned out to be a war novel. Edith Lewis explains:

> She was the last person to have set out deliberately to write a "war novel" . . . and it would not, I am sure, have occurred to her . . . except for an accident.
>
> It was the news, in May, 1918, of a favourite cousin's death at the head of his men in the battle of Cantigny—the first American offensive—that gave her the idea of writing *One of Ours*.[9]

Perhaps it was the novelty or shock of the news about her cousin that Cather first received as she read the *New York Times* in the beauty parlor.[10] But whatever convinced her to do it, at the end of the First World War, with the carnage still fresh in every mind, she decided, as a woman and a writer who had never been near military combat, to compose the story of a farm boy who goes to battle. She would explore his background, his psyche, his dreams. And in the interests of truth she would acknowledge several facts which veterans sometimes denied: that war can be a version of heaven, if one has left hell to reach it; that some men find in military action the answers they previously have futilely pursued; that one plausibly might prefer war to several familiar forms of peace; that some soldiers believe passionately in what they die for.

Composing this story took Cather four of her intensest and most difficult years. As both cause and effect of the effort, she came to identify intensely with G. P. Cather, the dead cousin after whom she patterned her protagonist, Claude Wheeler. Indeed, she seemed in this period to live so closely with him that Woodress reports,

> She felt a blood identity with her cousin, a Siegmund and Sieglinde sort of thing, and writing about him drained her power to feel things. During the first winter working on the book she never knew when he would come to her—at the symphony, at the tea table—and she got so she had to be alone in case he appeared. It was life at its best, complete possession, but he was an expensive boy to keep, she wrote Fisher. She had to travel with him, cut off every source of income to give him a perfectly undisturbed mind.[11]

The novel started well, but then bogged down repeatedly. Cather went back to Nebraska and then to France to research it further. She made use of the kind of factual background materials that came to her from interviews or research, and that she normally did not heavily rely on. Finally, having completed *One of Ours* at what must have seemed massive expense, Cather sent the

4

manuscript off to her new publisher, Alfred A. Knopf, and was quickly assured that it was "masterly, a perfectly gorgeous novel." At this happiest point in her life, Woodress tells us, "She was enjoying being lionized, and for this brief interlude ... she seemed accessible to everyone."[12]

That calendar year of 1922 was extraordinary by any standard. In the course of it, Cather wrote parts or the whole of at least three major novels. She was certainly reading proofs and galleys of *One of Ours* as the year began. After several false starts, she had in hand by spring the first complete draft of *A Lost Lady*. Then in April of 1922, she threw down in the pages of the *New Republic* a kind of critical gauntlet with her provocative essay "The Novel Démeublé." In midsummer she taught successfully at Breadloaf, and in late summer, while vacationing at Grand Manan, she finished a short story that was apparently "Tom Outland's Story," the centerpiece of *The Professor's House*.[13] Thus, from a reader's point of view the year was almost miraculously productive. A chaplain at Bard College in former years reportedly prayed over each graduating class, "God deny you peace and give you glory." From the evidence at hand, we might surmise that Cather's 1922 was what he had in mind.

By 1923, however, the critics had begun their assault. Cather must have felt besieged and savaged. They derided her for everything in *One of Ours* that she had dared to do at such "enormous expenditure of time and energy"[14]: for presuming to write about men's activities; for technical ignorance of modern warfare; for hubris. They misrepresented the book itself, and they dismissed the taste of those who enjoyed it. Receiving the Pulitzer prize for *One of Ours* in 1923 was clearly no compensation for the negative publicity Cather's novel had received:[15] "the Pulitzer was more annoying than it was pleasant. She gave thanks to the Lord that she had been in France at the time hers was announced."[16] From her point of view, the damage had been done. It was as if "the world broke in two in 1922 or thereabouts."[17]

This narrative certainly makes a plausible story, but nothing in a real life is quite so simple. In fact, biographers Woodress, Robinson, and O'Brien all stress the troubled, erratic, and anxious beginnings that led to 1922. For that matter, the year's extreme productivity could have been the result of anxiety as easily as stability. In any case, Cather, a very slow starter from several perspectives, was by 1922 nearing her fiftieth birthday, though she was publicly lying about it. Her parents' fiftieth wedding anniversary celebration on December 5, at the end of the pivotal year, would further remind her of her own birth date, a year and two days beyond their marriage day. Furthermore, in spite of her recent accomplishments, her life as 1922 arrived felt less than triumphant. She was sick with one thing or another throughout most of that winter, and when she herself was not sick, she was worrying about the illness of her mother. She was haunted with forebodings about the critical reception of *One of Ours*,[18] anticipatory anxieties that the September publication would prove only too well-founded.

The first question to ask from this darker angle, then, is What first aroused Cather's fears about that novel she would later claim as her favorite? Rather, what created her anxiety as she wrote it? Several possibilities are worth considering. For one, she may have been grappling with a specifically menopausal depression at the time; for another, she was certainly aware of the literary risk she was taking. Cather, as most humans, was ambivalent about such risk. On the one hand, she liked answering a dare, but on the other, she was deeply frightened of failure. Moreover, she had achieved the varieties of success we have noticed partially because she was so driven by the specter of failure. The fear of critical contempt had so haunted her that she published much of her earliest writing under pseudonyms. And years before, newly arrived in Pittsburgh, she had remarked that she understood Lamb's quip, "Gad, how we like to be liked!"[19] As O'Brien says, "Cather increasingly wanted to triumph in public as well as in personally chosen terms." Determined to succeed at her first full-time job, she adopted as her credo, "if it was trash they wanted and trash they paid for, then trash they would have—the very best she could produce."[20] The point, of course, is that while Cather by 1922 had long since outgrown a willingness to compromise her talents in order to appease public taste, she had not outgrown—Does anyone?—her desire for public approval.

Another reason *One of Ours* must have been difficult to write is that it required Cather to face—head on—her most frequently recurring nightmare: physical mutilation. Numerous critics have remarked that a mutilation seems to occur in almost every Cather novel. For Cather, the idea of mutilation had the power of darkness to appall. Yet mutilation is the very essence of war, and war is the essential setting for her character study. The subject of war, in and of itself, triggered Cather's debilitating anxieties and slowed down her writing. O'Brien insightfully summarizes the situation:

> "Lop away so much as a finger" Cather had written in "The Profile" (1907), "and you have wounded the creature beyond reparation."... As we have seen, Cather's preoccupation with injuries to the hand reflects her literary anxieties. The hand which holds the pen is the physical agent of creation, as Cather noted in speaking of the creative process as the "voyage perilous" from the "brain to the hand." ... But the severed hand in "Singer Tower" suggests a more serious concern than Cather's fear of literary inadequacy: it recalls the fear of retribution for writing shown in her early stories through images of mutilation, castration, and disfiguration.... Daring to claim novel-writing as her vocation, Cather merited punishment for her overreaching desire: destruction of her creative powers.
>
> Although it is possible that Cather's fear of mutilation had a biographical source in the childhood trauma she recounted to Edith Lewis—the story of the half-witted boy who threatened to cut off her hand—images of mutilation and castration in her fiction and real-life problems with her right hand and arm frequently occurred at times of professional and personal stress when she was attempting to "rise" as a writer. We see this pattern when she first began to write fiction ("The Clemency of the

Court"), when she took Henry James most directly as her mentor ("The Namesake" and "The Profile"), when she moved from the short story to the novel ("Singer Tower"), and when she wrote her first and only war novel, *One of Ours* (1922), a text filled with images of dismemberment, most often injuries to the hand and arm. After completing *One of Ours* and suffering the critical attacks she half expected for venturing into such masculine territory, Cather faced the punishment she had imaginatively anticipated in her novel: she experienced a painful attack of neuritis in her right arm and found herself unable to write.[21]

As O'Brien points out here, Cather had half expected some punishment for venturing into masculine territory at all. She had nevertheless ventured even further than a casual glance takes in; for she had set out in this story to plumb the mental and emotional reflexes of a male. Perhaps as an inevitable follow-up to Jim Burden's narration of *My Ántonia,* Cather determined to do in *One of Ours* what the preceding novel made unnecessary and inappropriate through its focus on Ántonia. She would compete with her masters James and Flaubert: she would prove that a woman could portray the psychological complexities of the opposite sex just as well as those men had done, and in much greater depth than she herself had tried in *Alexander's Bridge* or *My Ántonia*. In her previous efforts, she had focused either on a crucial event or a defining love. In *One of Ours*, she would penetrate a male psyche. She would, in fact, develop as detailed a treatment of a man as she had developed for a woman in *The Song of the Lark*. By the literary rules of the day, it was a punishable offense.

Still another strain can be detected in Cather's forebodings about *One of Ours*. G. P. Cather, her cousin whose life story provided the basic plot line of the novel, was the son of Cather's Uncle George Cather and Aunt Franc. Aunt Franc was widely recognized to be the prototype for Georgiana (the name, indeed, a giveaway for Mrs. George Cather) in "A Wagner Matinee." Friends and readers throughout Nebraska had been outraged at

Cather's presentation of her home state after that story was published, and they had unequivocally let her know about it. Thus, Cather had had her first taste of public disapproval in connection with the relatives whose home she was now revisiting to take more fictional material. Her writing about the charged dynamics of her uncle's family would certainly have reminded her of the distressing protests she had once triggered. Imagining a reencounter with that anger again, now repeated on a national scale, might potentially have aroused vast anticipatory anxiety and possibly felt like being trapped in a recurring nightmare from which she could not awake or escape.

At this point in Cather's life story, several questions must be asked. Did she overreact to the criticism of *One of Ours*? If so, why? How can getting bad reviews—even terrible reviews—reasonably seem like the world breaking in two? How could Cather even remember the notices after receiving such a reparation as the Pulitzer prize? Elizabeth Shepley Sergeant makes the cogent point that Cather's tone in her published work first changed perceptibly *before One of Ours* appeared. Her next book after *My Ántonia* was actually the short-story collection *Youth and the Bright Medusa* (1920). These short stories comprised the first volume published by Alfred A. Knopf after Cather had initiated her own disruptions by leaving Houghton Mifflin and her old friend and editor Ferris Greenslet. The tone of the new stories—as well as that of *One of Ours*, which immediately followed them—signaled a new and darker Cather vision long before the critics gave her a personal sense of injury to focus her feelings on. In any case, her "hostile stance toward critics"[22] seems to follow the notices of *One of Ours*. But if Cather was really so bad a sport, must we not then severely question her maturity?

One concedes that even writers of such genius as Willa Cather's can seem deeply flawed under conditions that leave them feeling very vulnerable. It is not reasonable to demand divine serenity of a human artist, even when that human perfects a superhumanly effective English prose style. Beyond acknowledging Cather's lifelong ferocious competitiveness, and her fiercely high standards for herself, we can reasonably guess at how sharply she would feel the scorn in a critical whipping, especially since she herself had often brutally wielded the lash in her youth. But Cather was no longer young, and no longer given to public abuse of her inferiors. What she seems to have felt in 1922 may even generally have dated back to 1916 and the dismaying marriage of Isabelle McClung—the beloved friend "for whom all her books had been written."[23] But her feeling is specifically linked to the kind of effort *One of Ours* represented, and the subsequent reception that effort had elicited. She had taken a dreary life and a disgusting political morass and had transformed the hog wallow into beauty. Having dared—and, in her own view, achieved—the impossible, she was derided for trying. And Willa, like her protagonist, Claude, was "thin-skinned" and "couldn't bear ridicule very well."[24] She thus lost the energizing belief that the universe is just, and that her own best efforts would be rewarded. She also lost her illusions that she could control her own relations to her public, her work, and her artistic achievements. Such a loss has paralyzed many a smaller ego.

That Cather went on to write at least three, if not five or six, more masterpieces, is a reason for rejoicing. How she managed the feat is the question with which this book starts. I begin by assuming, however, that the story is worth telling—that is, it has meaning[25]—*because* it is a fully human story, comprised of pain and fury and suspicion and despair as well as the occasional sounds of widespread applause. I also assume that this most autobiographical of writers leaves traces of her intellectual struggles and passions in the texts of her novels. What I will do in this study, after a chapter discussing repeated themes and the techniques she habitually relied on, is to begin with that watershed novel *One of Ours*. I will then follow Cather sequentially through her later novels, as she very slowly works out her own salvation. I believe that her desire after 1922 was to find a way to weld her world whole again. Her intense struggle makes her effort remarkable, as if her story "had never been said before." Thus Cather models one answer to the age-old question: What does one do when the world breaks in two; what then?

CHAPTER TWO

Distinguishing the Artist: Recurrent Techniques and Themes In Cather's Fiction

It was, he said, the most wonderful voice he had ever taught; it was capable of everything but certainty, precision, that unfailing exactness which distinguishes the artist from the amateur. . . . It is perhaps the most wonderful contralto voice in the world, but there is no mind to direct it.

—————— WILLA CATHER *The World and the Parish* ——————
from the *Courier*, January 6, 1900.

In *The Professor's House* Godfrey St. Peter thinks morosely, "Nobody saw that he was trying to do something quite different—they merely thought he was trying to do the usual thing, and had not succeeded very well."[1] To study Willa Cather is to surmise why a character as similar to her as Godfrey St. Peter might have drawn the Professor's cynical conclusions: repeatedly readers have dismissed her exact, meticulous sentences as oversimplifications and her controlling intelligence as simplistic sentimentality. Her precision has seemed too certain to hold attention.

"Art, it seems to me, should simplify," Willa Cather pronounced clearly.[2] Following this tenet, Cather purified her prose as Mondrian refined his paintings until she had reduced each scene to the quintessential shapes and lines necessary to achieve her purpose and to convey her vision. Such a process of intensification through reduction inevitably confounds or irritates the frivolous passerby. Underemphasis that would escape the notice of a careless reader, however, was an effect Willa Cather was prepared to pay for in order to create her kind of clarity. As she asserted, "Fine quality is a distinct disadvantage in articles made for great numbers of people. . . . Amusement is one thing; enjoyment of art is another."[3]

One can say that any artist or human being repeats particular patterns and arrangements. As did Mondrian, Cather devised her inventive compositions by using freshly those lines, figures, and combinations that sprang most naturally to her mind. Her typical figures and forms, as well as her central questions and concerns, can in fact be found in her first published pages as well as her last. She observed early in her novelist's career that life develops only two or three old stories that keep repeating themselves as if they had never happened before.[4]

When Cather tells such stories, the significance resides, not in a basic plot line, but in her distinctive ways of telling. She always strove for "the one thing that survives all arresting situations, all good writing and clever storymaking—inherent, individual beauty."[5] She was therefore willing to throw away many good stories in order to perfect one intense or complete artistic moment. In fact, she habitually boiled down her broth to its strongest palatable form, or to use another cooking metaphor (for food is always appropriately associated with Cather), she sacrificed many an egg white to clarify an elegant consommé.

Cather also tried and created something new in each new work. But she relied from the beginning through the end of her career on a repertory of trusted devices to get her to her desired new goals. Her tactics are like those of an experienced trekker, whose zest for trying new trails in order to discover new scenery depends on having at hand both familiar clothes and reliably tested equipment during the climb. Cather had her own reliably tested supply of fictional techniques that got her dependably to the carefully projected ends she intended to reach.

Occasionally readers confuse Cather's innovations with old ideas badly rendered because she sometimes returns to old ideas in order to reverse her conclusions. Normally, she *does* depend on tried and true equipment when she heads for a new destination. Or to return to the previous metaphor, she always uses egg whites to clarify consommé—as a master chef would—no matter how novel the flavor planned for the broth. She does not use prepackaged substitutes when she sets out to cook.

This chapter will describe some organizing principles and practices, some recurrent objects and effects, some typical symbolizing acts, and some reappearing themes that recur throughout Cather's novels from beginning to end, and which comprise her equipment. The purpose is to establish what one can say *in general* about Cather's fiction, before we ask what is new and distinctive and different about each novel Cather wrote after 1922. Thus, when convenient I will refer to novels that preceded, as well as those that followed, *One of Ours.* Emphatically, I am not suggesting that Cather's fiction can be reduced to a formula. Rather, I am trying to establish a few basic facts about what her imagination clutched in order to climb. I list the equipment we also must possess and know how to manage efficiently, in order to follow her successfully up the Himalayan trails of her art.

The first important study of this general kind was Richard Giannone's *Music in Willa Cather's Fiction,* published in 1968. In this breakthrough work of criticism, Giannone not only demonstrated the complexity of Cather's fiction but also documented two crucial facts: first, every novel included a reference to some kind of music; and second, those seemingly throwaway musical gracenotes deliberately enlarged the central themes of the works. Thus, one could explore the central themes of each novel by locating and thoroughly analyzing its musical allusions.

The most recent similar study of which I am aware is Marilyn Berg Callander's *Willa Cather and the Fairy Tale,* published in 1989. As Giannone did, Callander points out that when Cather allows an apparently casual allusion to remain in her text, she does so because it has, and serves, a purpose. One ignores her references to fairy tales at one's critical peril, though one has almost as wide a choice about how to interpret the reference as one has in the folktale itself. There are, in fact, no casual excrescences in Cather's fiction; each phrase is purposeful, though patterns reappear in the service of contradictory ends.

What both these scholars have demonstrated is that any item that helps one to grasp a nuance in a single Cather novel is likely to reappear as a help in another novel as well. Cather's work has a continuity in which symbols and themes and techniques repeatedly resurface, if only because the author has changed her mind about some facet of their meaning. As we sometimes argue with one possibility a text suggests, so does she. Some dialogues, arguments, or explorations extend through several books.

To begin, Cather alludes to many art forms in adding resonances to her central concerns or dominant themes. Besides music, she uses the visual arts (the special focus of Jean Schwind's work), architecture, jewelry, and pottery, as many have now noticed. Particularly, she mentions other works of literature—drama, poetry, and philosophy, as well as other fiction—to underscore, parallel, contrast with, or intensify her own fictive moments. If she does relatively little with dance, she certainly uses movement and motion to define her characters. Her references to the arts, however, hardly dint the list of her repeated patterns. And though each work contains a musical reference, artwork, and literary analogy, just as each human body contains a liver, stomach, and heart, yet one reduces bodies to those organs or functions at peril of one's comprehensive understanding of the whole organic system. The bodies of Cather's novels, like human bodies, are more complicated. What is finally most important is each individualized entity. Which fact does not erase the truth that real and fictional bodies live and function effectively because particular organs are present and working well. We study these parts in order to be ready to understand the independent novels that appeared after 1922.

One Catherian practice widely recognized already is Cather's reliance on symbolic or meaning-full names to define her characters. Among her most obvious names are *Ivy Peters, Nellie Birdseye,* and *Lucy Gayheart.* Cather's fondness for this device is so marked that one generally does well to assume a name has meaning until all attempts to find one have failed. Another significant organizing habit is her reliance on evocative juxtapositions, so that scenes, lines, or facts placed side by side change each other.[6] Though Cather's juxtapositions do not differ from those of Hawthorne, Dickens, James, Chekhov, or any others from whom she could have learned the device, they seem to me to differ in the degree of importance they assume in her evident plan. She seems to depend *more* on the chemical changes two separate ingredients can produce when exposed to each other. She may well have known of Kuleshov's experiments just after the Russian Revolution of 1917, which established that perceived meaning is profoundly determined by juxtaposition: juxtaposed pictures of a neutral face and a bowl of soup suggest hunger, for example; the same face juxtaposed with a coffin suggests sorrow. But Cather was relying on her reader's ability to register the quiet explosion in the brain that juxtaposed volatile elements can produce long before the Russians taught filmmakers Kuleshov's truths about editing techniques.

While each of Cather's novels can illustrate her profound reliance on juxtapositions to create special effects, my favorite examples appear in *My Ántonia*. It is a novel based in the most elaborate ways on juxtaposed oppositions, particularly on the opposite qualities embodied in Jim and Ántonia. Polarities determine the story's structural units, both large and small, and the principle dictates the shifting components of all nineteen subsections of the first book, "The Shimerdas." My favorite of these smaller units is subsection 7, which begins with Jim's complaint that Ántonia takes a hateful superior tone with him because she is four years older. The section then outlines the equalizing adventure they experience in the late (and fortunate) fall of the year and of their childhood.

Ántonia is headed to Russian Peter's house to borrow a spade, when Jim offers her a pony ride through air "heady as wine." The atmosphere is so exhilarating because the day follows a night of "black frost."[7] Passing over roads along which the bordering sunflowers have been annihilated, the two reach Peter's snug cabin

15

and find he has harvested ample provisions. For Peter seems to the children to live as orderly and sociable a life as do the prairie dogs in dogtown. In fact, the analogies between human lives and the lives of prairie dogs, owls, and snakes have already been drawn several times by this point. Returning from Peter's homestead, the children decide to use his spade to dig down below the surface in the extensive dogtown that is located behind the melon patch. Almost immediately, they sight a snake so large he seems the incarnate and eternal grandfather of evil. But Jim uses the spade to kill the snake; Ántonia leads a triumphant procession home to display the conquest; and ever thereafter, she treats Jim with respect.

What Cather achieves with this sequence of occurrences beautifully illustrates the way she uses juxtaposition. First, she reminds us that days "heady as wine" follow nights of "black frost," as well as vice versa. Further, she prods us to register that while sunflowers die, foodstuffs can be stored and preserved. Then she reminds us that towns ostensibly constructed on the most orderly and sociable behavioral patterns inevitably include sickening evil. Finally, she presents the fact that Nebraska prairies may seem to produce ample harvests or to run over with the juicy sweetness of youth's easily digested melons, but there are, nevertheless, terrifying snakes in this or any childhood garden. On the other hand, the evil snakes on these prairies can be destroyed. Yet Jim survives his encounter at all, much less emerges heroic, because he has the chance good luck to strike when a huge old serpent "had forgot that the world doesn't owe rattlers a living" (MA, 49). Only by chance does Jim join the ranks of the dragon slayers in history's most fanciful stories. Still, history does boast such a list for him to join.

Noting such mutually affecting and meaning-engendering juxtapositions prepares us to appreciate another pattern that dominates Cather's fiction from *Alexander's Bridge* to *Sapphira and the Slave Girl*—that of constant, almost compulsively created, reversals in every element of the composition. For example, at the end of *Alexander's Bridge* Bartley Alexander rushes toward the Canadian site where his newest bridge is being built. He is determined to take control, right wrongs, eliminate defects, and move honorably. Such resolve requires his writing his wife of his infidelity, and he carries the unmailed letter in his pocket as he rushes into action. He is urging workers off the cracking structure of his half-built bridge when it plunges him and them into the river below. Though a powerful swimmer easily able to save himself, Bartley drowns when others cling to his neck. In his last moment, the powerful builder and active agent suddenly feels that his reliable wife has let *him* go. His gasp triggers his drowning. But after his body is recovered, his letter is illegible, so his widow "doesn't drift" as she lives serene in the memory of their marital relationship.[8] Bartley resolves on honor but fails to complete the honorable act, resolves on action but fails to complete it honorably, resolves to save others and instead is destroyed by them, relies on his wife and drowns as he projects his own unreliability onto her, cracks and crashes from his worry about wounding and losing her, and loses her only to retain her serene love forever. Ironies abound.

Cather intensifies such rapidly flipping reversals and ironies in *Sapphira,* for in her last novel she plays wickedly against the commonsense, standardized assumptions and literary expectations of her readers. She sets a beautiful young slave named Nancy on an isolated farm, makes her the personal servant of the owner who sleeps in a millhouse apart from his invalid wife, and establishes that the healthy miller is fonder of Nancy than of anyone else. Then Cather allows the farm's mistress to import her profligate nephew expressly in order to debauch young Nancy. Having established a situation of total sexual vulnerability for Nancy, however, Cather allows her virginal slave to escape unharmed and then, years later, to return from Canada, prosperously wed and triumphant. Especially in this final novel Cather seems mischievously to be asking her readers to name who is actually the more morally inadequate—a nineteenth-century Southern slaveholder or a judgemental twentieth-century contemporary who assumes the worst reflexively. The novel unequivocally asserts that slavery is terrible, but also suggests that male slave owners sometimes behaved honorably, at least where slave seduction was a possibility; that slaves survived to marry legitimately, as well as to hold their heads high. Here, the horrors of slavery remain horrible *without* the "inevitable" seduction of a slave woman by her white master.

As a matter of fact, this dependence on opposition or reversal in Cather's work extends to more than plot. She often establishes character by contrasting opposite types, then by pulling her straight line between the two opposite points into a triangle. Her books seem repeatedly to start with a clear opposition, only to become a study in triangles or intersecting triangles. For example, *O Pioneers!* begins with resourceful Alexandra Bergson and her dependent little brother Emil; it then quickly introduces Carl Linstrum, the dependable friend against whose contrasting strengths and weaknesses we can measure all the Bergsons. It also quickly introduces Marie Tovesky, who is too pretty to ignore. Carl and Marie each become third parties for triangular patterns here, though they themselves do not interrelate closely enough to suggest a quadrangle. Or Marian Forrester, the center of *A Lost Lady,* is known in one sense or another by a cluster of gentlemen who keep playing against each other for her attention: Frank Ellinger pulls her away from her husband, the Captain; later Ivy Peters replaces Ellinger as an illicit lover; and Niel Herbert pulls ineffectually against them all. It should go without saying, however, that the most powerful triangle in Cather's oeuvre forms the basis of *My Mortal Enemy,* the novel in which three characters' lives are so intricately intermeshed that they seem to form a three-armed pinwheel that revolves dizzyingly to make one whole circle.

We start to understand Willa Cather's compositions, then, when we acknowledge the most common strokes she uses for filling in her initial silhouettes: she suggests the first outlines of an idea through reverberating references to other art forms, through symbolic names, evocative juxtapositions, compulsive reversals, and an inclination to start with opposition and turn it sooner than later into triangulation. She complicates such sketches by including particular objects and effects, many of which become trademarks reappearing in each one of her completed canvasses. Her most frequently chosen effects capitalize on light, color (especially grey, which is also no-color), and movement—or its opposite: stasis and tableau. Her favorite items seem to be jewels, flowers, interiors, meals, moons, landscapes (especially trees, rocks, and rivers), and connecting paths.

Locating Cather's connecting paths is easy as a child's map game, for every novel has at least one. Perhaps the most vividly symbolic path, however, is the one street up or down the cliff, in *Shadows on the Rock*, which connects the Lower Town of merchants and tradesmen with the Upper Town of the Governor and the church. Halfway between the two built-up sites is the apothecary's shop where the book's central characters reside and work, within easy access of all elements of the settlement.

As flowers define Marian Forrester in *A Lost Lady*, so jewels most centrally define the character and concerns of Myra Henshawe in *My Mortal Enemy*. After Myra's death at the end of Cather's bitterest novel about the failure of human relationships, Myra's amethysts (jewels thought to be anti-intoxicants) remain with Nellie as a keepsake, though wearing them gives her no joy and leaves a chill around her heart. But when in the next novel, *Death Comes for the Archbishop*, Cather recovers her faith in friendship, the archbishop treasures his amethyst ring; it is a bequest to him from his beloved Joseph and reminds him of their happy boyhood days together. Emil Bergson of *O Pioneers!* and Tom Outland of *The Professor's House* both bring turquoises back from the Southwest to give to those who provoke their generosity; Louie Marsellus gives ostentatious emeralds to his wife, Outland's ex-sweetheart, thereby outraging his sister-in-law; and the lost lady Marian Forrester removes her rings before assignations with the outrageous Frank Ellinger. Jewels signal subtle messages for them all.

In her heyday Marian Forrester fills her house with flowers, but especially with roses, classic symbols of love. When Ivy Peters begins to invade her husband's territory and to plant his wheat on the captain's bottomland, however, he characteristically brushes "through the rose plot where Captain Forrester was sitting in the sun . . . without looking at him, as if there were no one there."[9] Making points in a similar fashion in *One of Ours,* the flowers each spouse prefers define the difference between the personalities of frustrated Claude Wheeler and his frigid wife, Enid. Claude wants a gourd vine to keep his porch cool, while Enid, recoiling from such common growths, prefers clematis (*OO*,153). What she grows best is sweet peas.

Cather's particular genius for evoking landscapes has been remarked many times, though it seems almost impossible to praise this exceptional talent too strongly. Considering her gift, few should be surprised at the use she makes of her landscapes from book to book. Among Cather panoramas, however, the landscapes of *O Pioneers!* particularly stun a careful reader. Whether one is registering the sexually charged atmosphere as Emil mows steadily toward Marie perched in a cherry tree or the killing cold and ironhard resistance of Nebraska fields in winter, Cather evokes in this novel human life's most basic experiences and responses when she depicts natural places. In a later book, when Lucy Gayheart sets out to go skating on too cold a day, and is shocked by Harry Gordon's rude refusal to give her a ride, we register how appropriate to Lucy's emotional confusion is her attempt to walk over too hard a road on too harsh a day after too little attention to hometown events. As a further irony, she is ignorant of the fact that the river she skates on has changed its channel. Thus Lucy miscalculates the ice and drowns.

Balancing the highly charged descriptions of natural sites that Cather fashions are her equally evocative renditions of interiors. The rooms in which her fictional people live provide one of Cather's most dependable characterizing devices. Thea begins to "find herself" in *The Song of the Lark* as she lies in the moonlight in her attic bedroom, which she decorates exactly her way; and Godfrey St. Peter very nearly loses himself in his poisoned, spartan attic study in *The Professor's House.* Of all magically evocative rooms in Cather's fiction, however—and again, each novel is furnished with at least one—my favorite remains Latour's study in *Death Comes for the Archbishop.* Here the air always smells of incense from the piñon-wood logs burning in the fireplace, the adobe walls reflect care, from being shaped by the palms of Indian women, and the whole unit relaxes its owner because it provides him an "agreeable shape" (*DA*33). The room captures all that restores and nourishes Latour's life as he endures the trials of church administration.

Latour's life in *Death Comes for the Archbishop* is concerned with many different kinds of light. But if one takes her dozen novels altogether, Willa Cather's art seems as centrally concerned with capturing light and motion as do the canvasses of the French Impressionist painters she loved. Indeed, Lucy's pointed comments on Impressionist art in *Lucy Gayheart* force our attention to this connection. Lucy asserts, some pictures "are meant to represent objects, and others are meant to express a kind of feeling merely, and then accuracy doesn't matter."[10] Lucy responds to Harry's emphatic assertion, "anatomy is a fact . . . and facts are at the bottom of everything," with an ambivalent, "Are they Harry? I'm not so sure" (*LG,*101). We have no reason to be sure facts alone are at the bottom of *any* of Cather's scenes, for she always seems more interested in capturing something infinitely harder to hold than mere facts.

From first to last in Cather's novels, light shapes our appropriate attitude toward a scene. For example, her first novel, *Alexander's Bridge*, begins on a "brilliant April afternoon" as our sympathetic observer, Professor *Lucius* (the one who has the light here) Wilson approaches the Boston home of Bartley and Winifred Alexander. But as Wilson moves through the "thin sunlight" of April he seems to descend into "cooler depths of grayish shadows" (*AB,*2). In this house Bartley's life has reached its professional prime but has lost its emotional zest. Bartley rediscovers that quality in London with his youthful sweetheart Hilda, with whom he also experiences bright sunlight. Thus we learn through such lighting effects about the tepid dimness of middle-aged marital love, the initial sweet intensity of the recovered London love affair, and the terrible guilt when the lovers part in the cold, late night rain of New York.

Light and motion, seemingly equally evanescent, are equally challenging to capture in words; but Cather obviously loves and returns to such challenges in every work. Because her mind works in oppositions, she sometimes approaches the challenge movement poses by freezing motion in a scene that functions like a snapshot or tableau vivant. Indeed, in *One of Ours* Enid approaches as close as she ever will to drama when she plays a blind Christian martyr at her church's tableaux vivants (*OO*, 108). The most famous of all such "stills" in Cather's fiction is the plow magnified to giant size by the light of the setting sun, in *My Ántonia*. But other frozen moments are noteworthy too—Latour's kneeling before a cruciform tree, Tom Outland's discovery of a screaming mummy, the intertwined corpses of Emil and Marie lying under the mulberry hedge, the anatomical contours of Panther Canyon where Thea Kronborg lies in the sun, Captain Forrester's unblinking admiration for his wife's penmanship on the envelope to Ellinger he forces Niel Herbert to inspect. In such "snaps," the recording camera of Cather's prose seems to freeze the action for a moment, to add symbolic weight to a particular frame or detail. Myra Henshawe's lips curl like a snake's; Lucy Gayheart's running footprints remain in a concrete sidewalk; rhododendrons bloom forever in the road's double *S* on Sapphira's Back Creek.

Permeating one's response to any survey of Cather's techniques or preoccupations must be a growing awareness of her intense sense of symbol. Exactly because she is so insistently using simple objects and events to suggest many things at once, Cather makes us realize that the most ordinary things can become the most powerful symbols. Gardens and meals are among her most intensely charged places and events, just as eating and gardening are among the most important activities of her characters. Her most complex characters garden—Godfrey St. Peter, Archbishop Latour, Captain Forrester, and Sapphira, for example. Those who don't garden are often defined by what or how they eat. In fact, young Cécile Auclair in *Shadows on the Rock,* as aging Joseph Vaillant in *Death Comes for the Archbishop,* retains our affection because of the care expended on cooking. The importance of cooking vessels thrown by Indian women is recognized in *The Song of the Lark,* as Claude Wheeler's or Thea Kronborg's emotional emptiness is clear when they don't pay attention to what they chew. Alexandra's incompleteness is symbolized by her inappropriately decorated dining room, as Myra Henshawe's glamour is conveyed by the way she sets her table.

All such symbols, however, serve Cather's handful of crucial themes: the importance of desire, and of the passion it produces as an anarchic force without which life is worthless; the centrality of art, and of its highest expression in religion; the quintessential value of cultural continuity, and hence of tradition that produces a sense of history; the horror of failure, one symbol of which is physical mutilation; and the possibility of miracle. These themes or ideas, I believe, energize Cather's work, for all appear at least peripherally in most of her novels.

The problem, then, is to illustrate these themes efficiently without degenerating into dry-as-dust cataloging. My strategy here will be to cluster the novels as they seem centrally concerned with each theme. For example, the destructive potential of desire seems most obviously illustrated by the life stories of Bartley Alexander, Lucy Gayheart, and Emil Bergson. But the equally destructive consequences of the failure or absence of desire can be explored through the stories of Godfrey St. Peter, Myra Henshawe, and Claude Wheeler. Other novels explore the imperative need for passionate desire if anything significant is to be accomplished at all—Thea Kronborg's story, or Ántonia's and Alexandra's, for example, or even the two bishops' passionate ambitions for the advancement of the church.

The intricate interrelatedness of art and religion is a truth Cather's Professor St. Peter articulates, but which is intricately explored in the three novels that follow. The subject shades into the value of cultural continuity by the time Archbishop Latour comes to dominate his diocese; the succeeding novel, *Shadows on the Rock,* however, makes the case for historical continuity most explicitly. Yet Cather explored the importance of cultural continuity from the time she began depicting ethnic groups in her early novels. And in the last novel, Sapphira dies happy partially because she has so steadfastly maintained her own cultural and class standards; her own way of keeping the faith with tradition has been her refusal to "lower her flag."

Cather's reverence for possible human accomplishment, when one is given enough energizing passion and desire, also produces an opposite line of thought: her horror of failure. The specter of human failure haunts Cather's novels from the beginning, as Bartley Alexander's terrible public and physical crash dramatically illustrates. Cather explores this nightmare centrally in the careers of Claude Wheeler, Marian Forrester, Myra and Oswald Henshawe, and Lucy Gayheart, and through the ruminations of Professor St. Peter. The nightmare's clearest symbol is physical mutilation, and mutilation or severe disability reappears in some form in every work, as several critics have observed. Conversely, however (for in this fiction the opposite is always true as well), Cather returns to the theme of the possibilities of human strength, especially the varied strengths of women. From the physical hardiness of Alexandra, to the professional brilliance of Thea Kronborg, to the race-founding fecundity of Ántonia, to the unforgettable grace of Marian Forrester, to the social ambition of Myra Henshawe, to the culture-preserving dependability of Cécile Auclair, to the frivolity of Lucy Gayheart, to the headstrong willfullness of Sapphira, Cather has rendered the varied potentialities of women more memorably than perhaps any other American writer.

Miracle is one of Cather's strongest words and a word she *never* uses loosely. And finally, what her humans prove, male and female, by their accomplishments and their experiences is the possibility of miracle. Miracle is for Cather that which is most intensely to be revered, "the actual flowering of desire."[11] Latour and Vaillant, her two bishops, understand miracle, as they understand all things, oppositely. For Joseph Vaillant, miracle is "something we can hold in our hands and love,"[12] something very concrete and flamboyant. But Jean Latour summarizes the possibility of such mystery made plain among us when he wisely concludes, "Where there is great love, there are always miracles" (*DA*,51). Great love never protects against terror, or mutilation, or catastrophe. But it provides the fertile ground in which miracle can still sometimes flower. In her rendering of human life with all its complexity, horror, despair, and beauty, Willa Cather's fiction most perfectly illustrates her definition of *miracle:* it flowers out of her passionate desire to tell a story as perfectly as possible. Her novels, viewed in toto, remain a stunning accomplishment. To read them is to encounter the miracle of enduring art. To appreciate them as they deserve, one must study them as they relate and connect with each other, and also as they stand autonomous and alone. We will do both in the chapters that follow.

CHAPTER THREE

A Manly Battle Yarn:
One Of Ours

*When a woman writes a story of adventure, a
stout sea tale, a manly battle yarn, anything without wine, women, and love, then I will begin to
hope for something great from them, not before.*

—— WILLA CATHER *The Kingdom of Art* ——
from the *Courier*, November 23, 1895.

For decades before she began working concentratedly on *One of
Ours*, Willa Cather had been contemptuous of most women writers. Patronizing women from a decidedly masculine perspective
in her youthful journalistic days, she had called for a woman to
write a manly battle yarn as proof of the sex's potential for creative excellence. Having announced such a criterion measuring literary worth, she was highly likely, sooner or later, to try and meet
it. Thus, though she may have had no particular battle yarn in
mind until she read the newspaper notice of G. P. Cather's heroic
death, she certainly would have wondered for years about how a
writer such as she would go about composing such a thing. A
manly battle yarn, for better or worse, was the proof of greatness
she had set. One suspects that one source of Cather's difficulties
with *One of Ours* was her fear of facing her own mediocrity if it
failed. Having felt she succeeded, however, she must have met
critical derision of her "womanly" attempts with exacerbated
fury.

Another conundrum to consider, however, involves the sources of the identification Cather felt with her cousin George. Is it possible, for example, that George—*because* he was young and male—became a repository for all the negative qualities Cather could project onto a shadowy alter ego? Did his story attract her *because* he was repressed, indecisive, sexually frustrated, and evidently full of self-destructive urges? And did she love his willingness to die as she loved her opportunity both to aggrandize and also to kill off such a projection of herself? Following such speculations, the book begins to suggest clearly autobiographical elements. It also becomes a reminder that the characters who most closely resemble Willa Cather are usually males—Jim Burden, Niel Herbert, Godfrey St. Peter—all of whom she presents in an intermittently negative or critical light.

In any case, as we begin the story of the second half of Willa Cather's creative life we must not forget the important continuities to be traced throughout all her work. While she often made her connections by yoking opposites in her fiction, her oppositions, inversions, and reversals still provide links.

Normally, any one of Cather's novels can be linked with another that it reverses. Her novels often stick together as opposite sides of a coin. For example, *One of Ours* reverses *Alexander's Bridge* by portraying an ordinary midwestern farm boy with no outstanding talents, who nevertheless longs for a life that would give him a sense of wholeness; *Alexander's Bridge* depicts a famous midwestern engineer who has come to symbolize a "tamer of rivers" (*AB*, 9) but whose life nevertheless falls apart. While conceding that over years of farming Alexandra grows hard and heavy, *O Pioneers!* more strongly suggests the creative opportunities a young woman develops in successfully cultivating her Nebraska farmland; while conceding some hopeful interludes, *One of Ours* more strongly emphasizes the deadening qualities in Nebraska farm life than destroy a young man's imagination. Reversing *The Song of the Lark*, *One of Ours* traces a young man's inchoate sense of failure, rendered more pitiful because he lacks words to express his frustrations; *The Song of the Lark* tracks the illustrious career of a Metropolitan Opera diva who conquers the musical world with her song. Or to describe the pair another way, *Lark* is the story of a young woman with nothing who achieves success and personal fulfillment as an artist, at the cost of almost everything deriving from personal feeling; *One of Ours* is the story of a young man with everything who feels little but failure until the moment of his heroic and therefore fulfilling death. *One of Ours* inverts Ántonia's story by tracing the abortive career of a young Nebraska farm boy who dies quickly in World War I, rather than the long and productive life of an aging Nebraska farmwife who resembles "the founders of early races" (*MA*, 353). In *My Ántonia*, Nebraska dominantly symbolizes fertility and constantly returning rebirth; in *One of Ours*, the state dominantly suggests brain death, meaningless waste and labor, and frustrating fragmentations. These inversions become the clear links between Cather's novels, which links in turn suggest her continuing concentration on her chosen personal material and her consistent willingness to consider that material from more than one angle. They also suggest how a writer such as Cather could keep using two or three stories that seem to keep telling themselves over and over as if they had never happened before: she endlessly explores other implications and possibilities and outcomes for those few basic plot lines. She seems tirelessly to trace what happens to the story when its teller changes one variable—for example, the gender of the protagonist.

Hereafter one assumption in this study will be that Cather never entirely finished a subject. She returned repeatedly to the matters she considered essential or the problems that would not disappear. She attacked the same conundrums repeatedly, renewing her own interest by changing her angle of vision. As she said of the novel that precedes *One of Ours*, "My Ántonia, for instance, is just the other side of the rug, the pattern that is supposed not to count in a story. In it there is no love affair, no courtship, no marriage, no broken heart, no struggle for success."[1] Having displayed "the other side of the rug" in *Ántonia*, Cather turned the rug rightside up again, replacing all those missing features and highlighting a great many more in *One of Ours*.

Before we can begin to understand Cather's Pulitzer-winning novel, we must accept the fact that a number of the things she said about the book, directly or obliquely, are not exactly, or not absolutely, true. There's no reason to ignore the fact that a great writer of fiction creates fictions. Take, for example, Cather's explanation for her chosen prose style, first published in 1931, a decade after she completed *One of Ours*, in her justly famous essay "My First Novels [There Were Two]":

> When my third book, *The Song of the Lark*, came along, Heinemann [a British publisher] turned it down. I had never heard from him directly that he liked *O Pioneers!* but now I had a short hand-written letter from him, telling me that he admired it very much; that he was declining *The Song of the Lark* because he thought in that book I had taken the wrong road, and that the full-blooded method, which told everything about everybody, was not natural to me and was not the one in which I would ever take satisfaction. "As for myself," he wrote, "I always find the friendly, confidential tone of writing of this sort distressingly familiar, even when the subject matter is very fine."
>
> At that time I did not altogether agree with Mr. Heinemann, nor with Randolph Bourne, in this country, who said in his review almost the same thing. One is always a little on the defense about one's last book. But when the next book, *My Ántonia*, came along, quite of itself and with no direction from me, it took the road of *O Pioneers!*—not the road of *The Song of the Lark*. Too much detail is apt, like any other form of extravagance, to become slightly vulgar; and it quite destroys in a book a very satisfying element analogous to what painters call "composition."[2]

This passage needs the closest, most skeptical scrutiny. For one thing, it suggests that after *The Song of the Lark* Willa Cather understood that the contrasting style of *O Pioneers!* and *My Án-*

tonia was her better and truer method, and never thereafter departed from it. The insinuation is patently untrue, for *One of Ours* is not only "full-blooded" but is also an attempt to tell everything, if not about everybody, at least about the central figure, Claude Wheeler.[3] All Claude's impulses, motives, and acts are explained and rendered plausible by the text. Claude is thoroughly researched and accounted for.

A second inference one might draw from the Cather statement above, however, is that Heinemann suggested the main thing wrong with a "full-blooded" method was its predictably confidential and distressingly familiar tone. If Cather hated to be wrong as much as Elizabeth Sergeant suggests—"When she had made her mind up, she wanted to prevail"[4]—then she may have decided deliberately to try the detailed style again, in the process doing it right by simply avoiding a confidential and friendly tone. In *One of Ours*, Cather keeps her distance, at least from the reader. In any case, Cather's final sentence in this statement needs careful attention. If too much detail is apt to become slightly vulgar, the slightly vulgar may well have been the effect she wanted for her slightly vulgar and decidedly ordinary protagonist. That too much detail destroys in a book what painters call "composition" may also have been a conscious effect in Cather's mind as she proceeded. In this novel, her stress is on disruption, and her details convey disorder.[5] It is certainly plausible to imagine that Cather deliberately chose a "full-blooded" and detail-chocked prose style because it synchronized with her subject: a young man who feels with dismay that his life lacks direction and meaningful form or purpose.

There are at least two other suspect statements Cather made when trying to explain her techniques in this book. Cather's abstract theory here seems to outstrip her actual practice; or else, she was not letting her organizing left hemisphere know what her performing right hand was doing. Cather told an interviewer: "I have cut out all descriptive work in this book—the thing I do best. I have cut out all picture making because that boy does not see pictures. It was hard to cease to do the thing that I do best, but we all have to pay the price for everything we accomplish, and because I was willing to pay so much to write about this boy, I felt that I had a right to do so."[6]

This statement, printed in an interview Cather gave the *Omaha World-Herald* just after she had finished writing *One of Ours* in 1921, is remarkable for its uncharacteristic defensiveness. It is more important, however, for the explicit assertions Cather made here that have befogged critical eyeglasses. Cather neither cut out the descriptions she did best nor did she avoid picture-making— quite the contrary. She *may* have avoided allowing Claude to perceive pictures, as Woodress shrewdly suggests,[7] but she certainly continues to write in her best style for her readers. *One of Ours* contains some of her most stunning pictures and some of her most effective descriptions, the latter easily rivaling those of *O Pioneers!*

As we remarked in chapter two, Cather habitually froze her action, as a movie projector is said to freeze a camera shot, in order to emphasize a "frame" that conveys powerfully and symbolically many layers of meaning. To me, the most shocking picture Cather ever created is cut into the end of *One of Ours*: the reappearing black corpse's hand that protrudes, as a fat boot also does, into the trench Claude's troop must defend at the time of his death. Both protuberances remind the inexperienced Americans that corruption will not stay buried, but reasserts itself into their space. Though the hand is repeatedly covered with earth, bombs shake the ground so violently that it keeps reappearing to clutch at the air. The buried enemy will not be ignored.

As this novel begins, a more often-noticed picture captures the transformation of five-year-old Claude into a screaming devil child: he accompanies his mother to pick cherries his father has promised them will be accessible and finds on the site, "The beautiful, round-topped cherry tree, full of green leaves and red fruit,—his father had sawed it through! It lay on the ground beside its bleeding stump. With one scream Claude became a little demon" (*oo*, 26). In its opposite way, this snapshot from Claude's memory book is as powerfully evocative as the famous magnified plow in *My Ántonia*. It records Nat Wheeler's sadistic humor, his profligate waste, his lazy antagonism to the desires of his family, and his malignant effect on Claude's maturation processes, specifically his sexual development. Willa Cather did not accidentally mention a cherry tree.

The novel is, if anything, an album more crammed with Cather pictures than her other works. For example, at the end there's the consumptive French mother who sits in the mud and tries with her last strength to nurse her German baby (*OO*, 306); in the middle there's the trapped bird who flew into Claude's half-built new house "and fluttered wildly about among the partitions, shrieking with fright before it darted out into the dusk ... and found its way to freedom" (*OO*, 152); and in the beginning there's the terrifying balance of Claude's car on the lip of a culvert, when Enid insists on driving them home through a terrible storm, merely because she does not like to change her plans (*OO*, 117).

In fact, pictures are often paired in this novel for ironic effect. Wandering aimlessly in the timber claim after his new wife, Enid, has departed for China, Claude spots a black barn cat mewing pitifully in the cold. He picks it up, and addresses it kindly: "What's the matter, Blackie? Mice getting scarce in the barn? Mahailey will say you are bad luck. Maybe you are, but you can't help it, can you?" Soon he adds, "Well, if you are bad luck, I guess you are going to stay right with me!" (*OO*, 193–94). Later, in France, Claude once again spots a kitten that this time belongs to a little Belgian refugee who has been deeply traumatized by the war: "As the two soldiers left the table and started for the camp, Claude reached down into the tool house and took up one of the kittens, holding it out in the light to see it blink its eyes. The little girl, just coming out of the kitchen, uttered a shrill scream, a really terrible scream, and squatted down, covering her face with her hands" (*OO*, 303).

While the reappearing black hand at the end of this novel is one of Cather's most ghoulish inventions, it pairs with its opposite—an image altogether delightful. The second is buried within a lyric description of spring farmlands, illustrating "what she does best":

All over the dusty, tan-coloured wheatfields there was a tender mist of green,—millions of little fingers reaching up and waving lightly in the sun. To the north and south Claude could see the corn-planters, moving in straight lines over the brown acres where the earth had been harrowed so fine that it blew off in clouds of dust to the roadside. When a gust of wind rose, gay little twisters came across the open fields, corkscrews of powdered earth that whirled through the air and suddenly fell again. It seemed as if there were a lark on every fence post, singing for everything that was dumb; for the great ploughed lands, and the heavy horses in the rows, and the men guiding the horses. (*OO,* 105)

Later the clouds of dust will contrast ironically with the falling dirt that shells spray over soldiers; the gay little twisters will contrast to the clouds forecasting rougher weather for the *Anchises* as it sails toward France: "Across the red west a small, ragged black cloud hurried,—then another, and another. They came up out of the sea—wild, witchlike shapes that travelled fast and met in the west as if summoned for an evil conclave" (*OO,* 250–51). The point is that descriptions, both lyrical and sinister, abound in this novel. They frequently include pictoral "slides" that capture specific symbols amplifying the narrative. Such slides or pictures are paired as opposites, for ironic effect, and emphasize the "breaking in two" of Claude's world and life.

Importantly, Claude actually prefers the second half of his life, which follows the radical disruption. The novel explains why. One reason is that Claude feels "a sense of physical well-being" not in Nebraska, but in France (*OO,* 297); in fact, on his twenty-fifth birthday he feels he "was having his youth in France" (*OO,* 349). Reviewing Claude's misspent youth forces us to acknowledge the last misleading information that must be reassessed before significant critical work can begin on this novel.

Willa Cather has sometimes seemed reactionary because of such reports as this from Elizabeth Shepley Sergeant:

> Her intolerance began to trouble me. She was truly
> skeptical about the post-war world. Take this Vi-
> ennese Freud: why was everybody reading him?
> Tolstoy knew as much about psychology—with no
> isms attached—as any fiction writer needed. I
> didn't agree. Freud was *here*; I had to try to read
> him, because I lived in today's world. But Willa,
> like the Pueblo Indians who—I had been told in
> New Mexico—had no word for "future," looked
> backward with regret. Our present lay about us in
> ruins but we had, she wistfully remarked, a beau-
> tiful past.[8]

The interpretive problem this passage creates does not derive
from misinformation or distortion. Indeed, Sergeant's phrases
("present lay about us in ruins") lead us immediately into the text
of *One of Ours*, and its clear references to *Paradise Lost*. What the
Sergeant passage produces is a deadly temptation to assume Willa
Cather is simple and straightforward, because her social manner
of speaking seemed to many to be so. In any case, whether Cather
hated Freud or not, and whether she felt Tolstoy had more to
teach or not, the fact is that she systematically set out to psychoan-
alyze Claude Wheeler with Freudian categories in *One of Ours*.
Whether she learned her important answers from Freud or Tolstoy, she used Freudian questions for the enterprise. When Cather
bragged, "I came to know that boy better than I know myself,"[9]
she may well have meant that she had found and provided a more
logical explanation for his impulses and acts—in the Freudian
mode—than she could provide for her own.

Cather supplied the details for a psychological case study
within this novel because she needed convincing answers to such
insistent questions as, Why would a lad go eagerly to war, and
why would he even die willingly there? How could he think
what he did was worth doing, when the overwhelming evidence
to the contrary finally convinces even such sheltered patriots as
Claude's naive and faith-filled mother? How could someone love
war, without being a moron or a sadist?

Cather starts her study as a shrewd Freudian would, with the childhood of the soldier in question and his place in the "family constellation." Claude is a middle child (thus, predictably insecure), the second of three brothers. He's the clear favorite of his weak and ineffectual mother, to whom he is so strongly attached that he always feels toward her an "almost painful tenderness" (*OO*, 43). When at one point his brother Bayliss criticizes Claude's friend Mrs. Erlich, she seems to serve as a "displaced object" for their antagonism. Bayliss actually criticizes Claude's close relationship with a mother. We are told that Bayliss has always been "bitterly jealous" of his mother's joy in Claude's reading to her (*OO*, 77), has in fact "a deep-seated sense of injury. He felt that he had always been misunderstood and underestimated" (*OO*, 78). In this family drama, Claude has played Jacob to Bayliss's Esau, and displaced Bayliss feels cheated of his birthright.

In her relationship to her son Claude, Evangeline Wheeler can be described as seductive. From his boyhood, they have spent their happiest hours together, and she is delighted to be left at home with Claude the autumn her husband is away with their younger son in Colorado: "'It's almost like being a bride, keeping house for just you, Claude,' she sometimes said" (*OO*, 69). The most passionate kiss in this novel is exchanged between Claude and his mother, when he leaves home for the last time (*OO*, 225).

Claude's father, Nat Wheeler (a natural wheeler-dealer), is physically the largest as well as the richest farmer in the area. He is not merely contemptible, as is older brother Bayliss, but he is certainly a destructive father to Claude as well. He mainly considers Claude "a fool" (*OO*, 150) and "often purposely outraged his feelings to harden him, as he had hardened Claude's mother" (*OO*, 25). In numerous ways—by ridicule, neglect, or overwork—Wheeler abuses Claude as he abuses his wife. Both appear to be incapable of opposing or defying the paterfamilias. In response to Wheeler's arbitrary displays of power, Claude can only feel impotent "rage and hate" (*OO*, 26).

With all the elements of this oedipal drama in place, it is not surprising that Claude is frequently uncertain, frustrated, or despondent, even wracked by feelings of self-hate. "Claude had come to believe that the things and people he most disliked were the ones that were to shape his destiny" (*OO*, 28). After some consideration, "He sneered at himself for his lack of spirit. . . . He could not assert himself against his father or mother, but he could be bold enough with the rest of the world" (*OO*, 29). Boldness, in fact, normally eludes him. "The boy felt bitterly about the way in which he had been brought up, and about his hair and his freckles and his awkwardness. When he went to the theatre in Lincoln, he took a seat in the gallery, because he knew that he looked like a green country boy" (*OO*, 30). By the time he is twenty-three, his mother "felt lonely for him. . . . She had begun to wonder whether he was one of those people who are always discontented" (*OO*, 183).

Given this meticulously elaborated psychological programming constructed for Claude, Cather takes great pains to emphasize repeatedly that he is physically normal and sound—that is, he is not effeminate, as is his brother Bayliss. In our first glimpse of him, his red hair stands up in peaks, "like a cock's comb" (OO, 3). He has all the physical attributes of a healthy male: "His good physique he took for granted; smooth, muscular arms and legs, and strong shoulders" (*OO*, 17). At college, a flirtatious art student "even coaxed him to pose in his track clothes for the life class on Saturday morning, telling him that he had "a magnificent physique," a compliment which covered him with confusion. But he posed, of course" (*OO*, 50). Explicitly, Claude is "a boy with strong impulses, and he detested the idea of trifling with them." While his sexual drive is strong, his associations with the family's hired hands has left him with "a sharp disgust for sensuality" (*OO*, 51).

Mostly, Claude is simply but deeply naive. His predicament is summarized with typical Cather finesse on the first page. Waking in the same bed as his brother (for he's just like everybody else) he rises early (for he's full of energy), to accomplish whatever work is necessary (he's not lazy) to get to the circus (the kind of amusement available to him). Having washed the family car in order to go in style, however, he's disappointed because, as a joke, his father requires him to drive in with the hired hands in the wagon. He's too diffident to protest or challenge his father's order.

Claude's awkward shyness is of course most evident in his relations with the opposite sex. In fact, he's never thoroughly comfortable except when around motherly women such as Mrs. Erlich, Mrs. Voight, or Mme. Joubert. Reared to respect girls, whether or not they are respectable, he stays too far from them to learn how to tell the difference. Thus, Claude predictably picks the wrong bride. He marries a frigid lover of Prohibition who enforces her rules a great deal more strictly than his mother, Evangeline, did. Too late, he learns the truth his father-in-law tried to tell him: "You'll find out that pretty nearly everything you believe about life—about marriage, especially—is lies" (*OO*, 130). Sexually frustrated, intellectually starved, and socially out of place, Claude is not half in love with easeful death: he leaps for it with eager ardor.

At this point, however, we do well to remember that we are dealing here with Willa Cather, whose simplifying art is always complex. Specifically, that means that her Freudian formulas are no sooner set up clearly than they are upended. Take, for example, the matter of Claude's visible and audible death wish. At his lowest point,

> The débris of human life was more worthless and ugly than the dead and decaying things in nature. Rubbish ... junk ... his mind could not picture anything that so exposed and condemned all the dreary, weary, ever-repeated actions by which life is continued from day to day. Actions without meaning.... As he looked out and saw the grey landscape through the gently falling snow, he could not help thinking how much better it would be if people could go to sleep like the fields; could be blanketed down under the snow, to wake with their hurts healed and their defeats forgotten.   (*OO*, 192–93)

The Cather twist here is that this clear death wish is a life wish. In Nebraska, on the farm, "Claude would become one of those dead people that moved about the streets of Frankfort; everything that was Claude would perish, and the shell of him would come and go and eat and sleep for fifty years" (*OO*, 134). But Claude wishes he were dead, or emulates the dead, only when he is at home. As soon as he escapes from his father's land, he is alive again. Thus, rushing into war is rushing toward life, freedom, maturity, and responsibility. Claude handles all those things "like a man," once he enters the army.

The key to Claude's desire is his yearning to find access to power, which means in this Freudian novel to find access to his father. What he particularly needs is a power that will defend him against his father's contempt. His uniform gives him that weapon which allows him to cut through his father's jokes into his father's presence and approval. In fact, his uniform functions as magic cloak, transforming Claude so completely that as soon as he dons it, he can deal coolly and effectively with the naughty boys who plague Mrs. Voight because she is German.

How Cather conveys this dramatic change of relationship between father and son, so crucial to Claude's well-being, is an interesting theme in itself. At the beginning of the novel, when Claude is unmistakeably allied with his mother against his father and younger brother, Ralph, Claude imitates his mother's disapproval or discomfort with new machinery. Ralph, conversely, wastes the funds that could cover a college education by purchasing machinery nobody wants, or understands how to use, simply because he enjoys buying it. The fast-accumulating junk piles up in the basement and represents for Claude a kind of witlessly wasteful family form of vulgarity. Representing a love of nature and living things, "Claude had always worked hard when he was at home, and made a good field hand, while Ralph had never done much but tinker with machinery and run errands in his car" (*OO*, 64). Claude admires the Erlichs because "They merely knew how to live . . . and spent their money on themselves, instead of on machines to do the work and machines to entertain people. Machines, Claude decided, could not make pleasure, whatever else they could do" (*OO*, 39). Machines, then, are associated in Claude's mind with males like those in his family whose values are life-denying. It is an irony that totally escapes Claude that a pair of mules run him into a barbed-wire fence and thus cause his terrible skin infection; while a machine may have frightened them into running, it was animals, plowing land, and protective property divisions that led to Claude's sickness and thus on to his terrible marriage. Or to take the point further, it was Claude's own furious overcompensation for his sense of masculine inadequacy that pushed him to overwork himself and thus infect his face.

As soon as Claude puts on a uniform, however, a great many things change, including his relationship to his male relatives and their machines. When he comes home dressed as a soldier, most of his friends are waiting to see him step off the train, including all his family. Thereafter, "Ralph ... stuck to his brother like a burr" even though "until now Ralph had always felt a little ashamed of him" (*OO*, 223). Soon his father begins giving Evangeline the neighborhood news he has withheld from her for years, so that she can pass it on to Claude. And Nat takes Claude over their farm and shows it to him, as if he is a stranger—as he is, for he has become an honored guest in his father's eyes. The most important change, however, has happened in Claude's own head: "now his own neighbourhood came to him with the freshness of things that have been forgotten for a long while,—came together before his eyes as a harmonious whole" (*OO*, 218–19). During his last morning at home, he by choice joins his father and brother outside where the women are excluded, and where the happily bonded males can tinker with the car engine right down to the last precious minute. His successful bonding with other males in the army, of course, leads not only to his greatest happiness but also to his death.

Once Claude becomes an admired and acceptable representative male to other males, at any rate, he no longer has any trouble understanding them or participating in their hobbies and pastimes. He no longer cringes at their machines; in fact, he feels happily at home on the *Anchises*, which can be explained to him by his friend Tod Fanning, who "knew a good deal about machinery" (*OO*, 235). He feels that "Two years ago he had seemed a fellow for whom life was over; driven into the ground like a post, or like those Chinese criminals who are planted upright in the earth." In the glorious present of the war, however, he asks wonderingly, "How had they come to be worth the watchfulness and devotion of so many men and machines, this extravagant consumption of fuel and energy?" (*OO*, 243). In his new and happy phase, then, Claude has no trouble accepting machines, waste, or extravagant consumption of energy—all the things that formerly appalled him. He is happy because he has found a community he fits into, an activity he does well, and a purpose he applauds and respects. He has also found that closest friend of his life—David Gerhardt. Such good things come to him from the army and the war. His death wish is to destroy his old homelife; his desire to live leads him into gunfire.

When Claude is happy, he has no trouble at all relating to the men around him, no matter how macho or sensual or even syphillitic. His happiness comes from his finding a way to be "one of them." He is most "one of ours" when illustrating this American desire to be liked; once enlisted, Claude immediately stands out among the others for his good-humored dependability. The discomfort he inspires in many readers does not derive, it seems to me, from his playing essentially female, nurturing roles.[10] It derives instead from his playing out a female plot: a passionate protagonist—hitherto depressed, repressed, or at least unhappy—finds something essentially forbidden to love and thereafter heroically and admirably advances toward self-destruction by a total and wholehearted commitment to it. This plot line covers a high percentage of literature's most memorable women—Juliet, Cleopatra, Isolde, Camille, Anna Karenina, to name a few.

The central fact about *One of Ours* that one must see in order to read it intelligently at all is that the book is bathed and saturated in irony. The fact Cather must have found intolerable about the critical response to the work is that her best friends, such as Elizabeth Shepley Sergeant, and best literary colleagues, such as Mencken and Nathan, missed her irony. And the irony is not all that subtle. For example, Cather makes it very clear that Claude is not a thinker. Since boyhood he has been easily manipulated, has played the "chump" (*OO*, 17) and fall guy for his brother Ralph's mischief. And he has never had any training in thinking, having been educated at a Baptist college that discourages it in favor of learning. He has never exhibited any startling or striking insight in his early manhood. With these facts repeatedly emphasized for the first three-fifths of the novel, it is astonishing to find readers who suddenly take Claude's generalizations seriously once he lands on foreign ground. He himself has already dismissed his own head as "a perfect block-head" (*OO*, 17). He is not meant to be a spokesman for serious people. He is meant to be a representative foot soldier. And that symbolic function must have seemed amply clear to Willa Cather, when she named her last section with a line from Vachel Lindsay's bombastic, jingoistic, crudely chest-thumping and repetitive poem about "Nebraska's shout of joy," entitled "Bryan, Bryan, Bryan, Bryan." With hindsight, one wonders who could take seriously anything directly linked to such verse as this:

> Oh, the longhorns from Texas,
> The jay hawks from Kansas,
> The plop-eyed bungaroo and giant giassicus,
> The varmint, chipmunk, bugaboo,
> The horned-toad, prairie-dog and ballyhoo,
> From all the newborn states arow,
> Bidding the eagles of the west fly on,
> Bidding the eagles of the west fly on.[11]

Two ironic patterns in this novel need particular attention. The first involves Claude's name. He repeatedly objects to his name, which seems to him "a 'chump' name, like Elmer and Roy; a hayseed name trying to be fine" (*OO*, 17). This objection is mentioned first during the period when Claude is objecting to everything about himself, especially including his head, which seems "uncompromisingly square in shape" (*OO*, 17). When Claude, much later, can bear to admit what has bothered him most, he concedes to David Gerhardt, "Well, it's a sissy name, if you mean that" (*OO*, 299). What Claude objects to most in relation to his name, however, is hearing the detested preacher, Weldon, or his own wife, Enid, call him *Clod* (*OO*, 114, 179). If he objects to their singular pronunciation, he must hear the name properly articulated the more standard American way: *clawed*. In any case, for three-fifths of the book, until he gets to France and hears another pronunciation of the hated name, we must assume he is either *clod* or *clawed*. The sounds themselves make a major thematic statement. Almost down to the publication day and against objections from her publisher and friends, Cather planned to name this novel *Claude*, to call attention to that theme.

Another pattern injecting both interest and irony into this novel is Cather's use of the homophones *sun* and *son*. The sun is so central and symbolic an image here, in fact, that more than once a sentence reminds us of sun-loving Flannery O'Connor. Descriptions of the sun hint at the predicaments or moods of the son, or "enlighten us" about his situation. A dozen or more suns rise or set in these pages, illuminating crucial moments in Claude's life, but a few examples will illustrate the symbol system. On the first page, when Claude wakes up excitedly anticipating a day at the circus, "The sun popped up over the edge of the prairie like a broad, smiling face" (*OO*, 3–4). During a bumper harvest in which Claude outdoes himself working in the fields,

> Every morning the sun came up a red ball, quickly drank the dew, and started a quivering excitement in all living things. . . .
> The sun was like a great visiting presence that stimulated and took its due from all animal energy.
>
> (*OO*, 136)

On shipboard, Claude and a friend

> found themselves standing side by side that evening, watching the broad purple sun go down into a violet coloured sea. . . . Claude was thinking how his mother would be standing at the west window every evening now, watching the sun go down and following him in her mind. (*OO*, 241)

Happy in a French forest, Claude finds that "suddenly the sun broke through and shattered the whole wood with gold" (*OO*, 300). At the end, when troopships return after Claude's death,

"The sun is sinking low, a transport is steaming slowly up the narrows with the tide" (*OO*, 387).

One of Ours is no naively sentimental story of the happy war dead. It is a deeply ironic treatment of war, and of what sends soldiers willingly to die. Cather does not make martial activity itself a pleasure, but she does portray a young man who dies satisfied with his fate, and whose fate, his mother knows, is kind to allow him to do so. In more places than this novel, Cather develops the thesis that some are born unlucky, and for them there is nothing to be done. Claude Wheeler is one of those who unluckily was born in the wrong place to the wrong people. The novel itself is happy, however, in giving Claude a disruption to his unlucky life that changes his fortune. He dies a successful leader of men, who loves the men he leads, the country in which he leads them, and himself, for having the youth and chance to be in France when he was needed there. Cather's depiction of this young man provides insights that were selectively forgotten in the aftermath of World War I.

The most important question Claude Wheeler asks through the story of his life is, What makes life worth living? He finds significant answers in wartime:

> The sound of the guns had from the first been pleasant to him, had given him a feeling of confidence and safety; tonight he knew why. What they said was, that men could still die for an idea; and would burn all they had made to keep their dreams. He knew the future of the world was safe; the careful planners would never be able to put it into a strait-jacket,—cunning and prudence would never have it to themselves.... Ideals were not archaic things, beautiful and impotent; they were the real sources of power among men. (*OO*, 357)

From the first pages of this novel, insecure Claude has longed for a sense of personal power. When he comes to recognize it in ideals that trigger acts, and to accept his own manliness that is capable of action, he successfully finds the real source of power in himself.

43

Claude's anguished search for potence—physical, familial, public, or professional—is certainly one of the likely bases for Cather's acknowledged identification with him, as well as her anxiety about this unfolding novel. Her task as novelist, after all, is in her public performance to prove she is everything Claude fears he is not. Claude serves as her "shadow" and has the psychological advantage of being expendable: she can kill him off and thus bury their shared inadequacies. But it necessarily creates anxiety to lop off the offending member of her family or part of herself.

At this point, then, one legitimately asks what reward there was in the task of writing *One of Ours* for Willa Cather. We have already noticed that the novel is actually organized to dramatize what a Nebraska blockhead feels when facing the fact that his world has broken in two. The novel's structure highlights that shattering as strongly as possible; the paired images further reinforce the sense of before and after. For Cather, one advantage of writing such a story is that it leaves her in control of the disaster. By structuring and describing it, she controls the falling apart. In fact, to develop her elaborate sun-son symbol system is to control the sun by controlling the son.

Once the smash can be controlled through structure and description, and the account of ensuing emotions controlled by guided accounts, the falling apart itself becomes something tolerable, embraceable. If Cather entered this writing period already fearing that the world was falling apart for her, she survived the crash by shaping the story through a controlled fiction. The final sign of control is the fact that Cather provides her fiction about the world's breaking in two with a happy ending, for her protagonist dies a happy death, as he deserves. It is affirmation of a sort, to suggest that a splitting world may bury a good-hearted Nebraskan, but not ignominiously. Romance-loving Cather provides a fine end for a story of breakage—a swashbuckling last gasp of the heroic available even to a middle son of Nebraska who was born unlucky and still lived to see France.

CHAPTER FOUR

The Measures of Loss
and of Ladies:
A Lost Lady

*The possibilities of analytical fiction are limited;
it can go on until it has lost all poetry, all beauty,
until it reaches the ugly skeleton of things, there it
must stop. The human mind refuses to be dragged
further even in the name of art. We will all sicken
of it some day and go back to romance, to romance whose possibilities are as high and limitless
as beauty, as good, as hope. Some fine day there
will be a grand exodus from the prisons and al-
leys, the hospitals and lazarettos whither realism
has dragged us. Then, in fiction at least, we shall
have poetry and beauty and gladness without end,
bold deeds and fair women and all things that are
worth while.*

—— WILLA CATHER, *The Kingdom of Art* ——
from the *Journal,* March 15, 1896.

We begin this chapter with one reminder: nothing Willa Cather
ever wrote is as simple as it looks. Nothing looks simpler, however, than Cather's description of *A Lost Lady:* "I didn't try to
make a character study, but just a portrait like a thin miniature
painted on ivory. A character study of Mrs. Forrester would have

been very, very different. I wasn't interested in her character when I was little, but in her lovely hair and her laugh which made me happy clear down to my toes."[1]

Cather's authorial warning against considering the depiction of Marian Forrester a character study is immediately interesting after we have explored *One of Ours*. In a predictable Catherian reflex, she reversed her former goal (a character study) and mode (realistic psychological analysis) after writing Claude Wheeler's story, and quickly—almost purgatively—wrote its diametrical opposite. *One of Ours* was a thorough and detailed Freudian character study of an affluent and depressed young male bumbler of the early twentieth century, who went off to war and died. *A Lost Lady* is a deft sketch of an ebullient and graceful nineteenth-century hostess who creates elegant entertainments, loses her wealth, and survives. After the four-year ordeal of producing *One of Ours,* Cather bragged that "*A Lost Lady* was written in five months." The subject, she said, came to her "whole" as she rested on a bed in the home of Isabel and Jan Hambourg.[2]

According to James Woodress, the conception of *A Lost Lady* can be traced back to Cather's reading the obituary of Lyra Garber Anderson, a woman she said she "loved very much in my childhood."[3] The lady died March 21, 1921, and was remembered in a Red Cloud newspaper Cather happened to read. Lying down to rest after the shock, she imagined the story from beginning to end in one productive hour. She actually wrote the book during the winter and spring of 1922, between her return from Nebraska and her one teaching stint at Bread Loaf. The dates are important here, for they help us anchor the actual events and activities that occurred in Cather's watershed year. They also remind us that many tributaries fed the flood of feeling Cather chose to objectify or symbolize with that 1922 date.

Woodress tells us that she had finished *A Lost Lady* before announcing her literary principles in "The Novel Démeublé," which appeared in April of 1922.[4] Thus, Cather's advice about "defurnituring" fiction, which still occasionally provokes a dismissal of *One of Ours,* was in the hands of critics by the time some wanted an effective stick with which to beat Cather's war novel. Her "démeublé" principles cohered immediately *after* Cather finished *A Lost Lady,* the writing of which had gone fast enough to seem an exhilarating compositional method that involved discarding all but the truly essential.

In several ways besides speed, however, Cather seemed to revert to earlier patterns in writing *A Lost Lady.* For one thing, she again focused centrally on a woman, as she had in *My Ántonia* or *The Song of the Lark.* For another, she wrote again in the "romantic," not the "realistic," mode. From her earliest years as a teenage critic, Willa Cather had made clear her preference for romance, "whose possibilities are as high and limitless as beauty, as good, as hope." As Elizabeth Shepley Sergeant phrases it, *A Lost Lady* belongs to the "late eighties perhaps?—when good was good and evil evil. Though written in the beginning of the Freudian age and by an author who now could present a cool cheek to a heroine—make her irresistible and yet not be herself overdazzled—it had no modern implications."[5] Nearly a half century after Sergeant spotted the pre-Freudian cast of mind in this novel, we see that Cather *returns* to the pre-Freudian world, after the Freudian patterns she built into *One of Ours.* At this later point, however, the modern implications are startling.

For the purposes of this narrative we must also realize that in *A Lost Lady* Cather turned (not re-turned, for she in some sense had never been there) to a conventional woman's theme: "refined" female sexuality. The novel arranges several men around Marian Forrester and uses them to characterize the social attitudes this subject is most likely to provoke. They walk around her and provide angles of vision, as around the famous jug on Sergeant's table:

> "I want my new heroine to be like this—like a rare object in the middle of a table, which one may examine from all sides."
>
> She moved the lamp so that light streamed brightly down on my Taormina jar, with its glazed orange and blue design.
>
> "I want her to stand out—like this—like this—because she *is* the story."

> Saying this her fervent, enthusiastic voice faltered and her eyes filled with tears.
>
> Someone you knew in your childhood, I ventured.
>
> She nodded, but did not say more.
>
> So I sometimes wondered, later, whether she was thinking of Ántonia or Mrs. Forrester. Often she thought about her heroines for years before they appeared in a book.[6]

Cather focused attention on a lady who chooses consciously to be a sex object. When the lady's sexuality defines her, as it does here, then female sexuality is what the circling men are reacting to. Thus, Niel Herbert denies or rejects it, Ivy Peters exploits it, Frank Ellinger serves it, the Blum boys accept it, and Captain Forrester honors it. The roses mentioned repeatedly in the novel, as Susan Rosowski beautifully and thoroughly summarizes,[7] are the Western male's oldest publicly acceptable tribute to such sexuality. At the least, Cather hits here on a subject of widespread interest.

Through gesture after gesture, Cather reminds us of Marian's sexuality. Even Niel recognizes that she enjoys an "ardour" and a "wild delight that he has not found in life" (*LL,* 171). While she literally strikes sparks with Ellinger (*LL,* 60), she exercises her power reflexively in the presence of any male of any age. She brings sweets to the boys picnicking on her grounds, and provocatively confides to them that she sometimes strips off stockings, hikes up her skirt, and goes wading, but fears that a snake will bite her toes (*LL,* 18). Poor Niel, sweating a broken arm, is placed in her bed, beside which she kneels and ministers so lovingly that he can see inside "the lace ruffle of her dress" where "her white throat [was] rising and falling, (*LL,* 28)—that is, she bends over him so that he can look down her cleavage. She daringly greets the president of the Colorado and Utah Railroad "en deshabille" (*LL,* 118), and entertains in "a house well known from Omaha to Denver for its hospitality and for a certain charm of atmosphere" (*LL,* 9)—a phrasing oddly suggestive of a brothel. Virtually every encounter or gesture Cather records reasserts Marian's contagious sexual energy. "Mrs. Forrester looked at one, and one knew that she was bewitching. It was instantaneous, and it pierced the thickest hide.... Something about her took hold of one in a flash" (*LL,* 35). In fact, any scene that features Marian seems to mention her touching, teasing, brushing, or patting a man. According to Cyrus Dalzell, such encounters "put fresh life into us all" (*LL,* 96–97).

Willa Cather herself explained that the point of her effort to write this narrative was "to get her [central character adequately depicted] not like a standardized heroine in fiction, but as she really was." The motive for trying, Cather explained, was to re-create a presence who "made me happy clear down to my toes."[8] Such magnetic charm, of course, is itself erotic and itself springs from sexual energy and power. Marian Forrester needs reciprocating men to provide her with a social cast of characters and financial backers in order to secure a stage for her own triumphs; but she also needs men as living proofs of her personal power to capture and hold attention. That is perhaps why she seems to feel so "safe" after intercourse with Ellinger in the woods (*LL,* 67). His sexual response is a reassuring reminder of *her* undiminished power, as well as of her ability to have her cake and eat it too—to preserve her marriage as well as her illicit sexual opportunities. Finally, the central theme of *A Lost Lady* is power, and how the two sexes most normally exercise it.

Before we proceed further into a detailed analysis of *A Lost Lady,* we indulge in two speculations. First, in this novel Cather seems deliberately as well as subversively to have set out to give the public what it wanted. She deliberately chose the subject that pleased that public most—the romantic entanglements of glamorous heroes and ladies, or as she had one phrased it, "bold deeds and fair women." Her choice was immediately rewarded. The book, published in September of 1923, went through five printings by November; two movies quickly followed (after which Cather forever forbade filming any of her works.[9] In this, as in all her other novels, however, Cather demanded that the venture meet her personal high standards, to do which it would have to serve her subtle purposes. And that leads to our second speculation: the possibility of deliberate subversion of her own text here. The first edition of the novel was dedicated to Jan Hambourg, whose name Cather later removed, though naming him again in the dedication to *The Professor's House*. One must wonder what part of this story Cather was initially connecting with her beloved Isabelle's husband. The ironies "felt upon the page without being specifically named there"[10] may help explain the novel's vast academic appeal as well as its continuing popular success.

Names give us our first indicators of the novel's central dynamic. Marian functions as the "Maid Marian" of a band of railroad magnates and robber barons who "came from the Atlantic seaboard to invest money and to 'develop our great West'" (*LL,* 10). Forrester's strength of character makes him the most appealing representative of the group. He is, in fact, their engineer. Three times we are told that he drives a "democrat wagon" (*LL* 12, 31, 104); he also protects the interests of the poor who will be defrauded, unless his money is given in restitution for theirs, when his bank fails. He thus robs the rich—himself and his wife, Marian—to give to the poor, as any honorable Robin Hood of the forest could be expected to do. He is repeatedly compared to a mountain (*LL,* 41, 48) because of his psychological strength.[11] His "Maidy," however, is no helpless spouse but a full-fledged member of the band. She functions effectively as a lawless agent in her own right, with her own code that largely ignores the conventional mores of the nearby town.

Place-names resonate in this story as provocatively as character names. In Greek slang, a "strayed" woman is said to be "of the sweet water." In this novel of loaded names, the bridge between Sweet Water and the Forrester place is fragile and can wash away. But the place in its prime is associated with Marian. The first sentence tells us how "much greyer today than they were then" such towns are, without the Forresters. At the Forrester place "the people who lived there made it seem much larger and finer than it was" (*LL,* 10). The name of Sweet Water resonates through the novel as powerfully as does the first name given Marian's beloved Denver: Cherry Creek.

The name Niel (so carefully misspelled to draw attention) sug-

gests *nil, nihil,* or *kneel,* as Herbert suggests a lowly *herb* to the
Captain's *forest.* In contrast to Herbert, Forrester can look, even
after his debilitating stroke, "like an old tree walking: (*LL,* 115).
Niel never makes so substantial an impression. Niel Herbert can
kneel to, or worship, a remote and abstract idea of Marian as
traditional lady, or mistakenly honor her less significant facade—
missing her face in his obeisance to her form. But he can understand nothing essential about her, if only because he himself
enjoys little life-force. He's handsome but stiff (*LL,* 63), moody,
reserved, and cold (*LL,* 33, 34). He feels "an air of failure and
defeat about his family" (*LL,* 30), and seems to compensate with
a tendency to challenge others (*LL,* 34). He lives with "monastic
cleanliness and severity" (*LL,* 33) behind offices of the law. His
proper and rule-bound life, like his father's, amounts to little.

Cather stated Niel was not so much a character as a "peephole
into that world."[12] His recurring interest for critics traces legitimately, I believe, to the peep he provides into the world it is
forbidden to describe. While he is certainly not to be identified
with that mature Willa Cather who writes and shapes this book,
he seems closely related to the point of view of a much younger
Willie Cather, who once asked fiction for "poetry and beauty and
gladness without end ... and all things that are worthwhile." I
simply insist here that Cather knew what he was when she fashioned him to peep at Marian: "I wasn't interested in her character
[that is, the character of Marian's prototype, Lyra Garber] when I
was little, but in her lovely hair and her laugh which made me
happy clear down to my toes." Niel's essentially childish view is
still the novel's most intensely felt one, the one through which
Cather gets her lady "just as I remembered her and produce[s]
the effect she had on me and many others who knew her."[13] As-
sociating Niel with an outgrown point of view that Cather still
remembers vividly perhaps explains the number of readers who
identify more strongly with him than with the other characters:
peephole though he is, his vision is *felt* more vividly because it
was rooted in Willa Cather's childhood reality. Though she punishes him for it, Niel's child's vision is one that peeps and spies at
adult secrets, then recoils, traumatized by primal scenes.

While we will necessarily return to Niel repeatedly, we observe here that soon after the action begins we see him lying "weak and contented" (*LL*, 28) in Marian's "own bedroom" (*LL*, 26) where she treats him not so much like her baby as like a child she is permitted to pet. The extraordinary subtlety of this novel's symbols is clear in this scene, through Marian's caresses and the deftly understated details about Marian's rings. As Niel regains consciousness and sees Marian's "white throat rising and falling so quickly," we are told, "suddenly she got up to take off her glittering rings,—she had not thought of them before,—shed them off her fingers with a quick motion as if she were washing her hands, and dropped them into Mary's broad palm" (*LL*, 28).

The detail is small and revelatory. For we have already seen Marian drop her rings into Mary's ready palm (suggesting habitual gestures for both of them) when we read, "It gratified . . . [the captain] to have his wife wear jewels; it meant something to him. She never left off her beautiful rings unless she was in the kitchen" (*LL*, 40). We are perhaps only semialert when Marian takes off her rings and earrings in her bedroom, before returning to the parlor for a late-night conversation with Frank Ellinger. When we follow Marian and Frank on their Christmas sleigh ride, however, few miss the point the rings provide:

> Ellinger took off his glove with his teeth. His eyes, sweeping the winding road and the low snow-covered bluffs, had something wolfish in them.
> "Be careful, Frank. My rings! You hurt me!"
> "Then why didn't you take them off? You used to. Are these your cedars, shall we stop here?"
> "No, not here." She spoke very low. "The best ones are farther on, in a deep ravine that winds back into the hills."
> Ellinger glanced at her averted head, and his heavy lips twitched in a smile at one corner.   (*LL*, 65)

We know that Marian removes the rings that symbolize her ties to Captain Forrester whenever her activities require more latitude than those ties permit. Her sudden impulse to remove the rings while she is ministering to Niel suggests the eroticism engendered by their positions; the quick presence of Mary's broad palm suggests that removing the rings is a frequently indulged habit. Ringless, "Mrs. Forrester ran her fingers through his black hair and lightly kissed him on the forehead" (*LL,* 29).

Kathleen L. Nichols and Sharon O'Brien[14] both observe that Niel wants Marian as a surrogate mother. He certainly resents with the intensity of a child the straying of her attention to other men. Just as childishly, until he actually hears Frank's voice in Marian's bedroom, naive Niel imagines only that Ellinger is guilty of a lapse of good taste (*LL,* 83). Once he has reached a supposedly informed maturity, however, Niel lives on "the most pretentious brick block in town" (*LL,* 33). Cather seems to link his monastic cleanliness and severity with pretense. His resolve to be a bachelor—that is, his sexual recoil—seems part of the pretentiousness. What he pretends is that his childish vision of the world has, or once had, validity for active adults.

What Niel cannot understand is Marian's exercise of her powers in service of herself and her own life's needs and desires. He hates her willingness to leave his pedestal for her dark forest. Thus, one must disagree with David Stouck's interesting conclusion that "*A Lost Lady* is a pastoral of experience because it brings its hero from childhood innocence to adult awareness and acceptance of life."[15] What Niel accepts in the end is not "real life" but the valid intensity of his childish delight in Marian Forrester. But the confusing pain of the attraction-repulsion Marian evokes in him leaves us sympathetic to Niel, as Stouck wisely sees, because these tensions are the unanalyzed pulses of the writer's childhood as well, when she herself tried to understand the power of Mrs. Silas Garber. His continuing celibate fastidiousness about such power may equally represent some part of the aging author of which she herself does not entirely approve, and that she certainly does not advocate.

Every evidence in this book suggests that the Forresters know each other well and admire each other loyally. The fact that the Captain "values" his wife with full knowledge of her adultery shocks uncomprehending Niel, who believes a wife should be the chaste and subdued possession of her husband—a trustworthy extension of him and his house. Niel resents the fact that Marian "was not willing to immolate herself . . . and die with the pioneer period" (*LL,* 169). Marian steadfastly "preferred life on any terms" (*LL,* 169), though she honors the Captain unflaggingly, in her own fashion, and even when engaged in flirtations, adulterous affairs, or another marriage.

The point is not merely that Marian has enough power to control males as effectively as "the brawniest tough in town" (*LL,* 27), or that she effortlessly emits such a magnetic sexual energy that even the youngest boy can recognize her as "different from the other townswomen" (*LL,* 19). The point is that her husband honors and admires her for that power: "it gratified him to see men who were older than himself leap nimbly to the ground and run up the front steps as Mrs. Forrester came out on the porch to greet them" (*LL,* 12). A man of few words, Captain Forrester "told Judge Pommeroy that he had never seen her look more captivating than on the day when she was chased by the new bull in the pasture" (*LL,* 13).

In this novel, in order to exercise with greatest impact that sexual power which is the source of Marian Forrester's joy in living, she needs not only men who can respond to her but also money. This need even Niel can recognize: "He dreaded poverty for her. She was one of the people who ought always to have money" (*LL,* 83). Her troubles begin when her financial base is eroded.

Initially, the Captain provides all her needs—for sex, financial security, and a varied audience to play to. But even before they met, in her youthful search for what he will eventually provide, she has always been something of an adventuress. Her story begins with scandal and a murder. Several weeks before her first wedding date, her wealthy fiancé was shot and killed in San Francisco by the husband of another woman. Marian was hurried to the mountains to escape the ensuing publicity. Shortly thereafter, she had a near-fatal accident with another young man, whom she had tempted to unwise risk taking. He fell to his death when their rope broke, while her own fall, which broke both her legs, was arrested by a tree. She was rescued by the party led by Captain Daniel Forrester, a widower twenty-five years older than she. While the men took turns carrying her down the steep trail leading out of the mountains, "she noticed that she suffered less when Captain Forrester carried her, and that he took all the most dangerous places on the trail himself." She is originally attracted to him by his vigorous masculinity ("I could feel his heart pump and his muscles strain"), his reliability ("I knew that if we fell, we'd go together; he would never drop me" [*LL*, 165–66]), and by his age—he's more seasoned than the two young men who had let her down. This attraction deepens as he becomes her "mainstay" through painful leg operations and through her recovery period. He steadies her as she begins to walk again. "When he asked me to marry him, he didn't have to ask twice. Do you wonder?" (*LL*, 166). She marries him, not out of gratitude, but out of a need for the dependable support and trustworthy care it seemed only a mature and vigorous man could give her.[16] Later, of course, he too will let her down.

Her youthful traumas appear to have created in Marian a basic insecurity. From the time of her first fall, she cannot, figuratively speaking, stand alone. Her need of male support even explains her choice of pleasures. She tells Niel that while she enjoys dancing, especially waltzing, "I don't skate . . . my ankles are weak" (*FF*, 77). After her husband's fall from a horse, when he is no longer sexually active, she pursues an affair with Frank Ellinger; after Ellinger "drops" her to marry, she grows distraught; after her husband's stroke, she falls to pieces; and after his death, "she was like a ship without ballast, driven hither and thither by every wind" (*LL*, 152).

Ellinger functions in this novel as more than willing stud or provocation for Marian's indiscretions. Besides being an L-shaped right angle, an *ell* is a measure of length. Through Ellinger's presence, the novel measures and attacks the double standards through which the behaviors of men and women are judged. For example, in spite of his womanizing, Frank, always forgiven, remains an acceptable—even a sought after—member of the "best" society. All elements of society condemn Marian's extramarital sexual activity. The jokes about Ellinger are hearty—for example, Nell Emerald's quip that she "had no respect for a man who would go driving with a prostitute in broad daylight" (*LL*, 50). The latter-day jokes about the Merry Widow's going "after the young ones" (*LL*, 153, 156) are hostile and derisive.

At some point in the novel, both these lovers are recognized as models of a sort. Before his mother's death, Ellinger is "a model son" (*LL*, 50); before the Captain's death, even Ivy Peters concedes that Marian "takes good care of him. . . . she never neglects him" (*LL*, 105). Ellinger and Marian Forrester are usually discreet about their sexual encounters, and both represent power: his is "wild muscular energy" and hers is that voice even Ivy Peters is afraid of (*LL*, 27). Both marry for money, though he lives in what was once Cherry Creek (*LL*, 52) and she lives in the "hole" that was once aptly Sweet Water (*LL*, 126). Such equals would clearly seem to deserve an equal public regard that is not forthcoming. When the narrator states laconically that "Morals were different in those days" (*LL*, 49), however, she teases the careful reader to observe that morals were not different at all; only social consequences were different for the different sexes. Possibly somebody would argue that the unequal (and therefore unfair) standards for judging the sexual behaviors of gentlemen and ladies "were different in those days" instead.

Once Captain Forrester exhausts his personal assets to protect the investors in a bank of which he is president, financial security is constantly on Marian's mind. She does not complain of her husband's grandiloquent gesture, but two years later she advises Niel to "hurry and become a successful man" because "Money is a very important thing. Realize that in the beginning; face it, and don't be ridiculous in the end, like so many of us" (*LL*, 114). She replaces the honorable Judge Pommeroy with the rascally Ivy Peters as her lawyer, knowing full well that Peters is crooked. She feels she must have money quickly to live at all, and acts under duress as Maid Marian naturally would—outside convention—to recover her power base and her effective image of herself. She relies on the only male at hand who offers her a financial opportunity: the detestable Ivy Peters of "unnatural erectness" (*LL,* 20).[17]

Ivy Peters is so unpleasant a presence in this novel that trying to ignore him is, for me, a temptation. But he, too, is necessary to complete the circuit that encloses Marian Forrester. Most obviously, he prevents a comfortable smugness about superior present-day understanding of sexual dynamics. Ivy presses us to acknowledge the indiscriminate force behind the fact of Marian's sexual needs. When she mates with such a clear inferior, she violates present-day expectations as clearly as she did her own time's. Ivy is detestable from every perspective the novel provides. Cather forces us, through him, to acknowledge that strong female sexuality cannot be refined to "proper" boundaries by any class system.

Worst of all, Ivy reminds us that some male heterosexual activity is actively misogynist. From his boyhood he clearly dislikes females in general and Marian in particular. He first describes her as a "stuck-up piece" (*LL,* 22), then injures her surrogate, the female woodpecker. In fact, he invades the cottonwood grove where boys are picniking partially because he "liked being ugly" (*LL,* 22) and partially in order to offend the Forresters. He obviously likes gratuitous cruelty and suggests the variety of his ways of being offensive when he observes, "There's more ways of killing dogs than choking them with butter" (*LL,* 22). He carries Niel's limp body in order "to get inside the Forrester's house and see what it was like, and this he had always wanted to do" (*LL,* 26). Once evicted by Marian, he resents "something final about her imperious courtesy,—high-and-mighty he called it" (*LL,* 27). Ivy is the sexual conquistador, seducing in order to dominate a female force he resents and hates. He finally accomplishes Marian's basest humiliation: he dishonors her by his behavior, destroys her reputation entirely, and then discards her to marry another. His presence in her life measures the anarchic intensity of her sexual need. He forces the reader to take seriously Niel's priggish question: "What did she do with all her exquisiteness when she was with a man like ... [him]? Where did she put it away? And having put it away, how could she recover herself, and give one—give even him—the sense of tempered steel, a blade that could fence with anyone and never break?" (*LL,* 100). Ivy dramatizes the malevolent contempt that can lurk behind the seduction of a "lady."

At this point, however, we must return to the Captain to ask what *his* gestures seem to mean. For if the Captain has offered to meet all his wife's most basic needs and desires, she has offered the same to him. They have made a clear and mutually advantageous pact. In fact, when he announces, "Maidy, I've come home a poor man" (*LL,* 88), he acknowledges that he has betrayed her financially at the same moment in which Niel became aware she had betrayed him sexually. Marian takes the Captain's announcement with a brave smile, and he accepts her infidelity in the same spirit. For if he is necessary to her self-definition, she is necessary to his: "Forrester? Was he the one with the beautiful wife?" an acquaintance asks (*LL,* 121).

The Captain explains his own life in terms of a simple desire and plan: "I planned to build a house that my friends could come to, with a wife like Mrs. Forrester to make it attractive to them" (*LL,* 53). He too once unwisely mated another—a first, invalid wife inadequate to his vision. The site for his dream house was an Indian encampment when he first found it, and he took possession of that land with less quivering of conscience than Marian displayed over Ivy's plans to profit from Indian lands (*LL,* 123).

From the beginning the Captain has put his power over other men before his wife. That he exercises such power is a fact both of them accept, as they both accept *her* power. Nevertheless, from the first years of their marriage, he has left her, whenever trouble blew up, with the words, "Maidy, I must go to the men" (*LL,* 49). That his first obligations are to men, not wives, neither questions. In the bank's debacle, even Judge Pommeroy concedes that the Captain has several legal options for saving some of his money—among them "certain securities, government bonds, which Captain Forrester could have turned over to you [Marian]" (*LL,* 89). He has chosen not to do so, since the gesture "would have been at the expense of the depositors" (*LL,* 89). When the moment finally comes in which he must choose *between* men who trust him and a wife who does also, he reflexively chooses to support his public role, that is, he chooses his men.

If Marian Forrester requires a man's support to play her role effectively, her husband equally requires a woman to prove his power. "It gratified him to have his wife wear jewels" (*LL,* 40), and he "bought them for his wife in acknowledgement of things he could not gracefully utter" (*LL,* 51). The two, in their primes, make a perfectly matched couple. They are as equally mated as Marian is in her next marriage to "a rich, cranky old Englishman ... [who] had been married twice before, once to a Brazilian woman" (*LL,* 173).

Neither of the Forresters blames the other for what they are or for what they become. Neither does Willa Cather seem to blame them in this novel. The blame here emits from Niel, whose absolutist idea of the way to aid an injured female bird is to kill her and put her out of her misery (*LL,* 25). The same impulses govern his reaction, years later, when he finds Marian resting in a hammock and thinks, "How light and alive she was! like a bird caught in a net." He reflects, "If only he could rescue her and carry her off like this,—off the earth of sad, inevitable periods, away from age, weariness, adverse fortune!" (*LL,* 110). Again we observe that the only way to get Marian that far away from adverse fortune is to kill her.

Niel's knowledge of life comes mainly from books, reading that makes him feel "he had been living a double life, with all its guilty enjoyments" (*LL,* 81). The life he discovers between such covers is that of "the great world that had plunged and glittered and sumptuously sinned" (*LL,* 81). Curiously, reading the classics makes him wish to be an architect—that is, one who contains or encloses the private secrets of such lives. In Niel's one moment of physically expressed affection, when he takes Marian in his arms, hammock and all, he manages to contain her, bed and all. But he can't hold her for long. Thereafter, he impulsively wishes he could take her out of the world. Niel serves Marian well only once—by "cutting her connection" with Ellinger (*LL*, 134). When he must disrobe her and put her in his own bed he *cuts off* her clothes, thus at least minimizing touch.

Niel's greatest sense of peace arrives when he restores the ordered vision of his childhood through restoring the order of the Forrester house (*LL*, 142): "He liked being alone with the old things that had seemed so beautiful to him in his childhood" (*LL*, 142). Thus, Niel "had the satisfaction of those who keep faith" (*LL*, 142). The faith he keeps is preadolescent, not a faith this novel seems to advocate for all; but at least Niel has the satisfaction of keeping it.

It is very important to remember that Niel does, in fact, keep a faith and find a satisfaction in this novel; so do Marian and Daniel Forrester. The subtlety of the novel rests in part on the recognition it forces of the number of faiths one might find to keep. Keeping faith does not eliminate heartache, of course, and the summarizing statement of Niel's fate conveys mostly frustration: "He has known pretty women and clever ones since then,—but never one like her, as she was in her best days. Her eyes, when they laughed for a moment into one's own, seemed to promise a wild delight that he has not found in life" (*LL*, 171). In one sense the consequence of Niel's keeping his strong child's absolutist faith is terrible: he is the only person in the novel who misses his dream.

Captain Forrester asserts, "what you think of and plan for day by day, in spite of yourself . . . you will get. You will get it more or less. That is unless you are one of the people who get nothing in this world. There are such people" (*LL*, 54). Every major character save one achieves his sharpest desire. Marian achieves a gracious life provided by a wealthy husband who loves her—twice. The Captain achieves the perfect home on the ideal site with the perfect hostess to entertain his friends. Constance Ogden achieves a marriage with Frank Ellinger, and Frank Ellinger achieves a wealthy wife. Ivy Peters achieves the Forrester estate and the money to transform and reshape it in his own image. Even Judge Pommeroy sees honor reborn through the heroism of his friend

Daniel Forrester. The only one who ends getting nothing he strongly values is Niel.

Finally, Niel's cold-eyed judgments convey that Marian embodies every nuance of "lostness." At some point she's confused, disoriented, misplaced, surrendered, endangered, unrecoverable, or damned. But after all her lostness and losses, before she dies, "she seemed to have everything. . . . It was remarkable, how she'd come up again" (*LL*, 173, 174). By contrast to Marian and the rest of them, Niel can only judge and peep at other's sins. Niel radically lacks the capacity to risk a dream. Rather, his romantic belief in "poetry and beauty and gladness without end" shatters when he realizes that "beautiful women, whose beauty meant more than it said" could also be women whose brilliancy sprang from "something coarse and concealed" (*LL*, 87). Never have the facts of life seemed more devastating.

While Captain Forrester's philosophy promises that consistently dreamed goals will usually be achieved, he does not promise that anybody can keep what she or he has once gotten. If everybody but Niel achieves his or her primary dream, most characters in turn lose what they have won. Thus the novel starts and ends pursuing the question of what happens to the perfect Forresters after their dreams disintegrate. What happens to Marian Forrester after her world breaks in two—in the telling, at least, in 1922 or thereabout?

Looked at in a widely Catherian context, Marian Forrester's story tells of a lady who fell dramatically, publicly, privately, terribly, and repeatedly, and still rose to dance again. It's a plot any author or reader might wish to appropriate. If the lady breaks both her legs, she survives it. Unlike Niel, Marian is a woman of the most questionable judgment. But she has indomitable spirit and can report that things have turned out well for her at the last. The statement reassures one that even after the worst social sins in society's eyes, things can end well.

Cather's novel acknowledges acceptingly a man and a woman who play traditional sexual roles, and fully exercise the potential power in each, to their mutual satisfaction. What Cather points out is that such exercise, such play, cannot last forever. Because it is natural, it is mutable. When the older mate falters and falls, the younger does also. But while both man and woman are in their primes, they enjoy a power that seems, in each, almost magic. And if magic, like human life, is transitory, its momentary effect is to produce the "promise [of] wild delight" (*LL,* 171). If Niel's long-lost lady must die, she still has conveyed "an excitement that came and went with summer" (*LL,* 31). To deny the value of that power is to deny the magic of summer itself. Marian Forrester faces winter with terror; yet she bravely stays by her husband's side, as long as he lives. He, in turn, fills their house during snows with hyacinths. A hundred years after this story takes place, what may seem most lost is the magical power of their particular kind of joy. What remains is our sense of their power.

CHAPTER FIVE

Dwelling in Possibility:
The Professor's House

*Youth and art! the two fairest things the sun
shines upon—and the two most unmateable!*

——————— WILLA CATHER, *The World and the Parish* ———————
from the *Courier,* January 28, 1899.

*Nobody yet ever knew anything thoroughly
through study, much less are they able to adequately impart that knowledge by a purely intellectual process. To know anything about any class
of people, one must ascertain how and what they
feel, and to do that one must not only observe but
feel himself.*

——————— WILLA CATHER, *The World and the Parish,* ———————
from the *Leader,* June 17, 1899.

*Whatever civilization has done, it has not been
able to expand by one inch the individual's capacity for enjoyment.*

——————— WILLA CATHER, *The World and the Parish,* ———————
from the *Courier,* August 24, 1901.

63

As *A Lost Lady* was ostensibly simple, *The Professor's House* is undeniably complex. In passing, some may suspect that the whole novel was constructed to display the exquisite Taormina jar of "Tom Outland's Story" (the last major composition Cather completed in 1922). But whether or not the first drafts of books one and three were initially imagined as pedestal—to set off, by contrast, the story of the consuming passions of youth—the completed novel encircles fierce enigmas and expanding ironies. All quicken, in embryo, inside that jar. The chief metaphor system maintains a tension between enclosures and expansions, compactings and boundlessness.

In *The Professor's House* Cather circles the hardest human questions, and ones acutely present for her as her life passed its half-century mark. For example, How do people summon the spirit to live? What makes some superior? What catastrophes can overwhelm them? How does one live with and without delight? How closely linked are delight and desire, and if very close, what then can a middle-aged person do about it? What are art, religion, possession, pleasure, justice, happiness? What ideas and objects have meaning and what are empty forms? What is more important than death and glory? Why does a human lay down habits of a lifetime and move out to perish? Wherein might one find some salvation? Are any satisfactory answers even rarely or miraculously possible? What is an appropriate style in which to ask these questions? The questions themselves—and the human facts that trigger them—were not new to Willa Cather; they had merely intensified in her emotional crisis time. In daring to ask them as a centrally integral part of her next fiction, however, Cather again accepts a Faustian challenge. As Zora Neale Hurston might have put it, she jumps for the sun.

To follow her action, even with our eyes alone and from a safe distance, we must understand something about her method. Cather hated finality, to base a somewhat final conclusion on all the signs. Like Emily Dickinson, she dwelt in possibility and devised a brilliantly effective manner of constructing fictions to keep possibilities open. By the time she came to St. Peter's story—which she designed to contain the keys to the kingdoms of art, religion, and personal fulfillment—her habitual mindset did not tolerate absolutes, no matter how much she sometimes wished they existed and she possessed them. Thus, she learned as a fictional method to create movement through tension, balance through suspense, choice through irresolution. She constructed a professor's house to include as many angles to every roomy question as possible. She does not draft these house plans assuming the desirability of perfect squares.

To grasp the psychological pressures under which Cather worked as she wrote this novel, we review the documented facts of her daily life. That such facts can be troublesome is a theme developed in all three books of this novel. In 1922–23 Cather was constantly in and out of hospitals and sanitoria, for influenza, appendicitis, neuritis, and such assorted illnesses. As *A Lost Lady* began to come out in magazine installments in the spring of 1923, she went to France to stay with the Hambourgs, and was attacked by neuritis in the right arm and shoulder. By September she took the desperate measure of spending a month in Aix-les-Bains for curative mineral baths. She returned to the States in November and began work (intensely? obsessively?) on *The Professor's House,* which she finished early. Between her return to the States and the time this novel was issued in 1925, she had not only suffered several more severe illnesses, but also had traveled for visits or vacations to the Poconos, to Nebraska (more than once), Michigan, Grand Manan, Arizona, New Mexico, Colorado, and Maine. These restless trips suggest drivenness, acute anxiety, or fearful flight. The psychic pressure cooker the facts imply, however, actually answers the reader's first question: simply, How did she write so much, of such extraordinary quality, in such a short time? Our common sense suspects that deep relaxation was out of the question; writing was a way of keeping her head above water. The speed of production, intensity of the fiction, and quality of the prose can all be traced to the same anxieties that simultaneously kept her moving; obviously, such anxieties are not unrelated to her health problems. Fiction gave her a world she could control. Her life crisis necessarily produced the questions she poses in *The Professor's House.* After its publication, "She called the novel a nasty, grim little tale and wondered why it seemed to be selling better than any of her books so far."[1]

The sequence of things written in 1922 is something we must again repeat at this point: first, *A Lost Lady,* so exhilarating to write because of the speed of its drafting and the method she developed for presenting a considered speculation on the world's most dangerous subject—female sexuality. That novel led, second, to a critical statement, "The Novel Démeublé," which announced Cather's esthetic criteria; especially, her essay stressed that what is felt but not glimpsed on the page can be said to be truly created. The doctrinal statement then led to further testing on an opposite subject—a captivating young male. "Tom Outland's Story" was therefore written in an even more obviously unfurnished style than *A Lost Lady* had been. A brightest and best young American, Outland seems initially as delightful and as universally adored in his thoroughly masculine way as Marian Forrester was in her feminine. One would be foolish, however, to assume in this increasingly troubled period that Cather would present Tom Outland any less ambivalently than she did Marian Forrester.

How do we look safely into this pressure cooker? Finding "broader contexts," we observe that *The Professor's House* ends one trio of novels that systematically utilized references to medieval culture;[2] it also abruptly begins a quartet of novels that centrally address questions about religion.[3] Both themes will reappear, ostensibly to culminate in *Shadows on the Rock.*[4] But wherever they go to or come from, linked questions bind what I consider four masterpieces—*The Professor's House, My Mortal Enemy, Death Comes for the Archbishop,* and *Shadows on the Rock*—each of which suggests different conclusions. Finding a starting point for the novel at hand, we begin where Cather began, with Tom Outland's story.

The text introduces Outland's story as "nothing very incriminating, nothing very remarkable; a story of youthful defeat, the sort of thing a boy is sensitive about—until he grows older" (*PH,* 176). The statement is singularly misleading and deceptive; Outland's story is every one of these things, as well as its opposite. It is incriminating about his treatment of Roddy, remarkable in its adventure and recorded accomplishment, a record of defeat in his attempts at preserving artifacts, and triumphant—unrepentantly ecstatic—at its conclusion. Its introductory sentence therefore reminds us that we cannot entirely or naively trust *any* sentence from the narrator who largely speaks from the professor's point of view. When the tale in Outland's first-person voice actually begins in book two, it is instantly electric and polished—a clearly stripped down rendition of a reality, dramatically different in style, as well as in every other respect, from St. Peter's enclosing sections. Though the narration is third person in books one and three, the syntax and style there is as complex as the Professor's mind—full of subordinate clauses and grammatical intricacies. Tom's story, conversely, like Tom, is straightforward, energetic, "primitive."

The style of "Tom Outland's Story" immediately captures attention because of its contrast to sections focusing on St. Peter. While his own work proceeds in a "shadowy crypt" (*PH*, 112), "St. Peter had noticed that in the stories Tom told the children there were no shadows" (*PH*, 123). The shadows in Godfrey's dialogue seem to emerge from that part of St. Peter which can say, "I like my closets" (*PH*, 34). Tom's tales, conversely, are devoid of hidden substances, subtle nuances, or shades. Cather achieves Tom's reportorial style—all events described as if seen in the open at high noon—by relying on a sentence structure that is predominantly subject-verb-object. She also limits the conveyed information to factual data (I did this and then I felt that). By repeatedly emphasizing the primary colors of red, yellow, and blue, she suggests essential and bedrock elements in the scene. Further, by using a clear plot or sequence of actions (this followed that in this time frame), she deliberately keeps most attention on externals. The fact is especially worth noting because in other contexts Cather sometimes denigrated fiction that relied on plot or action for its major impact.[5] By all these devices, she conveyed what Tom can and cannot do: He can explore new territory, act decisively, collect data systematically and dependably; he cannot interpret reliably what he finds. For analysis he needs to go to

Father Duchene or to Washington to find "an archaeologist who will interpret all that is obscure to us" (*PH, 222*). His need for a civilized, educated analyst who knows the past and who can comment with authority on Outland's story also explains Cather's creation of Professor St. Peter, the prizewinning historian. St. Peter's expertise includes his once having known a "primitive" as elemental as Tom: himself.

Tom's story begins in the middle of a conversation and stresses in the first sentence such words as "side-tracked," "late" and "accidents." More randomness in the second sentence—"It began with a poker game"—emphasizes the theme of chance that hereafter pervades the novel.[6] Tom's whole life seems shaped by random luck and accident. What he does with his chances, of course, defines him as a plucky waif ("a call boy in Pardee, New Mexico" [*PH,* 179] when we first glimpse him) who is a good deal of a southwestern adventurer himself. Tom's story includes strong male bonds, immense curiosity, an intense desire to know more, strong values, headstrong determination, pluck and luck, resilience, hard work, makeshift system, a respect for the future, and—as final reward—an exhilaration as satisfying as religious emotion. In the story's beginning, middle, and end, however, life is a gamble, a kind of poker game, in which luck is blind, justice a fiction, and the dirtiest and least deserving can take the jackpot, or good family men can be struck down and wiped out.

Action begins in the Ruby Light Saloon, a disreputable male gathering place off a back alley, where the game is in full swing and the stakes are high. The lurid name calls attention to all the charged associations with red lights, and must be linked with the phallic red tower that dominates the Cliff City:

> It was beautifully proportioned, that tower, swelling out to a larger girth a little above the base, then growing slender again. There was something symmetrical and powerful about the swell of the masonry. The tower was the fine thing that held all the jumble of houses together and made them mean something. It was red in colour, even on that grey day. In sunlight it was the colour of winter oak-

leaves. A fringe of cedars grew along the edge of the cavern, like a garden. They were the only living things. Such silence and stillness and repose—immortal repose. That village sat looking down into the canyon with the calmness of eternity.   (*PH*, 201)

The red tower's centrality to Tom's sense of life and eternity cannot be clearer in this text: "It all hung together, seemed to have a kind of composition: pale little houses of stone nestling close to one another, perched on top of each other, with flat roofs, narrow windows, straight walls, and in the middle of the group, a round tower" (*PH*, 201). It is a young man's vision of a new or old world. Cather does, it seems to me, deftly capture here the likely perceptions of a fresh, unanalytic, but sensitive young male.

It goes without saying, however, that all such perceptions are measured eventually against the adumbrations of the aging professor. St. Peter's aging male vision, by contrast, insists that great theologians and artists get their "splendid effects by excision. They reset the stage with more space and mystery, throwing all the light upon a few sins of great dramatic value" (*PH*, 69). The contrast of the two points of view reminds us that Cather had articulated her belief as early as 1899 that youth and art were "the two fairest things the sun shines upon—and the two most unmateable!"

Before, during, and after his defining adventure, Tom remains always conscious of the Blue Mesa's presence. In light of his constant awareness, it is interesting that he anatomizes the landscape of the mesa when he compares it to "the profile of a big beast lying down" (*PH*, 191). As with similar landscape analogies in *The Song of the Lark*, the anatomy of this landscape is female.[7] Such analogies grow clearer when we read that "the south flank ... looked accessible by way of the deep canyon that split the bulk in two, from the top rim to the river, then wound back into the solid cube ... like a mouse track winding into a big cheese. This canyon didn't break the solid outline of the mesa, and you had to be close to see that it was there at all" (*PH*, 191–92). Having discovered the possibility of penetrating the mesa by entering the deep canyon at the south end, however, Outland and Blake correctly infer that there must as well have been a path into the interior at the north end, along the face of the cliff. Penetration becomes an obsession for both. To intensify their desire, the wild cows they will eventually shoot for fresh meat appear like Sirens beckoning from the forbidden side of the river. The cattle emerge to drink from "that deep canyon that opens on the water level" at "the flanks around which the river curved" (*PH,* 190–191). More and more, the mesa holds the men's attention: "the closer we got to it, the more tantalizing it was" (*PH,* 191). Tom adds, "No wonder the thing bothered us and tempted us; it was always before us, and was always changing" (*PH,* 193). Tempted, teased, and tantalized, Tom eventually "got my nerve up, and I didn't want to put off making a try at it" (*PH,* 199). He swam the dividing stream and entered the forbidden canyon. For reward, he finds "a little city of stone, asleep ... still as sculpture" that was "set in a great cavern in the face of the cliff," and given "a kind of composition" by its organizing, central red tower (*PH,* 201). At the end, having ruthlessly expelled the rival male with whom he has had to share these treasures, Tom is left the Cliff City's—indeed, the whole beastly mesa's—sole owner: "Something had happened in me that made it possible for me to co-ordinate and simplify, and that process, going on in my mind, brought with it great happiness. It was possession" (*PH,* 250–51).

Tom equates the summer in which he possessed and was possessed by this object of his desire, the Blue Mesa, as the high point of his life. Alone with his beloved, he knows pure joy: "I had my happiness unalloyed. . . . It was my high tide. . . . I wakened with the feeling that I had found everything, instead of having lost everything. Nothing tired me. . . . I seemed to get the solar energy in some direct way. . . . There are times when one's vitality is too high to be clouded, too elastic to stay down" (*PH,* 251–52). Though Tom believes "Anyone who requites faith and friendship as I did, will have to pay for it," he does not seem to begrudge his doom: "You must take my word for it. Troubles enough came afterward, but there was that summer, high and blue, a life in itself" (*PH,* 253). At the beginning, Tom has described Rodney as one not "trained by success to a sort of systematic selfishness"

(*PH*, 185). When he himself is trained by the successful possession of the mesa, he revels in his systematic selfishness, and equates expanding into it with "religious emotion" (*PH*, 251). Indeed, an age-old young male's story.

Loving the mesa has taught Tom more than his own elevation. He has learned what identifies superior people. They "lived for something more than food and shelter" and "developed considerably the arts of peace." They "had an appreciation of comfort" and "unquestionably a distinct feeling for design." They obviously had great pride, for the "workmanship on both the wood and stone of the dwellings is good" (*PH*, 219). The mesa's occupants seem to have been "a provident, rather thoughtful people, who made their livelihood secure by raising crops and fowl," who developed a properly varied diet, "developed physically and improved in the primitive arts," and continued "working out their destiny, making their mesa more and more worthy to be a home for man, purifying life by religious ceremonies and observances" (*PH*, 220). The admiring descriptions do not acknowledge Mother Eve, the Mesa's screaming mummy whose preserved scream suggests domestic tragedy even in Eden. Conceding that omission, Tom's idealized Cliff Dwellers provide a measure for judging the others he meets at college, in Hamilton,[8] and in the Professor's house.

In several significant ways, Professor Napoleon Godfrey St. Peter in his depleted middle age is unlike Tom Outland as well as the mesa's superior people. Unlike Outland, who can move mountains (or at least the part of a mountain that has obliterated a trail down the face of the Blue Mesa), the Professor admits his "moving was over and done." While Tom's past summer is ecstatic, St. Peter's present summer is "low in energy" (*PH*, 269). While Tom loves his work on the mesa, St. Peter views his teaching with fatigue and distaste. While Tom has reveled in delight, St. Peter must learn to live without it, especially since he has endured "the saddest thing in the world . . . falling out of love—if once one has ever fallen in" (*PH*, 275).

All our principle players here—Tom, Godfrey, and the superior people—have "a distinct feeling for design" (*PH*, 219).[9] But

Godfrey, unlike the Cliff Dwellers, has a distinctly qualified "appreciation of comfort." He refuses to give up the "dusty air and brutal light of the empty rooms" (*PH,* 14) and insistently prefers his dark, badly ventilated, and badly lighted attic (in which he must work with a kerosene lamp or a hanging electric bulb) to more comfortable and available quarters.[10] Though he succumbs to temptation and accepts Louie's luxurious hotel suite in Chicago, he acknowledges the mistake. He seems to conclude that loving comfort imperils one, and that he might grow vulnerable as a Cliff Dweller for accepting it. (Of course, Godfrey actually grows vulnerable anyway and is nearly exterminated because he does *not* love comfort enough to replace his dangerous gas stove.) While the Cliff Dwellers "made their livelihood secure by raising crops and fowl" (*PH,* 220), St. Peter insistently prefers to create a nonproductive French garden (to the scandal of his German landlord). While Cliff Dwellers are commended for good workmanship, St. Peter, a deft hand with tools, has chosen not to fix things that "had made him wince many times a day for twenty-odd years" (*PH,* 11). While Cliff Dwellers were thought to have lived "caring respectfully for their dead, protecting the children, doubtless entertaining some feelings of affection and sentiment for this stronghold where they were at once so safe and so comfortable" (*PH,* 220), Godfrey's affections are for that attic where he is neither safe nor comfortable. Further, he is rather flippant about the landlord's dead wife, as we shall see, and as for children, "When a man had lovely children in his house, fragrant and happy, . . . why couldn't he keep them? Was there no way but Medea's, he wondered?" (*PH,* 126).

If there is a primary difference between St. Peter and the superior people Father Duchene imagined living in Cliff City, however, it becomes their hypothetical "working out their destiny, making their mesa more and more worthy to be a home for man, purifying life by religious ceremonies and observances" (*PH,* 220). Half St. Peter's problem as this novel begins is that he has recently lost his connection with either past or future,[11] hence does not wish to engage in the active choices that work out a destiny. He specifically contrasts himself with his wife, Lillian, herself "so occupied with the future, you adapt yourself so readily" (*PH*, 94). Lillian automatically makes an assumption that the professor does not: "One must go on living, Godfrey" (*PH*, 94). But Godfrey now feels cut off as well from the past: "I've put a great deal behind me, where I can't go back to it again—and I don't really wish to go back. The way would be too long and too fatiguing" (*PH*, 163). Thus, his life threatens to cease as abruptly as the Cliff Dwellers'.

The other half of St. Peter's problem, however, is that he is incapable of energizing the present moment by "purifying life with religious ceremonies." In fact, St. Peter is known in his lectures for saying "slighting things about the Church," according to devoutly Catholic Augusta (*PH*, 99). Scott McGregor remarks, "How you get by the Methodists is still a mystery to me" (*PH*, 70). Throughout his productive years, we are told, St. Peter avoided religious ceremonies by working and writing most intensely on Sundays (*PH*, 24). In the novel's present we see him spoiling the Sabbath through deliberate mischief, the day after the first family dinner in the newly completed house. It is one of the novel's subtlest sequences.

Sunday begins as St. Peter wishes "he could be transported on his mattress from the new house to the old" (*PH*, 46). He must respect family habit, however, and breakfast with his wife: "There was no way out; they would meet at compt" (*PH*, 46). The last phrase suggests St. Peter's apprehensions about the reckonings built into his marital Sunday breakfast games. He obviously fears his wife's skillfully made points. What follows is a conversation that could serve as model for husbandly evasiveness. St. Peter parries Lillian's every thrust about his previous night's inhospitable behavior and refuses to acknowledge any shade of personal wrongdoing in his last evening's "disapproving silence" (*PH*, 46). He remains ostentatiously good-humored, especially about personal silence and reserve—a quality he strongly praises and regrets that his son-in-law Louie Marsellus lacks. He thinks privately as the first scene ends, however, that his wife could not be said to have a mind, but only a "richly endowed nature" (*PH*, 50). Making his escape from her as soon as possible, he veers from the narrow path toward his working study, in order to seek out his landlord Appelhoff.

The conversation between Appelhoff and St. Peter is as permeated with subtle aggressions and witty hostilities as was his breakfast with Lillian. It is especially interesting for the light it sheds on St. Peter's fabled good manners. St. Peter seeks out his landlord on Sunday to discuss business—in itself, of course, a gesture of questionable courtesy. The purpose of this visit is to arrange to continue renting the old house for another year, a wasteful proposal Godfrey knows will irritate Appelhoff. At first, St. Peter addresses Appelhoff directly as *Fred*. He then asks about Appelhoff's fruitful garden, since gardens are clearly a long-standing bone of contention between them: Appelhoff replies slyly, "I don't like dem trees what don't bear not'ing" (*PH*, 51). Godfrey then asks intrusively—especially for one who has within the hour advocated keeping feelings private—whether his landlord misses his dead wife. In this question St. Peter consciously invades another's privacy, flippantly fails to honor the dead, and then deliberately patronizes Appelhoff by Anglicizing (and thus mispronouncing) Appelhoff's name—twice: "Pretty lonesome without her, Applehoff?" (*PH*, 52). And again, "We all come to it, Applehoff. That's one thing I'm renting your house for, to have room to think. Good morning" (*PH*, 52).

Having treated Lillian evasively and Appelhoff overfamiliarly, St. Peter next spots a colleague and third Sabbath victim. Horace Langtry, Godfrey's "professional rival and enemy" (*PH*, 52), is at the moment taking a Sunday stroll. Though in "twenty years the two men had scarcely had speech with each other beyond a stiff 'good morning'" (*PH*, 53), on this troublemaking Sabbath Godfrey outflanks, overtakes, and pounces on the luckless "Lily." Among other trials, St. Peter tempts Langtry to behave like a faculty cliché. He asks, "Don't you notice a great difference in the student body as a whole, in the new crop that comes along every year now—how different they are . . . in the all-embracing respect of quality!" (53–54).[12] In fact, Godfrey's attempts to disturb Langtry work so devilishly well that Langtry escapes him only at the sound of church bells—the medieval intervention device that could save the imperiled from the Devil. At this point we recall St. Peter's students call him Mephistopheles (*PH*, 13), and that he leaves behind him a smell of smoke (*PH*, 17). In reviewing *Faust* before the turn of the century, Cather had defined Mephistopheles as "the spirit that denies. A character as strange as Hamlet and as little understood, always shrouded in mystery and doubt." [13]

Most readers know what has triggered the professor's doubt: his house, the space in which Godfrey St. Peter lives or doesn't live, is now cold, empty, lifeless, and dead. All the living being done here anymore takes place in the "dark den" (*PH*, 16) of the third-floor attic study the Professor still works in; that is, what life he has left occurs in his upper story, in his head. The book is about the Professor's feeling in his head that the rest of his life is like his cold, dead, empty house. Further, even when he was feeling alive, his house, as his story, saw the intrusion of the mysterious stranger Tom Outland, who became his student: "the design is the story and the story is the design."

How Professor St. Peter has reached the sad plight of the novel's opening sentence—"The moving was over and done"—is also clear: at age fifty-two he has finished his ambitious life project—a "dazzling . . . beautiful . . . utterly impossible thing" (*PH*, 25); he has won a prize that made him rich and famous; he has lost interest in the superficial concerns of his family; his teaching career he thinks of in terms of "lost causes" (*PH*, 143); and thus he has nothing left to work for, therefore to live for. Cather summarizes that everything around him "seemd insupportable, as the boat on which he is imprisoned seems to a sea-sick man" (*PH*, 150). Since he's too young to die and too smart to stop prying at himself, he must now face these next questions, which are important to extrapolate carefully: Why do I feel so numb? Should I slog on? If so, how? St. Peter's existence is a kind of living death because he is emotionally comatose. Because so many readers identify with the charming Professor, they do not always acknowledge the intense anguish of his predicament.

Feeling a "diminution of ardour" (*PH*, 13) because his "heart" is dead, St. Peter is freed from any philosophical restraints. In a head more like a statue's than a man's (*PH,* 13) he coldly considers his intellectual options. We are told that in his swimming visor he looks "like the heads of the warriors on the Parthenon frieze" (*PH,* 71); the analogy should convey that he is both an aggressive warrior (his secret first name is Napoleon) and also frozen. In this state he decides that he owes nothing to anybody, including himself (*PH,* 281). He has no loyalties left toward which he feels an obligation. In Tom's chance-struck universe, randomness produces unexpected opportunity; in St. Peter's frozen wastes, randomness prevents control and produces defeat. Even confronting Langtry he concludes, "What was the use of keeping up the feud? . . . Couldn't Langtry see it was a draw, that they had both been beaten?" (*PH,* 57).

Both the Professor and his creator would prefer to be back in preadolescent youth. In fact, in St. Peter's condition, only youth itself can "command" or "kindle" him: "he loved youth—he was weak to it" (*PH,* 28). Moreover, he has lost his youth only recently, a phenomenon that distresses his wife: "You are not old enough for the pose you take. . . . Two years ago you were an impetuous young man. Now you save yourself in everything" (*PH,* 162). Engaged in such denials, however, both character and creator face the facts unblinkingly and critically. Mrs. St. Peter assures her husband, "You grow better-looking and more intolerant all the time" (*PH,* 35). Cather states, "St. Peter was very critical" (*PH,* 37). In fact, we observe St. Peter criticizing every character in the novel, including himself. Both he and Cather judge as harshly as the facts require.

The upshot is that Cather permits her Godfrey to be as wicked as he pleases. She may share with this protagonist his age, his background, and his situation, but she does not suggest, because they are similar, that he should therefore be assumed virtuous. She allows him, rather, to be free—free to ask the questions the two of them are facing simultaneously, in order to discover where they lead. He is God-free, meaning both free *as* God and free *of* God. His surname, St. Peter, suggests *both* possessing the keys to the kingdom of heaven and also possessing the power to judge, reject, exclude, and damn. The Professor must ask as the novel proceeds whether any rock exists on which one might eventually imagine erecting some systematic and sustaining faith. He has no such firm ground under him as the novel begins. It is important to remember throughout that the Professor is not only a historian—a definer and shaper of history—but also a destroyer. His wife remarks, "Your disapproving silence can kill the life of any company" (*PH*, 46). As we have seen, he rhetorically entertains the possibility of destroying his children as Medea did. And he certainly attempts to destroy the peace of mind of Appelhoff and Langtry, occasionally even Augusta, whom he loves to tease. He's as arbitrary as God *or* Devil.

Destructiveness, however, can be turned on its head or inside out as easily as any other characteristic. It goes hand in hand, at least, with the most basic artistic principles that St. Peter espouses throughout this novel and Cather asserts in other works as well. The most famous sentence on the subject is part of St. Peter's overheard lecture: "Art and religion (they are the same thing, in the end, of course) have given man the only happiness he has ever had." He adds, "The Christian theologians went over the books of the Law, like great artists, getting splendid effects by excision." He concludes, "With the theologians came the cathedral-builders; the sculptors and glass-workers and painters. They might, without sacrilege, have changed the prayer a little and said, *Thy will be done in art, as it is in heaven*" (*PH*, 69).

St. Peter is consistent in all his preferences. He strongly objects to Louie's "too fluent" support, as well as to his "florid style" (*PH*, 47, 48). He breezily associates restrained expressions of pleasure with "the Age of Chivalry" and adds, "It's a nice idea, reserve about one's deepest feelings: keeps them fresh" (*PH*, 48). Acknowledging that St. Peter's motives are mixed here—he advocates restrained expressions of pleasure at a point when he has no pleasure to express—his views on art, style, and manners express the same conviction. St. Peter hates redundance and excess. All excellence depends for him on scale. Thus, he wields a harsh yardstick when he concludes that both his daughter (*PH*, 58) and her jewels are "out of scale" (*PH*, 76). The same standard condemns unnecessary ugliness (*PH*, 142) and unnecessary discomfort (*PH*, 144). Such qualities, by being unnecessary, are in excess. One commandment supersedes all others here: "Too much is certainly worse than too little—of anything" (*PH*, 154). As early as 1920, Cather had reduced these principles to three verbs: simplify, condense, sacrifice.[14]

The presence of order that gives meaning is the common ingredient art and religion share, which makes them seem the same thing to St. Peter. In this novel, order, meaning, composition, arrangement all imply an arranger's or artist's hand, and create together the pleasure that can be as intense as religious emotion. Both art and religion, however, are equated with the artificial and the unnatural. After St. Peter considers the effects of autumn flowers displayed profusely in his new parlor, "It struck him that the seasons sometimes gain by being brought into the house, just as they gain by being brought into painting, and into poetry. The hand, fastidious and bold, which selected and placed—it was that which made the difference. In Nature there is no selection" (*PH*, 75). No wonder St. Peter can say the cathedral builders might have prayed without sacrilege, *Thy will be done in art, as it is in Heaven* (*PH*, 69).

Finally, the critical, analytic, distant Godfrey St. Peter considers his options in this novel, in light of his artistic taste, his aesthetic judgments, and his psychic possibilities. The novel furnishes good and bad role models, but each group breaks down into opposites, as each person comes to embody oppositions. His models come to seem as complex as he is. And St. Peter himself, as remarkable a mix as his "terrible women," is immensely interesting partially *because* he is so appealing and also so appalling.

The bad life models before him seem to include his family and colleagues, though at least one of the bad guys—his son-in-law Louie Marsellus—certainly turns into a good guy, "magnanimous and magnificent" (*PH*, 170). Defenders of his wife Lillian have also appeared.[15] But the two positive models who most obviously function as polar opposites in this novel are Tom Outland and the spinster seamstress Augusta. Each of these, in turn, seems as human a mix of the positive and the negative as their readers and scrutinizers always do.

The harder of the two to decipher is Tom Outland, for he, though the still-glowing symbol of youth for the Professor, is already dead when the novel begins. Outland, a "tramp boy" (*PH*, 257), lives in the novel's present only as a memory; and nobody in Hamilton, including the Professor, is necessarily a reliable or objective judge of this character. For McGregor, Tom is "a glittering idea" (*PH*, 111); for Godfrey, Tom is associated with "some fugitive idea" (*PH*, 132). Both make him into an abstraction. But if we assume in this novel that "the design is the story,"[16] then we must say that Outland becomes the great disrupter of this house of fiction. His story, inserted as book two, blasts the unities. His adventures on the Blue Mesa also provide the fresh breeze that blows through the Professor's stifling house.[17] He provides the *idea* of heroic action, the blue lake of the mind, that St. Peter must have to live in his badly ventilated attic. Outland is the mysterious stranger who once appeared bearing lavish gifts and who then estranged the St. Peter daughters, as well as the parents, from each other. The mysterious strangers of literature, however, are as often destroyers as saviors, and usually both.

Considered positively, Tom is the student who possessed the "one remarkable mind" (*PH*, 62) St. Peter remembers teaching. For the Professor he embodies promise, dedication, energy, and commitment to an idea—the qualities St. Peter summarizes in the word *desire*. He has been the one student whose achievement Godfrey feels he foretold (*PH*, 29). Tom not only discovers and "possesses" the past, frozen eternally in its living death within the ruins of the Cliff City. He also discovers the Outland vacuum and a gas that affects the course of aviation and the wars of the future. For his life he "got nothing ... but death and glory" (*PH*, 41), which Godfrey comes to envy, though he warns his daughter that envy destroys (*PH*, 84). For Godfrey, Tom is youth, joy, adventure, achievement, and a possessor of the kind of power St. Peter admires most: that which follows the intense demand of the most concentrated desire.

Considered negatively, Tom would have to say with Mark Antony, *"My fortunes have corrupted honest men"* (*PH*, 150). His discoveries trigger greed in all who look on them. The gas that he developed in Crane's laboratories figuratively poisons all the people who knew him. Only such men as Louie Marsellus, who never met Tom, escape poisoning to use constructively the ideas Tom left behind. Tom Outland is an appropriate hero for a pre-adolescent mind that has not yet accepted the need for compromise and the recognition of complex ambiguity required for living sensitively with others. Yet Tom inspires preadolescent dreams not only in Kitty, as a child, but also in her father, who is past fifty (*PH,* 131). Tom's purity of vision, his insistence on his own uncontaminated ideas, damn others who would "convert his very bones into a personal asset" (*PH,* 47). Of course he himself converts the very bones left on the Blue Mesa into a personal asset, as Roddy Blake resentfully observes before he disappears. St. Peter accurately suspects that Outland was lucky to die before he was required to submit to the inevitably less-than-ideal requirements of marriage, family, and career. St. Peter is also correct in surmising that the pure joy Tom experiences when alone in Cliff City could never survive a life lived among others, whose diverse needs always impinge on a private vision and alter a private exaltation.

In reporting the exhilarating solitude at the top of the Blue Mesa, Tom justifies St. Peter's weakness—a fear of intimacy. Inevitably, Godfrey begins to emerge as a charming performer who is unable to engage intimately with others, at least in the novel's present. He is unwilling to confront himself intimately, as well. He admits he has ceased to be his wife's lover (*PH,* 160), and is asked why he never has time to talk to her (*PH,* 48). His daughter is afraid of his distancing sarcasm (*PH,* 59), and he himself fears family dinners (*PH,* 106). Even when Tom Outland first appeared, we are told, "St. Peter held the boy at arm's length" (*PH,* 121). As Lillian observes, "this reserve—it becomes in itself ostentatious, a vain-glorious vanity." To which thrust St. Peter flippantly replies, "Oh, my dear, all is vanity!" (*PH,* 49). The plot, viewed from this angle, becomes Godfrey's steady approach to that point of intimate confrontation at which he must meet himself "at compt" (*PH,* 46). Throughout the novel, we have seen him in a steady series of unsuccessful maneuvers to evade intimate contact. In spite of his best efforts, however, he faces his wife, his family, each of his daughters and sons-in-law, his colleagues, and even his servant Augusta. Finally, in the novel's intensest intimacy, he must confront himself.

In the moment toward which the whole fiction moves, Godfrey's empty forms offer no succor. His domestic tragedy, unlike that which the Mesa's Mother Eve once endured, is a matter of distanced silences, not screams. His horror is not a violent and lethal assault but an impenetrable isolation. Godfrey's hard female forms are not petrified in agony for eternity; they are headless, gutless, and comfortless. They certainly offer no protection against the emptiness of his third-floor study. In that elevation, he must face himself and his core responses or basic reflexes and decide whether he cares to live or die.

Thus he comes, as his readers must also, to Augusta, whose name suggests the "Roman" who defined an Augustan age. That epoch symbolizes peace (the Pax Romana), practical improvements (roads and architecture), and the Augustan literature known for its restraint. Augusta is Outland's opposite, a "remedial influence" (*PH*, 280).

The descriptive phrases for Augusta are specific and compelling. She is "the sewing-woman, niece of [Godfrey's] landlord, a reliable, methodical spinster, a German Catholic and very devout" (*PH*, 16). Her sense of humor notwithstanding,[18] she walks with a "heavy, deliberate tread" (*PH*, 19) and essentially reduces to "the bloomless side of life that he had always run away from" (*PH*, 280). She can serve as a guide for the professor only when he concedes that henceforth, he must live "without delight." But she is "seasoned and sound and . . . for all her matter-of-factness and hard-handedness, kind and loyal" (*PH*, 281). Though Augusta can invest her resources foolishly and lose her worldly goods as rapidly as any other inexperienced gambler, she can also work beside the professor considerately, and with pleasure. She tolerates his smoke.

Previously, Augusta's steady devotion to recurring, humdrum duties has hardly attracted a man like St. Peter, a "tireless swimmer" who looks most attractive when stripped (*PH*, 12), while

Augusta's business is to manufacture clothes. Yet she is St. Peter's most effective instructor within this novel. While they have shared forms, practical Augusta has used them while St. Peter has abstracted them (*PH*, 278). Most crucially, Augusta has presence of mind and a strong arm (*PH*, 278). Those traits, not Tom Outland's brilliance, save a life on the brink of the grave, and sustain life steadily through the years. In the crucial moment of St. Peter's imminent asphyxiation, he remembers later, the thought of Augusta showed him what he should do. He lunges up, and falls with a thud. But the steadfast Augusta is at hand, hears his crash, and rescues him. Later, her presence brings him loneliness, that is, restores feeling and a desire for connection (*PH*, 279).

Tom Outland is the romantic hero who finds and conquers a world, and dies young while innocent of adult sins and riding on glory. It's a story line Willa Cather admired in her earliest critical statements. But Godfrey St. Peter's task in this novel is to shape a plausible life in his waning years. Thus, though it nearly kills Godfrey to do so, he must sacrifice the youthful image Tom represents, and let it die. Godfrey, *because* he is free as God, must relinquish his spiritual son to make further life possible—to stay in the game of living. The heartbreaking act requires what Cather called "letting go with the heart."[19] To cut his losses and stay in the game, St. Peter must allow that primitive youth he once was to die within him if he is to reattach his heart to some possibility in the present.

Augusta models for St. Peter the life that is possible in tireder years. She is "like the taste of bitter herbs" (*PH*, 280). But to feel that life can go on, at this point, St. Peter must join "a world full of Augustas, with whom one was outward bound" (*PH*, 281). The change is not abrupt, for Augusta's patterns have interpenetrated St. Peter's manuscripts for years (*PH*, 22). She is the one he wants to watch beside him in the dark night of his soul that begins at midnight in the final chapter. Unlike Outland, who for one brilliant summer finds a joy as intense as religious emotion, Augusta habitually worships every day. She thus retains a capacity St. Peter envies, to play "a principal in a gorgeous drama with God" (*PH*, 68). Tom finds a "miracle" in the Mesa's preserved artifacts (*PH*,

244). Augusta's life contains a daily "chance at miracles and great temptations and revelations" (*PH,* 68). When he finally accepts these possibilities—including the possibility of everyday miracle—St. Peter feels real again, as if his feet were on firm ground.

The coincidence by which Augusta arrives like saving church bells in the moment of her employer's greatest peril is as much a miracle as Tom Outland's chance discovery of Cliff City. Cather acknowledges the miracles possible in youth, but also in age. Life was richest, St. Peter has taught his dull students, when "The king and the beggar had the same chance at miracles and great temptations and revelations" (*PH,* 68). For "that's what makes men happy, believing in the mystery and importance of their own little individual lives" (*PH,* 68). In this "grim little tale" of middle-aged letting go with the heart, Cather still balances her miracles to affirm that each type and age-group has a lucky chance to find or experience them. And one's daily life need not be purified by religious ceremonies in order to be so miraculously saved. If overintellectual and disengaged, sometimes malicious and always critical, emotionally, physically, and professionally depleted Napoleon Godfrey St. Peter can be saved and live on, so can she. Miracles fall on the just and the unjust, the devout and the unbelievers alike.

Cather does not end any novel (even the one she will write next) without some hope. This one, which begins in startling stasis, is no exception. Its last sentence keeps the hopeful possibilities open, even in light of the fierce enigmas that the novel has acknowledged. "He thought he knew where he was, and that he could face with fortitude the *Berengaria* and the future."

The *Berengaria* is the ship, now inward bound toward port, that will return St. Peter's unwanted family to him. It is also the name of the actual ship in which Cather sailed home from Cherbourg in October of 1923.[20] But the italicized name, obviously, is the key to the final sentence of *The Professor's House.* A *berengarian* is a follower of Berenger of Tours, a heretic who denied transubstantiation—that is, who rejected the doctrine that, in the communion sacrament, commonplace substances become divine. The *Berengaria* returns to St. Peter those unbelieving family members who are immersed in worldly pleasures—including the pleasure of anticipating new life and birth. St. Peter realizes that he can now face those positive hopes and negative facts, can face the future, because he has found his intimate reality, and Augusta represents it. He has learned that bitter herbs can save life. Thus, at his request, Augusta watches with St. Peter through the chill midnight hour, announced by church bells, that they share in the professor's house.

CHAPTER SIX

Triple Complexities and Tour de Force Symmetry: *My Mortal Enemy*

It is now several years since this well-known actress [Clara Morris] began to contribute short stories to periodicals. In so far as I can see, Miss Morris plays her new role much as she did all her old ones, with a sort of ferocious violence which at once repels and fascinates. She is as crude in her literary methods as in her dramatic ones, and as effective. These stories of hers [A Silent Singer] have little beauty of form, but they have force; no symmetry, but considerable power. Mentally, the woman was always strong. She had a message, and a message which could only be spoken in her own way. When she went to New York, a frail slip of a girl, with big burning eyes and a great talent over which she had no power of control, Augustin Daly, who always trained where he could, let this woman alone. He realized that the raw, fierce genius of her would win its own way, and that she must speak her message through the violent, erratic, unartistic medium that was natural to her. In her stories one recognizes the same power, the same lack of restraint, the same strange combination of shrewd humor and violence, above all one recognizes that old tendency of hers for probing the depths of physical and mental an-

85

guish. She is never content to suggest, she must say it all. . . . It is a sort of ungloved method of attack, a tendency to lay bare the horrible and painful which amounts almost to a mania. The effectiveness with which Miss Morris does all this is evidence of her sincerity, but it is an unfortunate and a misdirected power. To use a pretty phrase of Stevenson's, it "sins against the modesty of life." There are certain extremes of all emotions over which it is well to draw a veil, certain paroxysms of pain, of which it is not best to speak. But Miss Morris never was known to let any detail of agony escape her. Hers was a realism which knew not suggestion. . . . The artist proper cultivates method to save himself, he makes his brain work, and learns to cherish and guard his emotional force. Miss Morris either could not, or would not, learn this; she burned the wick; and she burned it out quickly. She was a physical wreck when she should have been in her prime. Her violence wore her out, like the mill that grinds itself to pieces. Now, in an exhausted body, the old fierce soul of other days is still rampant, and she is seeking to let it out by a new channel.

———— WILLA CATHER, *The World and the Parish* ————
from the Leader, July 15, 1899.

When we move from *The Professor's House* (1925) to the abode of *My Mortal Enemy* (1926), we exchange a middle-aged male intellectual protagonist who feels emotionally dead for a middle-aged female protagonist whose volcanic emotions are likely to erupt even when she is dying. We also move from a protagonist whose life obviously resembles Cather's to a subject whose origins are much murkier. James Woodress reminds us that "the prototype for Myra Henshawe in this work has never been identified. Cather wrote in 1940 that she had known Myra's real-life model very well, and the portrait drawn in the story was much as she remembered her. Many of the real Myra's friends and relatives wrote, she said, to tell her they had recognized her immediately. The story, Cather added, was not written until fifteen years after this woman's death. E. K. Brown goes a little farther in identifying Myra as a woman, 'older by a full generation, whom Willa Cather had known well through connections in Lincoln,' but he was unable to name her."[1] One plausible explanation fitting these skimpy facts is that Myra Henshawe is modeled on the actress and author Clara Morris, whom Cather watched as a professional stage presence during her Lincoln days and later came to "know" as a writer of stories. Cather certainly felt she knew Morris well enough to publish an extraordinarily personal character sketch in the *Leader* in 1899. The facts in the epigraph passage uncannily fit the character of, Myra Henshawe. Even such phrases in the column as "a sort of ungloved method of attack" prefigure Myra's assertion that the Henshawes married "without gloves, so to speak."[2] Both Myra Henshawe and Clara Morris came to New York as girls with burning eyes and uncontrolled talents, were known for their shrewd humor and violent passions, and burned themselves out. As Elizabeth Shepley Sergeant said prophetically, "Often she thought about her heroines for years before they appeared in a book."[3]

It is also possible that Myra descends from such literary ancestresses as Chopin's Edna Pontellier and Flaubert's Emma Bovary, whom Cather discussed in print only a week before describing Clara Morris.[4] For example,

> Edna Pontellier and Emma Bovary are studies in the same feminine type; . . . the theme is essentially the same. Both women belong to a class, not large, but forever clamoring in our ears, that demands more romance out of life than God put into it. Mr. G. Bernard Shaw would say that they are the victims of the over-idealization of love. They are the

spoil of the poets, the Iphigenias of sentiment. The unfortunate feature of their disease is that it attacks only women of brains ... whose development is one-sided; women of strong and fine intuitions, but without the faculty of observation, comparison, reasoning about things. Probably, for emotional people, the most convenient thing about being able to think is that it occasionally gives them a rest from feeling. Now with women of the Bovary type, this relaxation and recreation is impossible. They are not critics of life, but, in the most personal sense, partakers of life. They receive impressions through the fancy. With them everything begins with fancy, and passions rise in the brain rather than in the blood, the poor, neglected, limited, one-sided brain that might do so much better things than badgering itself into frantic endeavors to love. For these are the people who pay with their blood for the fine ideals of the poets. ... These people really expect the passion of love to fill and gratify every need of life, whereas nature only intended that it should meet one of many demands. They insist upon making it stand for all the emotional pleasures of life and art; expecting an individual and self-limited passion to yield infinite variety, pleasure, and distraction, to contribute to their lives what the arts and the pleasurable exercise of the intellect gives to less limited and less intense idealists. To this passion, when set up against Shakespeare, Balzac, Wagner, Raphael, fails them. They have staked everything on one hand, and they lose. They have driven the blood until it will drive no further, they have played their nerves up to the point where any relaxation short of absolute annihilation is impossible. Every idealist abuses his nerves, and every sentimentalist brutally abuses them. And in the end, the nerves get even. Nobody ever cheats them, really. ... And next time I hope that Miss Chopin will devote that flexible, iridescent style of hers to a better cause.[5]

All three fictional ladies—Myra Henshawe, Edna Pontellier, Emma Bovary—overidealize love, demand more romance in life than God created for it, have brains and fine intuitions, and a habit of allowing everything to originate in the fancy. All make frantic and ultimately futile endeavors to love, and thus live out the negative consequences of the possibilities imagined by great poets and artists.

In her reviews of *The Awakening* and *A Silent Singer,* written a week apart, Cather focuses not only on character types but also on matters of style. In the case of Kate Chopin, she feels the style is superior to its subject. But Cather is even more distressed about Clara Morris's manner of writing. Interestingly, the list of Morris's stylistic defects is exactly opposite the qualities Cather deliberately incorporated into *My Mortal Enemy.* For example, while Morris lacks symmetry, *My Mortal Enemy* is the most rigidly symmetrical of all Cather's novels: books one and two each contain six chapters that resemble each other closely enough to be described as exactly parallel.[6] A final seventh chapter functions at the end as an epilogue, after Myra's death. Morris's lack of restraint contrasts to Cather's most starkly bare fiction.[7] Cather bemoans Morris's refusal to suggest anything; in contrast, Cather produces here her most suggestive work.

We surmise, with these parallel and opposite fictions in view, what Cather set out to prove in *My Mortal Enemy:* a real artist could produce every virtue Morris's fiction could claim—force, power, strength, probed anguish—while using a polar-opposite technique defined by rigid restraint. Put another way, *My Mortal Enemy* proved that one could write successfully an artistically exemplary work about a realistic subject. The enterprise, of course, would require making the primary female character more significant than Chopin's or Morris's kinds of realism had previously rendered her. In *My Mortal Enemy* Cather set out to invest this old subject with new importance, and to render that importance suggestively, not through multiplied realistic details. In so doing, Cather attacked the "realistic method" as it was commonly misunderstood in 1925 and 1926.

Even in 1899, however, Morris's *The Silent Singer* provided Cather the opportunity to launch another attack on the prose excesses currently justified in the name of realism. She returned to this subject frequently and vehemently: "Realism, BAH!"[8] Cather associated realism with banal facts of everyday life, with W. D. Howells, and with social studies: "Socialistic studies in the guise of fiction are usually unattractive, not infrequently dishonest, and almost never have they anything new to say. Usually they falter with painful indecision between the theme and the plot, and introduce a fragile and superfluous love story at the expense of sociology."[9] When she was forced to use the hated word in connection with someone she admired, such as Madame Modjeska, Cather described her as "a realist in the best sense of the word"—a sense associated with "the naturalness and simplicity of her method and its freedom from exaggeration."[10] Modjeska herself, so prominently mentioned in *My Mortal Enemy,* is associated with a style Cather labeled *romantic* because she admired deep feeling,[11] not *realistic* in the commonly understood sense, because Cather associated the latter with laundry lists.

We begin our discussion of *My Mortal Enemy,* then, by stressing that its unfurnished and restrained style and its symmetrical form appear deliberately designed to demonstrate the proper technique an artist should use to approach the subject of a passionate and unrestrained woman. As in all the works of this brilliant period, the novel quickly becomes something *more,* if only because the negative opinions Cather held of this chosen subject required that the subject itself be redefined. Cather inflates the significance of her subject, as we shall see, partially by expanding or reversing several themes—the links between religion and art, the possibility of miracle, the significance of possession, the relative strength of reflex as opposed to will—which she explored in *The Professor's House.* Predictably, however, she approaches all these themes from a radically new direction. The religion here, for example, is not the professor's Western mix of Methodism and Catholicism, but rather a pagan exaltation of the triple goddess—maiden / mother / crone—associated with the moon and the sea and named in one avatar, Diana.[12]

Writing *The Professor's House* was not cathartic. To judge by her next year's activities, Cather's distress had intensified. *My Mortal Enemy* stands in my mind as Willa Cather's most brilliant—in the sense of technically astonishing—tour de force. As Cather's crisis deepened, however, so too did her apparent anger, disgust, and sense of betrayal. After all, she had just acknowledged the possibility of miracle and certainly of everyday endurance and fortitude. No sense of relief or faith in survival seems to have followed. In her new novel, a controlled despair permeates the action. Consequently, in comparison to what followed it, *The Professor's House* momentarily looks like a simple three-room flat.

One key to the reading that will follow is imbedded in the fact that all the major characters of this fiction hail from Parthia, Illinois. Parthian identity derives from the fighting horsemen in the ancient kingdom famous for its military prowess. Parthia (in what is now Iran) developed the "Parthian shot" as a lethal military tactic. Its riders would fake retreat, luring their enemies to break ranks in order to pursue them. Then the Parthians would turn and coolly shoot the betrayed opposition down. For ancient Parthians, retreat was attack, and appearances were contrived to deceive.

My Mortal Enemy encapsules the story of a couple who risk all for love and eventually lose all, to the dismay of a young friend who tracks their downward plunge and later tells their tale. The last passionate groan from the novel's central character Myra Henshawe summarizes the primary theme: "I could bear to suffer ... so many have suffered. But why must it be like this? I have not deserved it. I have been true in friendship; I have faithfully nursed others in sickness. . . . Why must I die like this, alone with my mortal enemy?" (*ME*, 95). The theme concerns mortality and mutability that in turn link to injustice, inconstancy, and indignity.

Hearing Myra's terrible murmur, the narrator, Nellie Birdseye, adds, "I had never heard a human voice utter such a terrible judgment upon all one hopes for" (*ME*, 95). Following Nellie's lead, many a reader has felt in Myra's statement Cather's mean-spirited dismissal of everything valuable in human life. Further,

Nellie's response, appearing as it does in a work so spare that every syllable seems to count twice, has provoked two further questions: What *is* all one hopes for; and who is named here as Myra's mortal enemy? To answer either, we must understand the author's presentation of Myra Henshawe.

Myra—mythic, monstrous, magic—reflects many crucial characteristics of the triple goddess.[13] In the Parthian stories about her, she's the fairy-tale princess. Once ill, she claims to live off sea air. In the final pages, she is unequivocally the death-dealing and devouring crone. She also functions as Nellie Birdseye's surrogate mother (or wicked stepmother), and even as her own. Susan Rosowski identifies the work's most chilling line as Oswald's statement when Myra is dying, "These last years it's seemed to me that I was nursing the mother of the girl who ran away with me" (*ME,* 104).[14] But overlapping phases typify the goddess.

Like the goddess, Myra is always associated with power. She is the subject of "the only interesting stories" Nellie heard as a child, stories of Myra's girlhood (*ME,* 3). In their first encounter during Myra's middle years, Nellie says, "I felt quite overpowered by her" (*ME,* 6). Ten years later Myra appears "crippled but powerful" (*ME,* 65). In her dying moments Oswald says of her, "She can do anything she wills" (*ME,* 98). Myra herself remarks that hers "was no head for a woman at all, but would have graced one of the wickedest of the Roman emperors" (*ME,* 63).

The goddess's power, because it symbolizes female power in three essential phases or forms, is not only regal or imperial but also common. Thus Myra compares herself to "old Irish women" (*ME,* 85) and mimics an Irish brogue when she wishes to be caustic or cruel. She rewards the penny-whistle performer who plays *The Irish Washerwoman* (*ME,* 26). Father Fay observes, "She's not at all modern in her make up" (*ME,* 93). Oswald seems to summarize the paradoxes when he exclaims, "Ah, but she isn't people! She's Myra Driscoll, and there was never anybody else like her" (*ME,* 76).

As an avatar (or like Bellini's Norma, a priestess) of the moon deity invoked in the *Casta Diva* aria, Myra models an archetypally female story. It includes power, love, and marriage; but it is not unrelated to Cather's youthful absolute, "On the stage a woman has but one business, to be in love, and to have it mighty hard."[15] Attending a play in the novel, Myra watches from the audience, but finds, "The scene on the stage was obliterated for her; the drama was in her mind" (*ME*, 44). Whether she locates this woman's story on a physical or a mental stage, Cather seems to find mighty hard the plight of a woman whose one business is to love.

Beyond her power, Myra is defined by her differences. She is different in Nellie's eyes from Nellie's humdrum Aunt Lydia, and from all the other hometown folk. But she seems especially different from her husband, Oswald. Oswald is passive, while she is active. In Nellie's eyes he has a "gentle heart" (*ME*, 37), while she "greeted shock or sorrow with that dry, exultant chuckle which seemed to say: 'Ah-ha, I have one more piece of evidence, one more, against the hideous injustice God permits in this world!'" (*ME*, 65). To Nellie, Oswald suggests "indestructible constancy" (*ME*, 103), while Myra candidly concludes at the end of their romantic marriage, "It was money I needed" (*ME*, 75). Oswald tolerates bothersome neighbors who live too close, while Myra weeps that they trample like cattle. The point is that both Henshawes are *felt* by the reader more clearly because of the contrasting presence of the other. And while Myra remains intensely aware of Oswald at all points, it is not perhaps too strained to recall that Myra says Oswald "was always a man to feel women, you know, in every way" (*ME*, 91).

Myra also contains within herself significantly warring contradictions or oppositions. Her extravagance, for example, extends to more than her spending habits. She also loves and hates extravagantly, and sometimes does both simultaneously. While we see her wounding her friends, she is repeatedly associated with beautiful or generous friendships (*ME*, 43, 76, 95, 104). She admits, "People can be lovers and enemies at the same time. We were" (*ME*, 88). Myra's treatment of others can volley so swiftly from warmth to icy disdain that she seems to keep Nellie constantly off-balance. But Oswald thrives on her polarities and concludes after her death, "I'd rather have been clawed by her, as she used to say, than petted by any other woman I've ever known" (*ME*,

104). Recounting his love for his wife, Oswald concedes with satisfaction, "Of course, she was absolutely unreasonable when she was jealous. Her suspicions were sometimes—almost fantastic." Nellie adds, "He smiled and brushed his forehead with the tips of his fingers, as if the memory of her jealousy was pleasant still" (*ME,* 104). By the end, both Henshawes begin to seem like embodied oxymorons, full of brawling love and loving hate. In her last bitter days, Myra's priestly confessor compares her to saints of the early church; she, however, seeks those answers others find in religion by regularly consulting with a fortune-teller.

To keep her polarities from becoming as metronomic as the perfectly balanced parts of this book, Cather uses Nellie Birdseye as a triangulating agent. Nellie recalls, "Mrs. Henshawe got great pleasure from flowers, too, and during the late winter months my chief extravagance and my chief pleasure was in taking them to her" (*ME,* 71). Myra certainly remains the apex of this novel's triangular energies—the one on whom the other two wait in attendance. But Myra must be understood in relation to Nellie as well as to Oswald. And whether forming an equilateral triangle or not, these three, once joined, can be turned so that each becomes the point of strongest interest. Yet at Myra's death Oswald says desperately, "You don't know her, Nellie" (*ME,* 78).

The names themselves highlight the intricate relationships among the three of them. *Myra Driscoll* suggests the possessive *my,* as well as *mire, drizzle, cold.* The given name can also be pronounced with a short *i,* which homophone links the character even closer to the heroine of the opera *Norma.* Myra mirrors Norma's betrayal by her lover, Pollione, and Norma's bonding with a younger woman who also loves Pollione. The last duet between Pollione's two women begins, "Mira, o Norma. . . ."[16] The other two names obliquely direct attention back to Myra, too. *Nellie* may remind some of Emily Brontë's narrator Nelly Dean,[17] and others of Miss Birdseye in James's *The Bostonians.* Or she may suggest a little Nell, a girlish diminutive of Eleanor, one name for the triple goddess. But *Birdseye* reminds us that our narrator passes us information about the Henshawe story tinted by her own vision. And birds see from only one eye at a time—with less broad synthesis than humans are thought to achieve. Thus Nellie's name itself poses a question about how well the narrator sees the other two principals. And Oswald's first name refers to *King Lear,* for Oswald is the terrible Goneril's flunkey. A *shaw* is a strip of woods bounding a field; thus *Henshawe* suggests a hen's defining—or limiting—boundary.

In discussing the Henshawe relationship, David Stouck has already drawn attention to the fact that in Myra's New York apartment the sex roles are reversed and the women are the strong ones.[18] This power relationship, of course, is appropriately assumed in a goddess-centered pagan context instead of a Christian and Western patriarchal one. In any case, from the beginning to the end of the novel, Oswald plays a subservient and therefore (judged by patriarchal values) a female role. First, he's Myra's sex object, whom she courts with such overwrought passion that she lies all night on the floor longing for him. Later, he's Myra's spouse, about whom she says happily, "We're going home to Oswald" (*ME,* 26). Then he becomes Myra's betrayer, who accepts decorations and jewels from another lover—as only women are thought capable of doing (though for such duplicity women would demand more valuable pearls, Myra comments, than Oswald has accepted in his topaz cuff links [*ME,* 54]). Finally, he plays Myra's nurse. In the last role, he finally has her in *his* power, for which she cannot forgive him: "It's bitter enough that I should have to take service from you—whom I have loved so well" (*ME,* 92).

Loved, in this bitter statement, appears synonymous with *controlled* and *possessed.* Thus, the possession theme, expressed so ecstatically by Tom Outland on the Blue Mesa, sours and curdles in *My Mortal Enemy.* To Myra the active seeker, love is appropriately her gift to those she selects to receive it. Having freely given (and thereby possessed her beloved), she cannot so freely receive (and thus relinquish control). The reversal offends her because receiving love creates dependency. Oswald's last female role in relation to Myra, therefore, becomes providing life-support services, as mothers conventionally do, to one who is ungrateful. He mothers the mother of the girl he ran away with. After her death he obeys her instructions and prepares to scatter her ashes "somewhere in those vast waters" (*ME*, 103).

Nellie becomes aware, as soon as Oswald first appears in her aunt's parlor, that his "presence gave ... [Myra] lively personal pleasure" (*ME*, 8). Myra soon leaves him with the feminine task of entertaining Nellie, Lydia's awkward niece, while Myra herself exits for easier action outside the parlor. With no further prompting, Oswald entertains well. Nellie immediately notices that his eyes are "exactly like half-moons," which well they should be if Oswald, as we have seen, is by Western standards half a woman by virtue of playing women's roles in his marriage. In the course of their first evening together Nellie learns that Myra has given away Oswald's six new shirts because they give him a bosom (*ME*, 9). The feminine side of Oswald attracts this adolescent. Yet Nellie, seeking significant contact with female power, is also confused by Oswald's "perplexing combination of something hard and something soft" (*ME*, 10). She prefers him to his sharper-tongued spouse, however, because he doesn't frighten her as Myra does. Later, near Oswald's home, Nellie seems "moonstruck" (*ME*, 26). Throughout, the extent to which a character is associated with the moon, primary symbol of the triple goddess, measures that character's relation to power.

All the novel's characters, as we have said, exist as Myra's satellites. From the beginning, "All Myra's friends were drawn into the web of her romance; half a dozen young men understudied for Oswald so assiduously that her uncle might have thought she was going to marry any one of them" (*ME*, 14). Myra is the active agent, the one who "laughs at untoward circumstances, accidents, even disasters" (*ME*, 10). She is the one with a wit "none too squeamish" (*ME*, 12), who, as any adventurer entering the world to seek a fortune, has had the daring to leave her uncle's house with nothing but "her muff and her *porte-monnaie* in her hands" (*ME*, 16). Thus, she married "without gloves, so to speak" (*ME*, 85).

Myra accuses herself of being "a greedy, selfish, worldly woman" who "wanted success and a place in the world" (*ME*, 75). Measured against Oswald, however, these qualities appear unseemly not because they are unusual in the fairy tales Myra's life is compared to, but because the qualities should typify the prince. That is, the traits are appropriate to the fairy-tale lover who is conventionally the male. A prince in Western fairy tales is permitted to leave his guardian's kingdom in order to rescue and serve his princess with half-moon eyes. Princesses elicit jewels from their lovers. Myra's selfishness is real enough, but seems less shocking in the context of moon-goddess worship of a powerful female force.

Having acknowledged this thorough role reversal, however, we must then admit that Oswald and Myra are also very much alike. Myra describes them as "a pair of old foxes" (*ME*, 62) when Nellie finds them in California. And Oswald—as much as Myra—is associated with "personal bravery, magnanimity, and a fine, generous way of doing things" (*ME*, 8). Nellie often uses similar terms for the two. For example, as befits native Parthians, she describes both in martial images. She notices Oswald's "military air" (*ME*, 8) as soon as they meet, and ten years later notes his still-smart suit with a "military collar" (*ME*, 69). Later also, Nellie repeats Oswald's boast that Myra has "enough desperate courage for a regiment" (*ME*, 76). She also defines both Henshawes by the care they take for their physical appearances. At the end, Oswald is "the only man staying in that shabby hotel who looked well-groomed" (*ME*, 70), while Myra, bridging a small rupture with Nellie, is spotted "manicuring her neat little hands—a good sign" (*ME*, 78).

Both Henshawes are as careful of the other's appearance as of the self's. At the beginning, Myra gives away Oswald's new shirts because she can't bear him "in ill-fitting things" (*ME*, 9). Later, Oswald rises for work at 5:00 A.M. to have time to bathe his wife, make her bed, and help her dress attractively. While he may be sexually faithless, Oswald cares for Myra so steadfastly that he becomes Nellie's model of constancy (*ME*, 103). Myra, though wandering widely in imagination, stays physically faithful to Oswald to the grave. Both, then, remain true to each other in their fashion.

A crucial matter to consider in this novel, as Rosowski has

suggested, is the source of our information. We learn all we know from Nellie Birdseye. Thus, we come at the end to the teller of the tale. Her relationship to each Henshawe dictates her presentation. Her need to become a member of their wedding suggests a substratum of family drama in this plot. And when a child tells a parental story, it leads sooner or later to the child. In that light, one finds the opening sentence even more arresting than usual, if that can be possible in a Cather novel: "I first met Myra Henshawe when I was fifteen, but I had known about her ever since I could remember anything at all." The first sentence of *My Mortal Enemy* uses the first-person pronoun an unprecedented four times. One wonders how much more emphatically a novel démeublé could send this signal to watch the child, the last teller of the tale.

The first scene between Myra and Nellie is crucial. As the only interesting subject in Nellie's constricted small-town world, Myra suggests all the glamor for which Nellie longs. Yet as soon as Myra is introduced on the first page, we spot our first interesting discrepancies. Nellie's Aunt Lydia refers to our central figure as Myra *Driscoll,* the virgin; to Nellie, however, she is always Mrs. Myra or Myra Henshawe—the matron and surrogate mother.

Nellie has grown up hearing hometown stories of how Myra, a fairy-tale princess, defied the wicked king, her guardian, to marry a forbidden but handsome prince.[19] The old Driscoll estate in town seemed to childish Nellie "under a spell, like the Sleeping Beauty's palace; it had been in a trance, or lain in its flowers like a beautiful corpse, ever since that winter night when Love went out of the gates and gave the dare to Fate" (*ME,* 17). The last overwrought romantic phrase suggests Nellie's emotional age when she, as an adolescent, first meets the Henshawes. What she wants at that moment is to find that they have lived "happily ever after." That is, she wants to meet in Myra a successful model of female power as defined by a standard female plot. Instead, what Nellie meets are a couple who have merely been as "happy as most people" (*ME,* 17). Nellie notes indignantly, "the very point of their story was that they should be much happier than other people" (*ME,* 17). Nellie wants evidence of a magic marriage because she wants intimacy with the Henshawes *as a unit*. That is, she wants them as surrogate parents. She is ready to love and wishes to be included in every aspect of the Henshawes' married life.

Myra first glimpses Nellie in a mirror, not face-to-face. Nellie tells us, "She must have heard me, and glancing up, she saw my reflection in a mirror; she put down the guitar, rose, and stood to await my approach. She stood markedly and pointedly still, with her shoulders back and her head lifted, as if to remind me that it was my business to get to her as quickly as possible and present myself as best I could" (*ME,* 5). Several interpretations suggest themselves after this passage. For example, when *Myra* (or *mira*) glances in a mirror, what she sees is *Nellie*. Thus, Nellie is Myra's mirror image—both her duplicate and her opposite. Either may be seen as a psychological projection of the other. Or one might say that in their defining scene, Nellie is seen obliquely, not directly. Or further, the first Nellie to be seen is not the real lass but rather an illusion; one must look elsewhere to find the real Nell. These possibilities suggest in turn that any conclusions about the two women must reflect both their similarities and their mother-and-daughter-like opposition.

The initial account of Myra that Nellie provides appears to emphasize the distances between the two. Myra is forty-five, plump, attractive, peremptory, and cruel; Nellie is fifteen, shy, vulnerable, and eager to make contact. While Nellie wants Myra to like her, Myra seems sporadically caustic and judgmental about Nellie. Although we must rely on Nellie for the facts, we remember eventually the egocentricism of her first sentence. That opening sentence, as well as the first word of the title, signals that a major concern of *My Mortal Enemy* could be the speaker who delivers the story, especially in her relation to the Henshawes. That is, a major theme could be the disheartening possibilities a surrogate daughter is forced to learn from her closest adult models.

From the first scene, Nellie's imperative business is to get her eyes off the mirror where she is looking and on to the real Myra. Ten years later, Nellie arrives on the Henshawes' scene to hold

Myra's head between her hands, "making a frame for her face" (*ME,* 62). Our business is to ask how well Nellie goes about this framing business, and in how many ways she actually "frames" Myra. In asking the second question, we also ask how much of Cather is invested in Nellie.

It soon becomes a matter of interest that Nellie's vision (and therefore her presentation) is called into question by Nellie's own account. She says that she first sees Myra from a great distance, "at the far end of the parlour." She adds that her first reaction was bewilderment (*ME,* 5) and her first sensation to feel "stupid, hopelessly clumsy and stupid" (*ME,* 7). And again, "I felt I didn't have half a chance with her; her charming, fluent voice, her clear light enunciation bewildered me. . . . I was fascinated, but very ill at ease" (*ME,* 7). Nellie's repeated bewilderment calls into question her account of their first exposure to each other. Repetitiously she asserts that she is befuddled, vulnerable, defensive, and insecure. It is no surprise that when Oswald appears she turns to him with relief and not long after seems "moonstruck." We are allowed to heave no sighs of relief along with her, however, because she first asserts Oswald is "less perplexing" than his wife (*ME,* 8), and then mentions his "perplexing combination" of qualities (*ME,* 10). Nellie seems to know Oswald no better than she knows Myra.

When Nellie goes to visit the Henshawes in New York at Christmas, her vision does not clear. She is chaperoned by "the blurred, taken-for-granted image of my aunt that I saw every day" (*ME,* 43), while she finds herself "straining my eyes to catch, through the fine, reluctant snow, my first glimpse of the city. . . . The snow blurred everything a little, and the buildings on the Battery all ran together" (*ME,* 22). When the weather clears, however, Nellie's eyesight does not. As they step out of their hotel the next morning, "the sun shone blindingly on the snow-covered park" (*ME,* 32). Only a dangerously distorted vision could experience winter in New York City as a thoroughly temperate condition that "brought no desolation; it was tamed, like a polar bear led on a leash by a beautiful lady" (*ME,* 25). Madison Square "seemed to me so neat, after the raggedness of our Western cities;

so protected by good manners and courtesy—like an open-air drawing room" (*ME,* 24). This is simply not a trustworthy point of view, as New York resident Willa Cather certainly knew. Even more interestingly, on Christmas morning—the central Christian holiday—Nellie's eyes fix, not on a church spire or a Christmas tree, but on St. Gauden's golden Diana—the moon-goddess—stepping nakedly into the air off Madison Square.

Stronger doubts about Nellie's grasp of facts arise when she admits that Myra's "account of her friends was often more interesting to me than the people themselves" (*ME,* 40). Because she prefers Myra's vision to her own, Nellie finds that "when she addressed Aunt Lydia, for instance, she seemed to be speaking to a person deeper down than the blurred, taken-for-granted image of my aunt that I saw every day, and for a moment my aunt became more individual, less matter-of-fact to me. . . . her manner of addressing my relatives had made them all seem a little more attractive to me" (*ME,* 43). Having exaggerated Myra's magic, however, Nellie also exaggerates her malice. She reads Myra's social competitiveness as "insane ambition" (*ME,* 41). And entering a room where Myra, with justification, is thoroughly furious with her philandering husband, Nellie reports, "What I felt was fear; I was afraid to look or speak or move. Everything about me seemed evil. When kindness has left people, even for a few moments, we become afraid of them, as if their reason had left them. When it has left a place where we have always found it, it is like shipwreck; we drop from security into something malevolent and bottomless" (*ME,* 51). Remembering carefully this caution, we still judge reasonably that Nellie's reaction to a marital altercation seems as excessive as any of Myra's dramatics—unless Nellie is crediting Myra with the power of a goddess (or a fairy tale's wicked witch or stepmother). Nellie once thought of Myra's girlhood home as Sleeping Beauty's palace; here she herself seems to play the innocent princess who is immobilized for a century by the old fairy's poisoned words.[20]

Nellie tries to appropriate Myra's experience—including her romance—and to duplicate or supersede Myra herself. Even in her first fumbling encounter she has noticed that Myra was "no taller than I" (*ME*, 6). In New York, Nellie promptly falls in love with Myra's glamorous friends such as Madame Modjeska, who seems "by far the handsomest and most distinguished of that company, . . . beautiful in age, . . . a woman of another race and another period, no less queenly" (*ME*, 45). That is, Modjeska attests female power of a kind Myra can entertain. The stage people Nellie reports at the Henshawe apartment on New Year's Eve arrive with "traces of make-up still on their faces"; one displays "painted eyebrows [which] spread and came down over his eyes like a veil" (*ME*, 45). That is, she is still not seeing them as they really are, even up close. To her eyes, Modjeska's hands "were worldly, indeed, but fashioned for a nobler worldliness than ours; hands to hold a sceptre, or a chalice—or, by courtesy, a sword" (*ME*, 46). In short, hands of the goddess, the powerful female principle. It is also interesting that young Willa Cather's reviews of Modjeska repeatedly bemoan the fact that she must grow old.[21] Thus, it is imminently appropriate that Myra's party guests, including Modjeska, hear together the *Casta Diva* aria, the invocation to the moon, "which begins so like the quivering of moonbeams on the water" (*ME*, 47). The scene ends,

> For many years I associated Mrs. Henshawe with that music, thought of that aria as being mysteriously related to something in her nature that one rarely saw, but nearly always felt; a compelling, passionate, overmastering something for which I had no name, but which was audible, visible in the air that night, as she sat crouching in the shadow. When I wanted to recall powerfully that hidden richness in her, I had only to close my eyes and sing to myself: "*Casta diva, casta diva!*" (*ME*, 48).

When Nellie falls in love with Myra's marriage, the emotion necessarily involves loving Myra's husband as well. In fact, if Nellie is unconsciously presenting herself as an earnest duplicate of Myra, and therefore incidentally as an unreliable narrator, it is of some interest that she describes Myra, whom she duplicates, as one whose chief extravagance lay "in caring for so many people and in caring for them so much" (*ME,* 43). If three's a crowd, Nellie's act of joining the Henshawes suggests that she too cares for too many people too much.

Soon after Nellie arrives in the California apartment hotel the Henshawes already occupy, her life settles into a routine that includes pleasant nightly dinners alone with Oswald, Myra's husband. In her California duplication of the routine the Henshawes once followed in New York, Nellie seems content until she too encounters a younger rival who threatens to displace her. The rival is a young journalist who follows the profession Myra once recommended to Nellie. Nellie claims of the intrusion, "We enjoyed talking with her at lunch or dinner" (*ME,* 77) and then summarily dismisses the young woman as "perhaps eighteen, overgrown and awkward, with short hair and a rather heavy face" (*ME,* 78). A few pages later Nellie wonders how "That crude little girl [could have] made all the difference in the world to him" (*ME,* 91). Soon thereafter she notices that Oswald still wears the topaz sleeve buttons an illicit New York love once gave him. She appears, in the moment, as observant, as possessive, and as jealous as Myra.

Nellie herself once witnessed a jealous explosion Myra set off, during which she declared to her amused husband, "I will go through any door your keys open" (*ME,* 49). We register the Freudian image Cather has placed here. One door Oswald's key opened has apparently led to Nellie's heart. One key to the novel's ending may be the possibility that Myra, true to her word, has penetrated Nellie's heart to take a clear look around before she dies.

In their first New York holiday together, Myra chills in asking, "Oh, Nellie, . . . [i]t's all very well to tell us to forgive our enemies; our enemies can never hurt us very much. But oh, what about forgiving our friends?" (*ME,* 43). It's friends in the plural that Myra worries about forgiving. But this line, paraphrased slightly from Bacon's "On Revenge,"[22] also sets up the motifs of withheld forgiveness of friends and revenge as a factor in this novel's action.

We come to a consideration of the final pages understanding that Nellie's presentation is biased toward her own concerns. Nel-

lie is taking turns with Oswald in watching over Myra at night—
in seeing out an old life cycle in order to see in a new phase. She
is appropriately on hand when Myra protests having to die alone
with her mortal enemy. We note the presence of three people in
the room. While Oswald does not move or shudder, Nellie's reaction reverberates in our heads here: "I felt my hands grow cold
and my forehead grow moist with dread. I had never heard a
human voice utter such a terrible judgment upon all one hopes
for" (*ME,* 95). Part of Nellie's dread seems plausibly associated
with her guilt at replacing Myra. Partly, too, she reminds us of
her desire to be an integral part of the Henshawe family. But all
three can be assumed to hope for a final sense of coherent wholeness in their lives—a sense denied each of them. Beyond that,
Nellie has hoped from Myra for some access to the power of the
goddess, that is, the eternal female principle that promises the
eternal return of life and on which continuing human life depends. Unlike patriarchal Christianity which promises eternal life
to the individual, however, the goddess cults promise individuals
only death and a return to the body of the Earth; life in the
general sense returns only to the tribe. When Myra dies, Myra
and Nellie seem to embrace that alternate myth no more serenely
than Professor St. Peter did the Christian one.

Myra's mortal enemy is themselves, each of whom at this point
wears a face of the triune goddess. The goddess, in turn, represents that promise of female power Myra has wasted a life mis-
understanding and pursuing ineffectively. Profoundly possessive
Myra, who has engulfed the others in her own identity, finds her
betrayer in each of them, and also in herself. Oswald is the enemy
who tempted her to stake everything on one hand and thus to
lose. But the audacious predisposition to take the gamble was her
own from the beginning. And the less daring (such as Nellie or
Aunt Lydia) whose admiration encouraged her, certainly contributed to the debacle. Nellie and Oswald have both been necessary
pieces in Myra's game, but Myra moved the pieces and as queen
controlled their board. They all lose when she is taken. The real
facts of her life—including her love of Oswald, her sponsorship
of that adoring younger self, Nellie, and her aging body that re-

minds her of her entrapment in the flesh—are Myra's (as they are also Nellie's and Oswald's) mortal enemy. The three characters function together as the kind of three-winged pinwheel given to children for a toy. The object is made of three loosely attached arms, each of which is shaped like a triangle and functions like a sail, creating movement. When one blows life into the middle of the pinwheel, its three saillike arms catch the wind and revolve around each other and together, creating the optical illusion of a single whirring circle.

Oswald and Nellie mirror Myra. The two women, in turn, function as analogues of the cold and hot, passive and active parts of Oswald's personality. Each of the Henshawes in turn helps develop that character who emerges as our narrator. The implications of these relationships refract as dizzily as a moving object in a hall of mirrors. In the process, Nellie's reflections teach us that "violent natures like hers sometimes turn against themselves . . . against themselves and all their idolatries" (*ME,* 96). The turning against themselves and each other is the essential movement of this book, and suggests Cather's view of human life at this point, especially when seen from the female's perspective.

We have still, however, to unravel the most interesting conundrum in this book: the subtleties of Myra's last gesture. What is Myra up to when she drags herself to Gloucester's cliff to die? And how do the last scenes reveal the quintessential characteristics of our human pinwheel?

Much crucial information comes from Myra. She points out that she has two fatal maladies but prophetically declares of her close neighbors, "it's those coarse creatures I shall die of" (*ME,* 74). The creatures she momentarily has in her mind are the Poindexters, "all that slushy gush on the surface and no sensibilities whatever" (*ME,* 67). Nellie confirms that the Poindexters do make unnecessary noise, and they do ignore Myra's complaints. After protesting about them, however, Myra asks provocatively, "Why didn't you leave me out there [on the headlands], Nellie, in the wind and the night?" (*ME,* 74). Of course that is exactly what Nellie—another close neighbor—who figures out where Myra has gone to die, eventually decides to do.

With her two fatal maladies to contend against, Myra is still herself. Like Clara Morris, "she was a physical wreck when she should have been in her prime. Her violence wore her out, like the mill that grinds itself to pieces. Now, in an exhausted body, the old fierce soul of other days is still rampant, and she is seeking to let it out by a new channel." In Cather's novel Nellie describes Myra as "crippled but powerful . . . a witty but rather wicked old woman, who hated life for its defeats, and loved it for its absurdities" (ME, 65). Given her acknowledgment that absurdity is more likely to rule than justice, and her predisposition to stake all on one hand, Myra's behavior in her last days assumes new interest. First, her mind seems to be abnormally active. Second, she grows quite obsessed with "her old poets" whom she believes "shine on . . . into all the dark corners of the world" and "have no night" (ME, 82). That is, the poets seem to have had some access to an immortality that her body is presently denying her. Three old poets are singled out: Heine, whose poems about an anachronistic tear and a poor suicide's flower Myra applies to herself;[23] Whitman, "that dirty old man" who may save her and admit her into a new Parnassus (ME, 80); and Shakespeare, whom she quotes at length in her insomniac hours.

Myra herself explains that her attachment to Heine dates from the passionate days of her fresh romance. A rather notorious passage from Whitman's "Song of Myself" may explain Cather's repetition of the word *headlands* in this text (ME, 72, 100); Nellie's notice of Myra's "inexplicably mischievous" hand (ME, 63); and also what technically happened in Myra's last moments:

> The sentries desert every other part of me,
> They have left me helpless to a red marauder,
> They all come to the headland to witness and assist
>   against me.
> I am given up by traitors,
> I talk wildly, I have lost my wits, I and nobody else
>   am the greatest traitor,
> I went myself first to the headland, my own hands
>   carried me there.[24]

Certainly, while Myra carried herself to the headland, she did so because such sentries as Nellie failed to attend her closely enough, thereby assisting her in rendering herself fatally vulnerable to the "red marauder" of her diseases. But the poet we must concentrate on here is Shakespeare. Before doing so, we remember that Oswald identified Myra as having a will strong enough to do anything.

Poetry has been a key to Myra's thoughts throughout this book. As Myra drags herself to the headland she identifies as Gloucester's cliff, she seems full of some kind of desperation. In *Lear,* the cliff in question is the place where Gloucester wishes to die. To get there, however, blind Gloucester must rely on his disguised son Edgar for a guide. Edgar seeks to preserve his father's life, and so takes him to a safe spot he claims matches Gloucester's desired destination, where Gloucester falls forward after delivering his "final" speech:

> O you mighty gods!
> This world I do renounce, and in your sights
> Shake patiently my great affliction off.
> If I could bear it longer and not fall
> To quarrel with your great opposeless wills,
> My snuff and loathed part of nature should
> Burn itself out. If Edgar live, O bless him!
> Now, fellow, fare thee well. [*He falls forward and swoons*].
> (4.6.34–41)

In emulating Gloucester's act, Myra attempts to achieve Gloucester's result—a kind of rebirth, or miracle. Once again, she gambles everything on one hand and loses. In this gesture, she has tried to use immortal poetry to outwit mortality. Gloucester cheats death by forcing the issue of his own mortality in an apparently suicidal act, and then wakes to find himself alive. At that "resurrection point," he is told, "The clearest gods, who make them honors / Of men's impossibilities, have preserved thee" (4.6.73–74). Thereafter, Gloucester concludes piously, "Let not my worser spirit tempt me again / To die before you [gods] please" (4.6.213–14).

This reading that disturbs all the proprieties is justified by Cather's text. Myra herself concedes that in her latter days she feels herself drawing nearer the spirit of her uncle: "if he'd lived till now, I'd go back to him and ask his pardon . . . because as we grow old we become more and more the stuff our forebears put into us. I can feel his savagery strengthen in me" (*ME*, 82). Old John Driscoll's savagery has been that of an "old Satan" (*ME*, 81); but he has been nevertheless the man who appeared to have "escaped the end of all flesh . . . as if he had been translated, with no dark conclusion to the pageant, no 'night of the grave'" (*ME*, 18). Will-full Myra, her bodily reflexes failing, draws nearer to her uncle's satanic spirit, emulates him, and tries the same trick of seeming to die in the arms of the always-receptive church in order to escape the dark night of the grave. Or at least, Nellie is capable of imagining the possibility. Once before, she switched the two Driscolls in her mind. After her first glimpse of Myra Henshawe, she recalls, "I could not help feeling a little disappointed. John Driscoll and his niece had suddenly changed places in my mind, and he had got, after all, the more romantic part" (*ME*, 19).

Myra's latter-day Catholicism is not especially convincing, though in case her strategy is too sinful, she saves money to buy postmortem masses for herself and also hopes dawn will bring her "absolution" (*ME*, 73). The gesture has her kind of logic: "You know how the great sinners always came home to die in some religious house?" (*ME*, 73). More validity attaches to her belief that "in religion, seeking is finding" (*ME*, 94). The place she selects for her death, however, is a site sacred to the triple goddess of the tides, the moon, and the night. She does not designate the specifics of the religion through which she seeks, and observes that candles are *in general* religious, as indeed they are (*ME*, 94). Myra is catholic in a general sense. Her first California greeting to Nellie is, "It was in the cards that we should meet again. Now I understand; a wise woman has been coming to read my fortune for me, and the queen of hearts has been coming up out of the pack when she had no business to" (*ME*, 61–62). According to one expert, "For a woman consultant, [the Queen of Hearts] . . . means a rival [even though] she is unaware of it."[25]

Actually, the suit of hearts or cups is associated with water and refers to anything affecting the feelings or emotional relationships. The Queen of Hearts should combine the characteristics associated in more ancient decks with both the Queen and the Princess of Cups. The former represents Virginal and the later, Elaine; both are forms or representations of the moon-goddess, the triple-goddess, who is Snow White, Rose Red, and the Black Crone of death. Both are associated, too, with the ancient symbol of the cauldron, a pagan symbol of death and rebirth later associated with witchcraft.[26]

Myra, a Parthian, constructs a ruse to cheat death, her enemy. She retreats to the headlands to replay Gloucester's suicide. Thus, she invites the absolution from the gods as described through Shakespeare's art, and the renewal of life that Gloucester thereafter enjoys. To be successful, however, a Parthian retreat must provoke reflexive pursuit. What Myra forgets, of course, is that the Parthian strategy depends on gullible pursuers. But Nellie, her mirror image, protégée, and sister Parthian, who has literally watched by her bedside for days and nights, now can guess what is in Myra's head. Nellie recalls that Myra once asked to be left alone to die in the wind and the night. So she justifies her decision not to pursue, but to leave Myra alone on the headland, explaining, "I sat down to think it over. It seemed to me that she ought to be allowed to meet the inevitable end in the way she chose. A yearning strong enough to lift that ailing body and drag it out into the world again should have its way" (*ME*, 99).

It is a comfortable justification for letting nature take its course, disposing of Myra, and freeing Oswald. But Oswald is a Parthian, too; and he also decides against the pursuit of Nellie. As soon as Nellie accelerates Myra's dying, he smilingly turns in the other direction and packs for Alaska. The prospect seems to chill him less than staying near Nellie. Oswald actually seems to erase Nellie as he says, "I have always wanted to go, and now there is nothing to hold me" (*ME*, 104). His final statement is, "Nothing ever took that girl [Myra once was] from me. She was a wild, lovely creature, Nellie, I wish you could have seen her then" (*ME*, 104). In moments when she admires him most, Oswald stands before Nellie remote and untouchable, "like a statue" (*ME*, 47, 103). Thus, the hoped-for miracle fails to materialize for either woman, the anticipated link between religion and art fails to hold, and the pinwheel collapses.

Though Myra dominates it, the novel begins and ends as Nellie's story. Like Myra, Nellie is betrayed by Oswald, whom she has schemed to be near quite as desperately as Myra once did. Nellie has been faithful enough to the Henshawe unit, at least, to follow them both to poverty and California, where she had known they were.[27] But yoked as they all are to Myra's body, both are betrayed and abandoned, as Myra herself is, by Myra's bodily death. It is therefore no wonder that Nellie takes no comfort in the carved amethysts that are her only Henshawe keepsake, but which leave a chill over her heart.[28] The words that echo in the last sentence and in Nellie's head are the words that publicize Willa Cather's judgment upon the human life represented by these terrible three: "Why must I die like this, alone with my mortal enemy!" Terrible as the death and judgment are, however, we still note the stated probability that when her body failed her, Myra, the strong and courageous one, still found will enough to live until she could see the dawn.

CHAPTER SEVEN

Building a Cathedral:
Death Comes For the Archbishop

*A novel requires not one flash of understanding,
but a clear, steady flame and oil in one's flask beside. Not a mood, but a continuous flow of feeling
and thought and a vast knowledge of technique
and of the artistic construction of the whole.
Many a man can fashion an arch or design a spire
or carve a gargoyle, but to build a cathedral is
quite another matter.*

———————— WILLA CATHER, *The Kingdom of Art* ————————
from the Courier, November 30, 1895.

One of the greatest teasers in American literary history is the
question, How did Willa Cather write both *My Mortal Enemy* and
Death Comes for the Archbishop within a twelve-month span? We
have noticed the astonishing amount of travel and simultaneous
professional productivity in her life after her world broke in two
about 1922. We have noticed that such remarkable works as *The
Professor's House* were actually finished early. We concede that
Cather's mind, like Myra Henshawe's in her last phase, was "abnormally active" (*ME,* 93) during this period. But we also know
that *My Mortal Enemy* is permeated with Cather's intensifying
sense of disgust at human life's treacheries and betrayals. Yet, before *My Mortal Enemy* was even past the galley-proof stage,
Cather was busily and happily at work on *Death Comes for the*

Archbishop, again writing at top speed with total confidence in where she was going. The new book, published in 1927, became one of the nation's masterworks of triumphant serenity. It defies common sense that she could write it at this point at all, much less quickly.

The first task, then, is to suggest an answer to the riddle of how she did it. In my opinion (for like the Archbishop I find my miracles in nature and not outside of it), the new novel bloomed naturally out of the two spliced and parentlike novels that preceded it. At the end of *My Mortal Enemy* the heroine, Myra Henshawe, appears to glimpse the possibility of succor when she announces with characteristic passion, "in religion, seeking is finding" (*ME,* 94). Myra's assertion itself, however, relates to St. Peter's lecture in the preceding novel in which he reminds his class, "Art and religion (they are the same thing, in the end, of course) have given man the only happiness he has ever had" (*PH,* 69). And St. Peter's statement stands out in Cather's fiction for its grammatical and rhythmic awkwardness; it's a declaration he and we nearly choke on.

Myra, pretending to seek religious solutions to the hated facts she must face about her own mortality, is actually seeking a survival through art. She identifies a setting with Gloucester's cliff from Shakespeare's *Lear,* then sets up a disingenuous, Gloucester-like death scene, hoping with a kind of mad desperation to regain consciousness after the gods have spared her life as they did Gloucester's. Having thrown herself away with the same abandon as Gloucester did, however, Myra does not experience the same happy result. The scripted rejuvenation does not occur, and she dies.

What Myra has done in her last hours is to place a faith of religious intensity in literary art, which she believes can show her a way to double-cross fate, to hedge her bets, and to prolong her own life. What she fails to account for is the shrewdness of Nellie Birdseye, one of her loving friends and mortal enemies, who guesses where she is and what she is up to, and then decides to let Myra play it her way and die. Even Nellie, in reflecting on Myra's last moments, however, concedes that Myra has in all probability finally and successfully accomplished a heroic act: Myra has willed to live until she could see the dawn.

Like any great creative artist, Willa Cather plays all the major roles in her own dramas. She is, therefore, not only Myra and Oswald Henshawe but also Nellie Birdseye, the cold and unreliable observer. As Myra, Cather turns to art as her religion, to renew an increasingly pain-racked and diseased spirit; for Myra uses both art and religion as tricks to fend off death. Then, as Nellie does, Cather recognizes the trick, rejects it, and kills off that part of her driven and personally ambitious self which Myra represents, the part which also had such a passionate capacity for desire. After jettisoning Myra, however, Cather is left with Nellie Birdseye, the cold observer with the chilled heart. Thus, as Oswald, Cather decides to bolt. She has risen like Oswald to the occasions her life has handed her—and nursed her old concerns while any life was left in them. But when they positively cannot be lived with any longer and she has nothing left to hold her back, she jumps toward a new possibility. In thus acting, she wills, like Myra, to last until she can see the dawn.

Life as a Birdseye—lived on the periphery watching those at the center who enjoy greater vitality—is not a life worth living. So the Birdseye recorder in Cather, summoning Oswald's resilience, tries the whole trick Myra has courageously played. Cather's life at this point not only imitates art; it imitates her own art. She believes with Daniel Forrester that if you want something badly enough you will get it, at least for a while. She agrees with St. Peter's stumbling assertion that art and religion are the same thing in the end. So she tried Myra's artful literary strategy and invokes religion as she hurls herself into the void. With nothing worth preserving left to lose, she affirms that art and religion are the same thing—passionate attempts to understand mystery. She chooses to believe that through art one can find purpose and therefore reclaim joy. Abandoning other hope and letting go with the heart, she takes her own leap of faith off Gloucester's cliff. The trick works. She seeks and finds the confidence in human potential which gathers to a greatness in *Death Comes for the Archbishop*.

In the first chapter of the *Archbishop,* Latour is wandering in a triangle-dominated geometrical nightmare, a symbolic as well as literal desert landscape which could epitomize *My Mortal Enemy.* "The desert down there has a peculiar horror. . . . The very floor of the world is cracked" (*DA,* 7). As he wanders, he is sick and faint. His soul cries, "I thirst." The pain of that thirst is like Christ's on the cross. Living such a crucifixion, however, Latour is still a priest "trying to discover the logical relation of things" (*DA,* 9), who can acknowledge a connection between himself and a cross-shaped tree. He can also relate his own suffering to the *form* of significant suffering. His forms are not empty like St. Peter's or duplicitous like Myra's. He thus surrenders himself to the symbols his heart knows are valid (for the heart has reasons that the mind knows not) and "lets go with the heart." When he both gives up, as the Professor does, and also takes a leap of faith with the courage of a regiment, as Myra does, he is saved. He kneels to pray, submitting to the final logic of his own life and imminent death (not willfully subverting that logic as do *My Mortal Enemy*'s central three). Accepting his fate but continuing his search, he remounts his horse and finds hope within the hour. His exhausted mare and his pack mule both sniff water. Thus, he is carried—moving always in nature—to relief. He arrives to answer the prayers of those living in Agua Secreta, his "Bishopric in miniature" (DA, 32).

This first chapter introduces every philosophical question the novel explores: what is man; what is faith; what is significant form; where is hope; what is miracle; what results from desire; what forms contain significant art; and finally, how do desire, art, form, faith, and miracle contribute to ongoing life, to continuity? It also presents the novel's central motifs: the air, the light, the shapes around one, the church, the death one faces sooner or later. The imperative need for water implies the importance placed here on food and gardens.[1] In contrast to *The Professor's House,* which first asked similar questions through similar motifs, *Death Comes for the Archbishop* suggests some answers. It therefore must be judged the more awesome masterpiece.

That the heart has its reasons unknown to the intellect is a truth articulated most memorably by Pascal, who is identified in the last chapters as a favorite writer of the Archbishop's (*DA*, 267, 276). Both Latour and Pascal are from Auvergne, associated in French stereotypes with stubborn determination, obstinacy, and tenacity. Pascal is the authority whom Latour quotes often to his students. In this ostensibly casual, though repeated, reference, Cather adds to her work a significant resonance, the key, in fact, to all the literary references of this novel. For example, toward the end of the book Latour's three favorite writers are identified as Augustine, Mme. de Sévigné, and Pascal; and in his student days, Joseph has been reprimanded by an old priest "not untouched by Jansenism" (*DA*, 203). Pascal's first *Provincial Letter,* written to defend the Jansenists of Port-Royal against the Jesuits and the Pope, "exploded immediately like a powder magazine: one of the most staggering publishing successes of the Ancien Règime. It was greeted with roars of laughter all over Paris."[2] The Jansenists were partisans of Cornelius Jansen, Bishop of Ypres, whose work *Augustinus* was declared to contain five unacceptable propositions. While the Pope won this struggle, Pascal's letters were so brilliant that "From the provinces, Mme. de Sévigné begged her friends to send them to her." Apparently, "Mme. de Sévigné . . . found them delightful."[3]

As person and thinker, Pascal provides a model for Jean Latour. Cather may have been rereading Pascal at this time in her life, however, because as Turnell summarizes, "Pascal's primary concern was a lay apostolate to the unbeliever. The *Pensées* were written for the sceptical man of the world and for the earnest seeker after truth who cast a longing glance at the Church with the secret wish that it were all true."[4]

The historical figure Blaise Pascal distinguished himself first as a mathematician:

> At the age of sixteen Blaise Pascal put his abilities to the test among these old fogies. The Benjamin of the Mersenne Academy soon showed his colleagues that he was someone with whom they had to reckon. He offered for discussion his *Essai pour les coniques,* which was printed in 1640 as a

broadsheet on a single piece of paper. He stated clearly and simply the conclusions reached by Desargues, but added a new theorem which was named after him. He showed that the opposite sides of a hexagon inserted in the circumference of a circle meet at three points which are in a straight line. Then he went on to extend his theorem to any conic section. And he showed the gentlemen of the Academy that he could extract four hundred propositions from his theorem.[5]

Pascal's projective geometry, according to Brome, touches aesthetics as well as mathematics because it is concerned with perspective.[6] Further,

The problem of the repayment of stakes gave Pascal the idea of using very simple data to draw up a table of proportionate wins and chances which led to the invention of the famous arithmetical triangle. To tell the truth, the triangle existed before him.... But it is a fact that in this, as in the course of his experiments on the vacuum, Pascal displays his genius by the breadth of his views and the number of the deductions he makes from the data. With ... [others] he laid the foundations of the calculation of probabilities which in a letter to the Academy ... he calls by this title which he himself regards as staggering: "the geometry of chance."[7]

It is initially the cones, triangles, and geometry of chance that Cather seems to be linking directly to Latour. Cather's novel opens with the troubled bishop wandering lost in a featureless country, or rather one "crowded with features all exactly alike" (*DA*, 17). The country demands a projective geometry as well as an accurate calculation of probabilities. It is full of "conical hills" in which "every conical hill was spotted with smaller cones" (*DA*, 18). The landscape's "red sand hills ... the shape of haycocks" are so "exactly like one another" that Latour seems to be wandering in "some geometrical nightmare" (*DA*, 18). Cather insists, "The hills thrust out of the ground so thickly that they seemed to be pushing each other, elbowing each other aside, tipping each other over" (*DA*, 18). They confuse Latour, and he must close his eyes against "the intrusive omnipresence of the triangle" (*DA*, 18).

Like Pascal, who "flung himself into the most complicated figures because his imagination enabled him to see things in space,"[8] Latour is a man "in a thousand" (*DA*, 19). He can recognize in a natural object such as a juniper tree "the form of the Cross." (*DA*, 19) Pascal once wrote, "The perceptions of our senses are always true."[9] Latour perceives through his senses a significant form that signifies to him a profound truth. Unlike Myra Henshawe or Godfrey St. Peter, he is willing to surrender control of his life as he focuses his senses, and in such focus and surrender lies his salvation: "Empowered by long training, the young priest blotted himself out of his own consciousness and meditated upon the anguish of his Lord. The Passion of Jesus became for him the only reality; the need of his own body was but a part of that conception" (*DA*, 20).

Having endured the cross, Latour gains the crown and rises to new life. By submitting within this geometrical nightmare, he transcends it. The point is in no way casual. When Latour "blotted himself out of his own consciousness" he lived; at the end of the book, "He sat in the middle of his own consciousness" (*DA*, 290), and died. The book therefore quietly reinforces the association its two preceding fictions make between self-consciousness and death.

Conical hills are again referred to when Joseph leaves for Colorado (*DA*, 253) and when Latour's cathedral rises from such hills with a purpose so strong it was like action (*DA*, 272). Latour himself blends into the cone-shaped hills as much as his cathedral does. For Cather implies about lives what Latour accepts about architecture: "either a building is part of a place or it is not" (*DA*, 272). In fact, we read, "As he cherished this wish [to build a cathedral worthy of the naturally beautiful setting] and meditated upon it, he came to feel that such a building might be a continuation of himself and his purpose, a physical body full of his aspirations after he passed from the scene" (*DA*, 175). *To be part of a place*, however, may require a blotting out of one's own consciousness. To sit in one's own consciousness is to withdraw from one's surroundings.

Pascal the tortured believer and geometrician also furnishes one explanation for the singular structure of this novel, and perhaps for its style and central theme as well. In the older Brunschvicg edition of 1904, the *Pensées* begins with an explanation of "The difference between the mathematical and the intuitive mind."[10] In the mathematical, we are told, "the principles are palpable, but removed from ordinary use." In the other, "the principles are found in common use, and are before the eyes of everybody." Pascal explores at length the difference between these minds:

> The reason, therefore, that some intuitive minds are not mathematical is that they cannot at all turn their attention to the principles of mathematics. But the reason that mathematicians are not intuitive is that they do not see what is before them, and that, accustomed to the exact and plain principles of mathematics, and not reasoning till they have well inspected and arranged their principles, they are lost in matters of intuition where the principles do not allow of such arrangement. . . . And thus it is rare that mathematicians are intuitive and that men of intuition are mathematicians, because mathematicians wish to treat matters of intuition mathematically, and make themselves ridiculous. . . .
>
> But dull minds are never either intuitive or mathematical.[11]

Pascal obviously explores both types respectfully, although Steinmann reminds us, "In his eyes the ideal order is the mathematical order." A mathematical order does not cover every contingency, however: "Not everything is defined in it because there are some ideas which are so clear that all definition of them is useless and impossible. But we define everything that is not self-evident."[12]

What Pascal's thought on these subjects does for the Cather reader is to offer another explanation for Cather's decision to build *Death Comes for the Archbishop* around *two* protagonists, both sympathetically presented, though they are opposite to each other. Latour represents Pascal's mathematical, as Vaillant represents his intuitive, mind. Latour occasionally fails to notice commonplace details, and thus loses himself in the desert. But Vaillant occasionally fails to grasp overarching principles and thus faces financial misconduct charges before the Papal Court after he becomes Bishop of Colorado.

Cather's two equally admirable priests, Latour and Vaillant, are opposites in almost countless ways. Latour is a man of reflection, for example, while Vaillant is a man of action. Latour is careful and thoughtful, while Vaillant is impulsive. Latour loves a few very well, while Vaillant is sympathetic with many people. Latour is an organizer, while Vaillant is a developer and proselytizer. Latour is a scholar, and Vaillant is a preacher. Latour gardens, while Vaillant cooks. Latour identifies with the Indians, while Vaillant identifies with the Mexicans. Latour finds building a cathedral work for the head, while Vaillant seeks lost souls "without pride and without shame" (*DA,* 262). Latour thus erects a building that will embody his aspirations after he has passed from the earth; Vaillant builds a religious empire on earth and therefore deserves "a constellation" of stars in his heavenly crown (*DA,* 262). Latour tries to curb excesses, while Vaillant uses lax means for good ends. Latour acts expediently, while Vaillant is dogmatic. Latour sees faith as a spring of water rising miraculously out of the thirsty desert; Vaillant sees that "Faith, in that wild frontier, is like a buried treasure" (*DA,* 207). Latour dies of having lived and dies quietly as Indians squat silently in the nearby courtyard, while Joseph cheats death repeatedly and then attracts thousands to his funeral, which is not unlike a circus. Such a list of differences, though already long, could be extended much further. But what is important is that Cather, like Pascal, respects both her opposites; she concedes that neither is entirely self-sufficient and that each needs the other to function with maximal effectiveness.

Cather's choice of two opposite but equally worthy protagonists (though finally the Pascal-like Latour *is* the more important and central figure, as so many have asserted) is reflected in still another structural device. For Cather begins her novel twice, first with a prologue and then with a first chapter. The two openings—like intersecting triangles that provide the six points of a circumscribed hexagon—begin Cather's own interesting study in perspective. They provide paired yet opposite sentences. Through the points of intersection one can map the straight lines to the novel's final point.

The Prologue's opening sentence—"One summer evening in the year 1848, three Cardinals and a missionary Bishop from America were dining together in the gardens of a villa in the Sabine hills, overlooking Rome"—contains eight or ten (depending on how one counts) words or phrases that point toward important themes. In pleasant **summer twilight** (spared the glare and heat of an earlier sun), three **Cardinals,** privileged princes of the church, survey a much cruder **missionary** from **America** as they **dine luxuriously** in a **garden** overlooking the now-safely-domesticated **Sabine Hills** while keeping **Rome** in full sight.

Now consider the balancing opposite qualities of the first sentence in chapter one: "One afternoon in the autumn of 1851 a solitary horseman, followed by a pack-mule, was pushing through an arid stretch of country somewhere in central New Mexico" (*DA,* 17). Hour, season, light, motion, landscape, number, occupant, emotion, location, and effect are all antithetical to the opening of the Prologue; yet the kind of information given in the two sentences is the same. Thus, Cather's two beginnings provide intersecting points through which one can draw the lines that will eventually converge at accomplished mission points and at satisfied promises: "To fulfill the dreams of one's youth; that is the best that can happen to a man. No worldly success can take the place of that" (*DA,* 261).

From the "splendid finish" mentioned in the Prologue to the "purpose as strong as action" that the cathedral has begun to serve in the final chapter, Cather's structure appears as clear and carefully controlled as a geometrical figure. It is a figure that reverses normal order, moving from the finish to a new purpose. But as we have seen, one can imagine that a primary motive behind this particular fiction was the hopeful assertion of renewal after total exhaustion: that is, the assertion of rebirth. All the parts are significant, as in a legend that is totally opposite dramatic treatment. To be clear, however, it does not have to be simple, as the memory of Pascal's circumscribed hexagon prods us to recall.

In fact, several familiar explanations of this structure remain helpful. For example, her episodes move along as if they were panels from Puvis de Chavannes' life of Saint Geneviève in the Pantheon.[13] Or the novel's nine books parallel the nine strokes of the bell when the Angelus is rung correctly.[14] Or, in fact, the southwestern life Latour leads in the site of his potential martyrdom can be read, episode by episode, as stations of the cross, merely starting backwards with the near crucifixion in the desert. Or (if art and religion are the same thing in the end) the life in the service of religion turns out to be lived also in the service of art. That life holds as much art as a major cathedral. Each episode, in fact, contains some precious object or significant shape to which Latour is sensitive. All these keys quickly open up the novel, as if it were a cathedral, without necessarily admitting the touring eye to every chapel. To use another metaphor, once one recognizes the complexity of Cather's mind and structures, one does not expect a single geometrical figure to exhaust her blueprint. One may well demand, however, that all the figures within her completed circle intersect at some point to trace the line to her dominating themes.

Latour's stations of the cross begin as he experiences lostness and vertigo in that desert which gives every evidence that God has forsaken him. He is rescued by the animal instincts of his mount, only to find another station at Aqua Secreta. In this oasis where the residents "want our own ways and our own religion" (*DA*, 27), Latour finds an ignorance so dense that the occupants can hold only one idea in their minds at one time. Such natives illustrate for him the terrible needs he must fill, as well as the sources of his own refreshment in their folk art.

As he continues from station to station, not all the Bishop's days are filled with tribulations. He shares a restorative Christmas dinner with Father Joseph, hears the Angelus rung miraculously well on a beautiful bell, and even receives a beautiful mule for his future travels, thanks to Vaillant's zeal. But on the way to help refugees at Mora he comes near being murdered. Soon thereafter, in visiting Father Jesus de Baca, he encounters the remnants of a faith that precedes his own and a priest who is as superstitious as any native (*DA,* 86). Latour confronts frivolity in Gallegos of Albuquerque, Indian intractability at Laguna, clerical pride and personal ambition in the inappropriate church built at Ácoma, nature's threat to swallow him up in Jacinto's snake cave, undisciplined lechery and disorder in Father Martínez of Taos, and avarice and schism in Father Lucero. Still later, Doña Isabella Olivares teaches him something about personal vanity, the terror of aging, and his own cruelty. He must even face the pain of his own political expediency in his relation to Carson's treatment of the Indians, or to the issue of slavery. And Joseph's absence leaves him periodically prey to periods of coldness and doubt and to the recognition that Joseph returns his love much less intensely than Jean gives it. The discovery of gold beneath Pike's Peak doubles his responsibilities as well as expanding his territory, just as he begins to get his first territory organized; and when he finally survives all these ordeals, Latour must face, for having lived, death itself—extinction as ultimate reward. Truly he endures as many painful trials and tasks as his Master did. In enduring, he incorporates them into his living sacrifice as Jesus and his worshippers have been required to do.

Seeing Latour's life as a structure that he methodically builds allows one to understand why Cather places such stress, in the Prologue, on the need for the new bishop to have intelligence in matters of art, to be able to arrange. *Death Comes for the Archbishop* functions as its own gallery containing many pieces, the greatest of which is the portrait of Latour. Or one might say that the book itself becomes Cather's enclosing cathedral.

From the beginning Latour's taste defines excellence. But because his taste is exquisite, Latour displays "a kind of courtesy toward himself, toward his beasts," and toward all objects, even in the desert (*DA,* 16). Rescued, he is immediately interested in "the wooden figures of the saints, found in even the poorest Mexican houses," which are "much more to his taste than the factory-made plaster images in his mission churches in Ohio" (*DA,* 28). Upon his return to Santa Fe, he chooses his study for its "agree-able shape" (*DA,* 33) and lives in a kind of sacred space, perfumed by piñon-wood smoke that smells like incense (*DA,* 35). Much later still, he receives a present that will be good for the eye, as Joseph is given something good for the palate. In all these ways, in fact, Cather calls attention to the importance of beauty, of beautiful art objects and decorations, and of the Archbishop's ability to appreciate them.

The Archbishop also excels in his ability to appreciate natural phenomena—in fact, is able to build his cathedral as he dreams it because he can recognize the stone he needs for the edifice in a hillside. And finally, it seems to me, the extraordinary power of this book comes from its landscapes or descriptions of nature, which Cather is able to include because Latour can appreciate the things she describes best. The novel carries word-painting to its highest peak. Cather had publically acknowledged as early as 1921 that what she did best was "descriptive work" and "picture making."[15] She lets out all the stops here, removes all her own restraints. The result is page after page of "picture making" that for once matches the magnificence of the southwestern terrain and atmosphere. For example:

> Beautiful surroundings, the society of learned men, the charm of noble women, the graces of art, could not make up to him for the loss of those light-hearted mornings of the desert, for that wind that made one a boy again. He had noticed that this peculiar quality in the air of new countries vanished after they were tamed by man and made to bear harvests. Parts of Texas and Kansas that he had first known as open range had since been made into rich farming districts, and the air had quite lost that lightness, that dry aromatic odour. The moisture of plowed land, the heaviness of labour and growth and grain-bearing, utterly destroyed it; one could breathe that only on the bright edges of the world, on the great grass plains or the sage-brush desert.

> That air would disappear from the whole earth
> in time, perhaps; but long after his day. He did not
> know just when it had become so necessary to him,
> but he had come back to die in exile for the sake of
> it. Something soft and wild and free, something
> that whispered to the ear on the pillow, lightened
> the heart, softly, softly picked the lock, slid the
> bolts, and released the prisoned spirit of man into
> the wind, into the blue and gold, into the morning,
> into the morning! (*DA*, 275–76)

The capacity for appreciation is a matter of taste or style, however, and in those matters we again discern links to Pascal. The
fact that no absolutely correct order for the *Pensées* can be established suggests the need to learn to read that work without holding the note or assuming that its ordered composition will lead
to a specifically contrived effect.[16] But in regard to prose style
itself, Pascal's convictions predate Cather's: "He possessed the sec-
ondary quality of the poet which is completely negative: he detested rhetoric, despised Cicero and loathed emphasis. He made
fun of the inflated vocabulary, the flashiness and preciosity of the
verbal trumpery that ... his time called poetry. He himself had
given very little thought to such matters, but they aroused an
instinctive revulsion in him."[17] Part of Cather's gravitation toward
the understated style of a saint's legend may trace to Pascal's style,
which she was absorbing appreciatively as she was composing this
book. And Pascal taught, "The fact is that it is less important to
prove the existence of God than to make people feel his presence,
which is the most useful and, taken all around, the easiest job.
And in order to feel him, we must seek him in those feelings
which still remain in us and which are a legacy of the greatness
of our first nature.[18] In recreating a boy's exhilaration in the air
of the morning, Cather obviously helps readers to "feel his presence."

Religion is a major source of beauty and art in this narrative,
so that religion itself comes to seem, by the end, the highest art
of any culture. Thus, the novel leads to a deep respect for all
religion, as for all functional and indigenous forms of art. Truly

in this novel (whether skeptic Godfrey St. Peter can be thought to have adequately understood the fact or not), art and religion are the same thing in the end. As Padre de Baca's parish Christianizes the ancient parrot, so the Ácoma Indians paganize the painting of St. Joseph. But both artworks remain vital symbols because they are integral parts of their surrounding cultures.

Finally, art and religion are not only the same thing but also are forms of miracle. Pascal defined miracle as "an effect which goes beyond the natural power of the means employed to produce it." In another version, Pascal explains, "Thus I call it miraculous when illness is cured by touching a sacred relic, when a man possessed is healed by invoking the name of Jesus, etc., because the effects exceed the natural powers of the words used to invoke God or the natural powers of a relic, neither of which can heal the sick nor drive out devils." [19] The nature of miracle is a matter in which Pascal was deeply and personally interested. Pascal, in fact, conceded that heretics and unbelievers could perform a miracle to confirm a truth, an assertion that may have had more than passing interest for Willa Cather. In her novel, Jean Latour and Joseph Vaillant understand *miracle* in different and opposite ways, Joseph's miracle always running against—as Jean's occurs within the predictable bounds of—nature. Both, like Pascal before them, nevertheless recognize that miracles occur, and more often than many think. Pascal, in fact, once erupted, "How I hate those who profess to doubt miracles!" [20]

According to Joseph Vaillant, "miracle is something that we can hold in our hands and love" (*DA,* 50). Jean Latour confirms wisely, "Where there is great love there are always miracles" (*DA,* 50). For both these churchmen as for their predecessors, "Their way through the wilderness had blossomed with little miracles" (*DA,* 279). And finally this book, built as carefully as a cathedral, can be considered a kind of miracle. It creates an effect that exceeds the natural powers of the means employed. Besides providing a dependable source of inspiration for legions of readers, it rejuvenated an emotionally crippled writer. After completing it, she was once again able, for a little while,[21] to know delight.

CHAPTER EIGHT

Shadows and Lasting Things:
Shadows on the Rock

*Signora Duse . . . differs from all other women of
the stage. . . . She has moved through the crowd of
babbling Thespians without seeing or hearing
them, she has worn the motley as though it were a
nun's hood, she has gone from theatre to theatre as
though she were going from shrine to shrine to
perform some religious worship. . . . She has kept
her personality utterly subdued and unseen and
spoken only through her art. It is like the music
one hears in a convent where the tones awaken
and thrill, but the singer is hidden behind the
veiled grating of the choir. No one knows what
manner of woman it is that this music comes
from. . . . She is utterly alone upon the icy heights
where other beings cannot live. . . . In a calling
that is the least austere she leads the life of a nun.*

———— WILLA CATHER *The Kingdom of Art* ————
from the *Journal*, November 4, 1894.

*In response to a publicly published letter from
Duse stating "I am what I am," Cather continued
six months later:*

*You are right, Signora Duse, keep your secrets,
you might tell us all and we would never understand. . . . There is something wonderfully beautiful in that letter, it is so full of the loveliness and*

lovelessness and desolation of art. . . . Of the lone-
liness which besets all mortals who are shut up
alone with God, of the gloom which is the shadow
of God's hand consecrating His elect. Truly, it is
fortunate that genius is not often laid upon men,
for how many are strong enough to endure its an-
guish? Solitude, like some evil destiny, darkens its
cradle, and sits watching even upon its grave. It is
the veil and the cloister which keep the priesthood
of art untainted from the world.

—— WILLA CATHER, *The Kingdom of Art* ——
from the *Journal,* June 16, 1895.

By most accounts, Cather's decision to write *Shadows on the Rock*
came impulsively—without the long incubation period that
seemed to precede her other novels. She saw Quebec for the first
time in 1928, the year after she published *Death Comes for the
Archbishop.* As early as 1897, however, Cather was commenting
in print on a book subtitled *A Romance of Old Quebec,* and quib-
bling with those who thought that "Canada had no literature
because it had no national life; that it was like a plant whose roots
drew their nourishment from the other side of the Atlantic, and
they lost most . . . of it under the sea."[1] Thus, the *thematic question*
central to this novel—Where does such a transplant as Quebec
find the nourishment that keeps it alive?—had been lying dor-
mant in her head for more than thirty years. We also find in
Cather's early criticism first versions of several vivid images the
novel expands, especially for the Jeanne le Ber sections. Interestingly for our present purposes, in her devoutly admiring descriptions of the actress Eleanora Duse, Cather linked theater,
dedication to one's personal art, and religious vocation. The link
reminds us of Professor St. Peter's lecture, which builds an ex-

tended trope[2] linking medieval life and theatrical art with religion:

> As long as every man and woman who crowded
> into the cathedrals on Easter Sunday was a princi-
> pal in a gorgeous drama with God, glittering angels
> on one side and the shadows of evil coming and
> going on the other, life was a rich thing. The king
> and the beggar had the same chance at miracles and
> great temptations and revelations. . . .
> With the theologians came the cathedral-builders;
> the sculptors and glass-workers and painters. They
> might, without sacrilege, have changed the prayer a
> little and said, *Thy will be done in art, as it is in
> heaven.* How can it be done anywhere else *as* it is in
> heaven? But I think the hour is up.   (*PH,* 68–69)

Remembering Bernice Slote's admonition that clear correspondences exist between "the first things Willa Cather wrote and some of the last,"[3] we can say that the way in which Cather presented the central theme and the most memorable character of *Shadows on the Rock* can be traced back to ideas she was already beginning to develop before the turn of the century. Remembering the links we now expect to find between her novels, we can also say that a crucial speech in *The Professor's House* is elaborated upon in *Shadows on the Rock.* Part of this novel, then, emerges from longstanding opinions, and part, by Cather's own assertion, is something audaciously new.[4]

One impulse behind *Shadows on the Rock,* however, is as old as the species: to create the image of a safe place in which to live, or to find an image of life that one might associate with safety. Jacinto reminds Bishop Latour, "A man can do whole lot when they hunt him day and night like an animal. Navajos on the north, Apaches on the south; the Ácoma run up a rock to be safe" (*DA,* 97). Like the Ácoma, Cather runs up a rock to be safe when she writes *Shadows.* In fact, she made no bones about it. In the two-and-a-half years of its writing, she told more than one friend, "the book had been her rock of refuge, the only thing in her life that held together and stayed the same."[5] Why she felt pursued and hounded enough to need a rock of refuge is another question. But so is the kind of rock she elected to run up. Suffice it to say that as early as her days of travel in 1920, Edith Lewis remembered Cather's saying that "she wanted to live in the Middle Ages. And we did live in the Middle Ages, so far as was possible."[6]

The happy days that *Death Comes for the Archbishop* initiated lasted about six months, and reading proofs for the novel seemed "like having a gorgeous party all over again."[7] But by summer of 1927 the party was over. Cather was forced to leave her Bank Street apartment, an upheaval in her life she found traumatic. To avoid the turmoil she went west to visit her brother Roscoe in Wyoming, and coming back by way of Red Cloud, was on hand when her father suffered a heart attack. She canceled her planned trip to Europe and stayed in Nebraska until he recovered. When she finally returned to New York City she found that storing her belongings was "like having a funeral."[8] Two months in Jaffrey, New Hampshire, left her unrestored. She had no ideas for new work and experienced her first "let-down" or involuntary "let up" in five years. Her "temporary" New York lodgings were in the Grosvenor Hotel, but she was back in Red Cloud from Christmas until late February.

One week after she returned to the East, her father died. Cather reacted to this news so quickly and reflexively that she reached Red Cloud by train at 3:00 A.M.—in less than twenty-four hours. Her dead-of-night arrival gave her time to sit quietly alone with her father's body until daybreak. But after the body was moved to their Episcopal Church nearby, Mildred Bennett relates, "she paced frantically back and forth between the house and the . . . church . . . , wringing her hands, apparently unable to conquer the grief and panic which overwhelmed her. Acquaintances felt that her grief was not unmixed with still another emotion—fury—and a resentment that time, her greatest enemy, could affect such changes."[9] After her brother Douglass took their mother with him to California to recover from the shock of the death and the strain of the funeral, Cather stayed on alone in the old family house in Red Cloud for over a month, to find healing in the silence, as Myra Henshawe had once advocated. After a while, "She felt rested and strong as if her father himself had restored her soul."[10]

During this time of solitude, Willa spent hours getting the house ready for her mother's return and doing things as she understood her mother would like to have them done. When *Shadows on the Rock* finally appeared, the daughter's driving desire to follow an absent mother's system of housekeeping is crucial to the emotional thrust of the book. Finally, however, Willa embarked again for the East, stopping for a checkup at the Mayo Clinic. She arrived in New York at the end of April "absolutely tired." She had done no writing for six months and was in no physical shape to begin any. "Life does beat us up sometimes, she wrote [Mary] Jewett, and we must take our drubbing."[11]

By Edith Lewis's report, Grand Manan and their newly built cottage there "seemed the only foothold left on earth." For the sake of novelty, they decided to travel the long way—by way of Montreal and Quebec—and see new country. According to Lewis, "from the first moment that she looked down from the windows of the Frontenac on the pointed roofs and Norman outlines of the town of Quebec, Willa Cather was not merely stirred and charmed—she was overwhelmed by the flood of memory, recognition, surmise it called up; by the sense of its extraordinarily French character, isolated and kept intact through hundreds of years, as if by a miracle, on this great un-French continent."[12] In other words, at just the point when her homes disintegrated, Cather glimpsed a new psychological home, full of familiar and beloved things kept intact for centuries, as if just for her. She must have felt a little like Tom Outland discovering miraculously preserved Cliff City.

Cather began historical research on the place immediately, while Lewis experienced a fortuitously timed attack of the flu that prevented their traveling on. Eventually they got to Grand Manan, where their new and heretofore unseen cottage sat on their own Gloucester's cliff facing appropriately *east*, so that they could see the dawn and the sea simultaneously. The new cottage, like Tom Outland's Cliff City, was a place Cather could possess and return to. It represented potential stability and roots. It even had a floored attic workspace for Cather to use, not unlike God-frey St. Peter's. And with no plumbing or electricity, the place was an invitation to become "a primitive" again, as St. Peter had wished to do.

After two restoring months, Cather returned to New York. According to Lewis, "So far as I recollect, Willa Cather began writing *Shadows on the Rock* that Fall at the Grosvenor. At Thanksgiving she made a second visit to Quebec, this time alone. She was working with the energy and concentration she always brought to a new undertaking when, in December, she got word that her mother in California had had a paralytic stroke; and broke off her writing to hurry to the Coast and help her brother Douglass make arrangements for their mother's care." [13] It was another major shock and another terrifying reminder of the inexorable march of time.

By the signs we can read, then, in Quebec Cather spotted a new and interesting place that seemed to her to represent something she at that point yearned for: stability and undisrupted cultural continuity. In her letter to Governor Wilbur Cross, Cather said, "To me the rock of Quebec is not only a stronghold on which many strange figures have for a little time cast a shadow in the sun; it is the curious endurance of a kind of culture, narrow but definite. There another age persists. There, among the country people and the nuns, I caught something new to me; a kind of feeling about life and human fate that I could not accept, wholly, but which I could not but admire." [14] The kind of life she glimpsed there was not unlike the medieval one she coveted, in which a commonly shared faith or myth structure unified the most diverse elements of a culture. Discussing cycle plays, V. A. Kolve reminds us that "the Corpus Christi cycles owe much of their power, delightfulness, and variety, as well as the astonishing range of human experience they present, to this need to address a widely varied assembly. . . . we must renounce certain oversimple conceptions of their audience and their purpose. The plays were neither written by the unlearned nor staged exclusively for them. The medieval drama was catholic and comprehensive." [15]

Having seen Quebec, Cather began with immediately reviving

interest to imagine a tale set in the past that would capture a unified Kebecois kind of feeling about life. The tale would be a tribute to a coherent life developed by a cohering community that honored such citizens as a loving and daughter-nurturing father. She had barely started, however, when she was forced to confront the mortality not only of fathers but also of mothers.

The novel was eventually published within a month of her mother's death in 1931 and "became the most popular book in the United States during the next year."[16] It went through ten printings before the end of 1931 and ten more after that. It obviously in some way satisfied deep concerns of many readers.

The first thing one notices about the criticism of this novel is its remarkably good quality, and the second thing is the fact that the critics are thoroughly polarized. For example, Marilyn Callander describes the novel as Willa Cather's fairy tale and compares it to "a love-gift to a child." David Stouck notices "the preoccupation throughout the book with disease and death." Susan Rosowski sees in the novel "a saint's life to tell of the apotheosis of a French girl into a Canadian Holy Mother," while James Woodress finds Cécile "insufferably pious" and when out of her element "an intolerable prig." I believe they are all right. I also believe that Cather had in her own mind a metaphor for the communal life she was recreating; that she consciously shaped *Shadows on the Rock* on the analogy of a medieval miracle or saint's play. This analogy was not rigid, as if she were writing allegory. She described the book, in fact, as "a prose composition not too conclusive, not too definite: a series of pictures remembered rather than experienced."[17] But the analogy she was drawing, I think, contains and explains the book's apparent contradictions as well as the contrary critical responses that all prove illuminating.

Though lengthy, the following comments by Benjamin Hunninger prove immediately applicable to concerns now at hand:

> Theater is play—which defines it neither as real nor as unreal, neither as wise nor as foolish, neither as good nor as bad. Theater serves no practical purpose if judged by the standards of everyday life. It

is uncommon, separate. Exclusively for those who similarly separate themselves from life (its participants) does theater become truthful, important, orderly. This holds true, not only for theater, but for all art. It characterizes to a great extent also another human activity—the rite. Here lies our first and most permanent tie between the theater and art on one hand and religion and rite on the other. Everything which "does not belong," which serves no direct purpose in nature, which knows no function in society, which essentially escapes the intellect, belongs to the other side of life, to the "totally different," that has from primitive times been experienced as a supernatural force, usually leading into religion.

As an idea, "play" may escape the meshes of rational definition, but as phenomenon we see it everywhere, always a satisfaction to the human urge for pleasure and recreation. It is apparent that from it in spiritual activity the metaphor, for example, has developed and with that, the entire potentiality for abstract thought, which in turn indicates that not only religion, but also man's entire spiritual life, is unthinkable and impossible without play. Play releases man from the limits of matter. In stage-play, pleasure lies in imitation, originally of external and tangible existence. By the same metaphoric road, this imitation can reach the entire breadth and depth of human emotion. The theater and the rite meet again in such imitation: in primitive cultures, in fact, they are one, and the same.

Huizinga put the question of whether or not the peculiar relationship between play and beauty is the result of the very form and order created by play. It is true, at any rate, that play fences in an area of the imagination in which it creates absolute order, strictly guarded against anything which might disturb the *in-lusio,* the illusion. In every respect, the order it creates is contrary to the disorder of the imperfect world outside the play area: the contrast is so obvious that it seems willed and purposed. With that observation, play is revealed to serve not only as pleasure but also as protection: it creates order to bring a certain part of the chaotic world under control. Though still far from any practical purpose in everyday life, it acquires with this a certain social or perhaps more psychological function.[18]

Miracle plays grew out of the rites of the medieval church that themselves both established and celebrated communal order. They remained popular for centuries.[19] Miracle plays also, Cather's novel asserts plausibly, flourished in seventeenth-century Quebec. They are directed at the Ursuline school by Sister Anne de Sainte-Rose, who "had charm and wit and the remains of great beauty—everything that would appeal to a little girl brought up on a rude frontier. Cécile still saw her when she went to the convent on errands, and she was always invited to the little miracle plays which Sister Anne had the *pensionnaires* give at Christmas-time" (*SR,* 61). Such dramatic celebration of the Nativity and saints' lives and miracles was natural in a place like Quebec. Walking abroad in the autumn fog "was like walking in a dream. . . . Not even the winter snows gave one such a feeling of being cut off from everything and living in a world of twilight and miracles" (*SR,* 61–62).

Indeed, in every season, the Kebecois assume the possibility of miracles. Miracles occur daily here. Some, of course, are more flamboyant than others. When the town survives the bombardment of Sir William Phip's beseiging fleet, the church in the Lower Town is renamed "in recognition of the protection which Our Lady had afforded Quebec in that hour of danger" (*SR,* 64). But celebrating the miracles of Notre Dame was a primary purpose of the most popular miracle plays.[20] And on solemn feast days in Quebec, "all the stories of the rock came to life for Cécile; the shades of the early martyrs and great missionaries drew close about her. All the miracles that had happened there, and the dreams that had been dreamed, came out of the fog; every spire, every ledge and pinnacle, took on the splendour of legend" (*SR,* 95). As Frank reminds us, in a medieval ethos, "They could identify themselves with the sinners saved by acts of contrition; the lives and martyrdoms of the saints presented human values they could share. Dramatically considered, these miracle plays made use of an element of suspense lacking in the biblical plays; their action ranged far and wide and in so doing established a new freedom in the choice of persons, scenes, and emotions."[21]

Pierre Charron, one of the semiskeptical citizens of Quebec, believes in miracles because he has personally experienced them. Jeanne le Ber promised to pray that he would not die unexpectedly before having a chance to adjust his soul; he can assert, "I have certainly been delivered from sudden death" three times, as a result of Jeanne's prayers (*SR,* 180). The community's acceptance of miracle is a crucial point in this reading. R. George Thomas reminds us,

> comparisons seem incomplete because they lack the vital wholeness of context within which the pageants [which miracle plays provided] were enacted. The frame of mind of the spectator ... was not one of solely intellectual assent, or of participation in a ritual ceremony, or of tolerant amusement before light, if socially accepted, entertainment. ... Rather, the pageants were a confirmation—through the media of speech, action, song and spectacle—of the living faith and powerful assumptions of an entire community which believed itself to be an integral part of a wider community (or *ecclesia*) which encompassed all space and all time, and of which all spectators had some experience through the acts of worship, confession and communion which were as natural as breathing.[22]

It is exactly this worldview on which Cather insists, in depicting Quebec: "in this safe, lovingly arranged and ordered universe (not too vast, though nobly spacious), in this congenial universe, the drama of man went on at Quebec just as at home, and the Sisters played their accustomed part in it" (*SR,* 97).

In *Shadows on the Rock,* Quebec is not only that kind of coherent community out of which miracle plays developed; it also suggests the manger scenes that bring such drama alive: "Auclair thought this rock-set town like nothing so much as one of those little artificial mountains which were made in the churches at home to present a theatric scene of the Nativity; cardboard mountains, broken up into cliffs and ledges and hollows to accommodate groups of figures on their way to the manger; angels and shepherds and horsemen and camels, set on peaks, sheltered in grottoes clustered about the base" (*SR,* 5). Three-tiered Quebec in fact resembles the two- or three-storied sets of cycle-play pageant wagons: "The action of the cycles . . . frequently calls for two or more levels. . . . A stage with only one level would be psychologically unacceptable . . . [for the medieval audience] was used to seeing its ritual performed in several levels, at the foot of the altar and at the altar itself, on the porch and steps of the church, and even through the streets."[23]

What the physical characteristics of the town of Quebec remind its philosopher apothecary and us of, then, by the writer's intention, is the kind of backdrop familiar to the Norman French who not only founded Quebec but also originated the first trope-writing activities from which liturgical drama, and eventually medieval vernacular church drama, evolved. A simple but complete Shepherd's Play on the theme of the Nativity comes from Rouen (as do such Kebecois as the Pommier family, the Pigeon family, and Blinker). The Rouen Shepherd's Play still exists in a fourteenth-century manuscript. Arnold Williams explains, "The Rouen play is unique in its simplicity" and concerns Christmas as Normans celebrated it.[24] And from the first pages of Cather's novel, Quebec is associated with such Nativity plays and with a permeating Christmas spirit, even though the actual time when the novel begins is late October. But then, soon after that beginning Cécile reports to Count Frontenac, "Oh, everything we do, my father and I, is a kind of play" (*SR,* 58).

I take Cécile's assertion to be a book-defining statement. It leads us to make comparisons with those simple Norman theatrical tastes that Quebec citizens brought with them when they founded the town. It also leads us to remember Cather's remarkably reliable scholarly research. She researched this novel thoroughly, but she gravitated to this setting because she had been studying and reflecting on medieval Norman culture for years. Thus, she already knew the "basic facts" she would use:

> Extremely popular in the later Middle Ages, espe-
> cially in France and in the form of the miracle of
> our Lady, the saints' play is represented by eight
> extant plays, all dealing with Saint Nicholas. The
> legend of Saint Nicholas, little beholden to any as-
> certainable facts, characterizes him as a friend of
> the unfortunate and a reliever of poverty. He seems
> to be some sort of translated heathen god of gener-
> osity, and his feast on December 6 is sufficiently
> close to Christmas to explain why, as Santa Claus,
> he has displaced Father Christmas in the United
> States and Canada.[25]

No wonder *Shadows on the Rock* sometimes seems our nation's best Christmas book.

The metaphor of the miracle play directs episodes in this book and explains the pronounced oppositions David Stouck comments on, the folk elements Marilyn Callander catalogs, the emphasis on the Holy Mother that Susan Rosowski highlights, the unrelieved virtue of the central character that bothers James Woodress, and the conservative nature of the Catholicism John J. Murphy discusses: "The Catholicism [the novel] depicts is one of tradition, authority, ritual, miracles—an orderly, arranged, safe world—the kind Catholics have, fortunately or not, rejected."[26] A miracle play employs what by twentieth-century standards are flat characters, as well as a symbolic set that utilizes a good-at-the-top and sin-at-the-bottom topography consistent with the geography of Quebec. It also assumes that brutal mishaps and mutilations will be juxtaposed to better-than-life virtues, and insists on an order that includes miracles and saints.

One expected element in miracle plays is dramatic conversions, and we have several examples of them in *Shadows on the Rock*. When "an English sailor lay sick at the Hotel Dieu, Mother Catherine de Saint-Augustin ground up a tiny morsel of bone from Father Brebeuf's skull and mixed it in his gruel, and it made him a Christian" (*SR*, 125). But we have hardly begun the book when we find Cécile listening rapturously to the story of the *pécheresse* named Marie, one of Normandy's most abandoned sinners, who is so far past reclamation that she is driven out of town by respectable citizens and left to die in a solitary cave. Twelve years later, Sister Catherine de Saint-Augustin, who systematically prays for all the dying, is visited in Canada by a troubled soul from purgatory who asks why "I am the only one on whom you have no compassion." Sister Catherine establishes that the soul is "that poor Marie, the sinner, who died in the cave," but who was saved "thanks to the infinite mercy of the Blessed Virgin." At the last hour, "The tender Mother of all made it possible for me to repent," and now Marie needs only a few masses to release her from purgatory. Sister Catherine supplies them. "Some days later there appeared to her a happy soul, more brilliant than the sun, which smiled and said: 'I thank you, my dear Catherine, I go now to paradise" (*SR*, 37–39). Of special interest here is the fact that Cécile listens to this tale of miraculous conversion with admiration and rapture "almost like the glow of worldly pleasure" (*SR*, 40). The point, of course, is that such stories, or the dramatic forms that enacted them, provided more than religious pleasures, as indeed this book does also.[27]

Medieval cycle plays covered creation to doomsday and emphasized the crucial occasions in the church calendar year. In this novel Cather constructed a fiction around a year in the life of twelve-year-old Cécile Auclair. While Cather often used seasonal and cyclical time as a structuring device, this novel stands out as a carefully contained one-year-with-epilogue organization, analogous to the structure of the medieval cycle plays. Cécile may do little but her duty, and that well, but in the context we've now begun to understand we can see that she is fashioned to function as the hope of the New World. In her last year of life, Cécile's mother "would think fearfully of how much she was entrusting to that little shingled head; something so precious, so intangible; a feeling about life that had come down to her through so many centuries and that she had brought with her across the wastes of obliterating, brutal ocean" (*SR*, 25). In fact, "the character of M.

Auclair's house ... was really made of very fine moral qualities in two women: the mother's unswerving fidelity to certain traditions, and the daughter's loyalty to her mother's wish" (*SR*, 25–26). It is therefore no accident that this budding adolescent is as good in the novel's middle as in the beginning or the end. Cécile's personal growth is not necessary for this form. The novel celebrates communal growth, which is made possible by female stability and dependability.

Thus, unlike the two central clerics in *Death Comes for the Archbishop,* young Cécile Auclair never even encounters significantly trying temptations. Further, she never stumbles a single time, as Ántonia does in *My Ántonia*. She never wavers in her commitments, as Marian Forrester does in *A Lost Lady.* Further, Cather leaves young Cécile Auclair anchored in the same isolated Canadian place from which she does not long to return to French fleshpots. Unlike Lucy Gayheart, who follows her, she never even leaves home except for one truncated and well-chaperoned outing. Cécile remains what she begins: conventional, authority-accepting, home-loving, law-abiding, credulous, generous, and kind. Her purpose is to assure us it is possible to bring "a certain part of the chaotic world under control."

One thing this book did for Willa Cather, we therefore surmise, is to offer her a secure place, a world in itself, built like and with Peter's church, on a rock. It is shaped by mothers who pass along necessary knowledge before they die, and by fathers—natural, governmental, and clerical—who live to care for their own. As a side effect of this book, Cather may have relieved her own daughterly guilt by creating an offspring who was everything she had never been, and who therefore could be imagined to keep her important places safe. As a ritual penance she may have given idealized parents the perfect firstborn female that her own parents never had. But a more central motive was surely to relieve her own anxiety by creating a world time could not change or harm. She was still, however, whatever her personal motives, that same Willa Cather who always saw double.

The central event in a miracle play, after all, is a central miracle. For all the wonder of sinless Cécile, there's a more dramatic source of miracle here, which thrills all of Canada. And one feels somehow back in closer touch with the Willa Cather who wrote the other novels after one realizes that the greatest saint in *Shadows on the Rock* is also, by the novel's implied standards, its greatest sinner. Jeanne le Ber, the one visited by angels, is the one who betrayed her father's fondest hopes and broke his heart, denied her mother's deathbed wishes and refused a final kiss, rejected her lover's pleas, sending him into the forest, cut herself off from all elements of the community, embraced hunger and cold and discomfort—everything the colony works to conquer; and took on all the sin and misery of the continent. In short, the bad girl is the saint who provides the miracle that becomes the flowering of their corporate desire. In turning to her life of devotion, to her art, Jeanne le Ber lives out a lifeline that young journalist Willa Cather once ascribed to Eleanora Duse, the actress she profoundly admired. With no late-nineteenth century stage to run off to, Jeanne le Ber makes a stage of the chapel altar she has built with her marriage dowry. Her solitary performances there express "such resignation and despair!" Pierre Charron adds, "It froze everything in me. I felt that I would never be the same man again" (*SR,* 184). Hearing a sob in her supposedly empty auditorium, La Recluse maintains her perfect self-possession:

> "She was not startled. She stood still, with her hand
> on the latch of the grill, and turned her head, half-
> facing me. After a moment she spoke.
> "*Poor sinner,* she said, *poor sinner, whoever you are,
> may God have mercy upon you! I will pray for you.
> And do you pray for me also.*" (*SR,* 183)

It is interesting that ex-Baptist Cather so early associated a great actress with religious vocation. Later, creating the *religieuse* who is in many ways the most dynamic presence in this book, she associates that vocational energy with willful disobedience and with brilliant stage effects that hold the attention of all Canada. As reward for having "thrown the world away" (*SR,* 182), Jeanne earns a voice "harsh and hollow as an old crow's—terrible to hear!" (*SR,* 80). She wears "a stone face ... [that] had been through every sorrow" (*SR,* 182), and walks full of "resignation and despair" (*SR,* 183). But angels work for terrible Jeanne. And the news electrifies Canada. "The people have loved miracles for so many hundred years, not as proof or evidence, but because they are the actual flowering of desire. In them the vague worship and devotion of the simplehearted assumes a form" (*SR,* 137). The most important event in the novel, then, is not only one of a kind Cather has been mulling over for much of her life. It is also one that rewards the willful, family-disrupting and -rejecting daughter who takes on the awful knowledge of the sins of the world.

Shadows on the Rock asks what makes a place live. Cather posits a culture existing in conditions posing the greatest imaginable challenge to survival. From the first sentence's first syllable, she stresses different units of time—hour, month, season, year, century—all of which are running out. She begins by intensifying a sense of threat: "One afternoon late in October of the year 1697, Euclide Auclair, the philosopher apothecary of Quebec, stood on the top of Cap Diamant gazing down the broad, empty river far beneath him. Empty, because an hour ago the flash of retreating sails had disappeared ... and the last of the summer ships from France had started on her long voyage home." Beyond these public records of time's passage, the golden age of Cécile Auclair's childhood is also ending. Such a young, female, motherless child seems to tempt disaster.

Intensifying the threat further, Cather's emphasis from the beginning is also on a *place* being closed off. Here "winter ... [is] the deepest reality of Canadian life" (*SR,* 3). Before the first snowflake flies, however, *La Bonne Esperance,* The Good Hope, which is the last ship, sails away and leaves the remnants of French culture on "this rock in the North" (*SR,* 3) in the midst of the "Canadian Wilderness" (*SR,* 4). Their total isolation leaves no options but to go "back to their shops and their kitchens to face the stern realities of life" (*SR,* 3). Since the isolation will last eight months of the year, the novel purports to explain how the Kebecois lived through it. The answer must include every element of life in the town, from top to bottom, socially, religiously, and geographically. Here historical facts serve as symbols. Cather researched her material carefully, to make sure her surmises were historically accurate. Her answer begins with her permeating conviction that this survival requires an order that can only be supplied by a communally shared religion.

The actual topography of the town symbolizes communal hierarchical values. At first glance the most prominent sight is the chateau of Count Frontenac, but it is not literally the highest point. In fact a whole complex of ecclesiastical buildings—Recollet Friars' church, Ursuline convent, Jesuit monastery and seminary, cathedral and bishop's palace—all compose the "Upper Town" and witness to hierarchy made visible. The "Lower Town" at the foot of the cliff and along the riverfront is the place of worldly concerns, where merchants live as well as prostitutes. The connecting street has a few shops, most notably the apothecary's, belonging to Cécile's father, who is thus available to all, and represents an average citizen of median rank, or an Everyman.

Cather repeatedly stresses the crucial importance of the church to this colonial enterprise. Her insistence, in fact, led many to assume she had converted to Catholicism. She certainly insists that religion is crucial to the successful founding of a colony worth living in: "When an adventurer carries his gods with him into a remote and savage country, the colony he founds will, from the beginning, have graces, traditions, riches of the mind and spirit. Its history will shine with bright incidents, slight, perhaps, but precious, as in life itself, where the great matters are often as worthless as astronomical distances, and the trifles dear as the heart's blood" (*SR*, 98).

Having approached their rock with their religious values held close, the French of Quebec establish a village permeated with religious assumptions. One of the most moving scenes occurs around the celebration of the Nativity and the unpacking of a French crèche. A Quebec sailor has carved a beaver for little Jacques, the small son of his promiscuous mistress. Besides being a symbol of Canada, the object also suggests a lewd pun that Cather must have intended,[28] just as medieval actors deliberately incorporated the bawdy into their Nativity plays. But innocently, the boy still offers his one treasure to the developing Christmas display *"pour toujours."* It is accepted. "Our Lord died for Canada as well as for the world over there, and the beaver is our very special animal" (*SR*, 111).

As the crèche is arranged, the association of Quebec with Nativity plays is reinforced; the figures appear to be provincial, like the Kebecois themselves: "The Blessed Virgin wore no halo, but a white scarf over her head. She looked like a country girl, very naive, seated on a stool with her knees well apart under her full skirt, and very large feet. Saint Joseph, a grave old man in brown, with a bald head and wrinkled brow, was placed opposite her" (*SR*, 108). The French here stay so near their sources of inspiration that they can assert, "the angels are just as near to us here as they are in France"; for some, "they are nearer" (*SR*, 129). On holy days one can spot "families and friends in little flocks, all going toward the same goal,—the doors of the church, wide open and showing a ruddy vault in the blue darkness" (*SR*, 113). Book four opens with the whole town "gleaming above the river like an altar with many candles or like a holy city in an old legend, shriven, sinless, washed in gold" (*SR*, 169).

Quebec, connected by Holy Family Hill, centers its life in the family because of its worshipful reverence for the Holy Family. At the foot of the cliff is the best-loved church of the settlement, originally called the Church of the Infant Jesus. Its altar, where highest and humblest citizens love best to worship, features "by far the loveliest of all the Virgins in Quebec, a charming figure of young motherhood,—oh, very young, and radiantly happy, with a stately crown, and a long, blue cloak that parted in front over a scarlet robe" (*SR*, 65). Further, we read, "there is no other place in the world where the people are so devoted to the Holy Family as here in our own Canada. It is something very special to us" (*SR*, 101).

Under these circumstances, life itself, both individual and communal life, becomes a sacrament in which each element is an important and integral contributor to the whole. Because it is sacred in itself, each part of the Quebec day becomes ritualized, and therefore carries its own weight in the established order. We read what Cécile and her father do *habitually* in *every* waking hour. Because every detail of life is important, Cather carefully describes the architecture of the houses, the arrangement of the apothecary's rooms, the possessions on display in each chamber, the manner of setting a dinner table, and the typical menu of a standard meal (*SR*, 9–10). All are important objects in this set, for this play. And such details must be recorded because the facts they convey hold this world together and keep its culture alive. As Cécile's mother teaches her, "in time you will come to love your duties, as I do. You will see that your father's whole happiness depends on order and regularity, and you will come to feel a pride in it. Without order our lives would be disgusting, like those of the poor savages. At home, in France, we have learned to do all these things in the best way, and we are conscientious, and that is why we are called the most civilized people in Europe and other nations envy us" (*SR*, 24–25).

It is not merely any order, then, but the old tried-and-true order that Kebecois preserve and celebrate. The passion with which Cather's characters advocate such preservation recalls her contention to Governor Cross that "a new society begins with the salad dressing more than with the destruction of Indian villages. Those people brought a kind of French culture there and somehow kept it alive on that rock, sheltered it and tended it and on occasion died for it, as if it really were a sacred fire—and all this temperately and shrewdly, and with emotion always tempered by good sense."[29] Thus, this novel expresses intense reverence for tools of any kind, commercial or domestic: "These coppers, big and little, these brooms and clouts and brushes, were tools; and with them one made, not shoes or cabinet-work, but life itself. One made a climate within a climate; one made the days,—the complexion, the special flavor, the special happiness of each day as it passed; one made life" (*SR*, 198). Further, when visiting a disorderly and slovenly family, Cécile concludes, "They had kind ways, . . . but that was not enough; one had to have kind things about one, too" (*SR*, 197). Cather, in fact, would at this time have been especially sensitive to the need for kind things around one, with all of her kind things in storage. Serving her home as a priestess serves a sacred temple, Cécile must be about her father's and mother's business, preserving the kind things that make life worth living because they give comfort and therefore pleasure: they make a life.

The qualities Cather identifies with her most useful of life-making citizens, the apothecary, are instructive. Euclide Auclair (the clear measurer), is mild, thoughtful, urbane, conventional, and law-abiding. In the spirit of a morality play, he even advises the loose woman of the town at one point, "Do not quarrel with the Government, my girl. That can do you no good, and it might get you into trouble" (*SR*, 89). Euclide stays out of the worst forms of trouble because he is a man, not of action, but of reflection, and because, while dedicated to continuing his life as his father did before him, he is still capable, with his wife's encouragement, of moving the family apothecary shop to a new and strange continent. He is, however, a man of strong convictions who disapproves of fads, and he is capable of disregarding even a new bishop's authority when the bishop seems to him unwise.

Euclide, however, is not the exception but the rule, for the townsfolk on which this community depends are, for the most part, dedicated to performing humble chores well. One of the most interesting symbol systems in the whole novel centers on feet and the craft of making shoes to protect them. First, we have the wooden foot from which shoes for the great explorer La Salle were once fashioned. Though La Salle's foot "went farther than any other in New France" (*SR*, 83), we are still informed, "It went too far" (*SR*, 82). More often the feet of those who build this "city on a hill" go little farther than the town's clear boundaries. That is not to say, however, that feet that take small steps are unimportant. The whole hierarchy seems concerned about such tiny feet. Noticing the worn footwear of her young friend Jacques, Cécile knits socks for him, the Count buys shoes for him, the cobbler makes the best possible pair for him, and having spotted the infant weeping alone in the snow at night, the fierce old Bishop Laval carries him home, bathes his feet in an act emulating

Christ's, and kisses the feet and the boy as representative of "the least of these," whom Jesus commended to the charity of his true disciples.

Of course the world of new settlers must have its adventurers, too. A number of heroic explorers, of both secular and sacred vocations, people this novel. Most interesting is Pierre Charron, who is capable of becoming a surrogate protector for the Auclair family, once the count dies, and who eventually marries Cécile and rears a family of sons for New Canada. Pierre realizes "the romantic picture of the free Frenchman of the great forests which they had formed at home on the bank of the Seine" (*SR*, 171–72). His proud, vain, relentless, loyal, prejudiced character—a mixture of experience and sagacity—contrasts with the broken woodsman Antoine Frichette. But both witness to the key truth one learns in the wilderness: "In this world, who paddles must carry" (*SR*, 146). Not only every daily ritual but also every humble citizen must pull his own weight and care for his own canoe if the colony is to last.

In a study Willa Cather makes of goodness and continuity, one reasonably expects to find strong mention of their opposites. Such polar tensions are built into the very landscape here. Cap Diamant contrasts to Cap Tormente; nurturing river winds through horrifying forest; safe town is enclosed and almost engulfed by voracious wilderness. And rigidly ordered daily routines that become the very essence of the humdrum are interrupted by the miraculous—"there are so many sacred relics, and they are always working cures" (*SR*, 126)—as daily devotion is punctuated by bad faith.

Cather's town of two thousand is "always full of jealousies and quarrels" (*SR*, 20); "here much of the talk was gossip and very trivial" (*SR*, 22). Its citizens, from highest to lowest, are amply acquainted with grief. The Count was not rewarded adequately for his last campaign on behalf of the King; the devoted old Bishop Laval has lived to see his lifework undone by his successor; stalwart, masculine representative of the New World's best, Pierre Charron does not get the girl he loves first and most; little Jacques's heart's desire is denied when the sailor he loves fails to return. The cobbler's insistence on taking the time necessary for crafting perfect shoes merely irritates many of his customers, while the forest cripples the woodsman Frichette and the town lames Madame Pommier. Memories of the treacheries in European cities haunt the admired apothecary, while grotesque Blinker is terrified of the forest. All citizens honor the captains whose ships sustain them, but one captain admits he has no problems with pirating English ships. He shrugs and points out that the English have "no respect for good manners or religion" (*SR,* 220).

Perhaps the most interesting thematic opposition is that between the natural and the artificial. Nature is what surrounds Quebec on every side, and terrorizes her: "That was the dead, sealed world of the vegetable kingdom, an uncharted continent choked with interlocking trees, living, dead, half-dead, their roots in bogs and swamps, strangling each other in a slow agony that had lasted for centuries. The forest was suffocation, annihilation; there European man was quickly swallowed up in silence, distance, mould, black mud, and the stinging swarms of insect life that bred in it" (*SR,* 6–7). What Cather praises in *Shadows on the Rock* is the artificial. Cities themselves, she reminds us, are improbable and artificial excrescences in such a wilderness. If life itself is both sacrament and art, not to mention theater, it is anything but natural. Cécile's domestic efforts are an art, first bequeathed to her by her mother, then dispensed by her to her father and friends, and eventually to her sons. Her domestic skills are as much an art as the other admired and humanly shaped improvements on natural forms described here: the display of artificial fruit that Count Frontenac gives to Cécile before he dies, for example, or the artificial flowers that Cécile's favorite nun makes to decorate remote church altars. These are art forms Canadians have at hand, we realize, just as creating beauty or order or play is an art form they practice. And all art is artifice—man-made.

Appreciating beauty becomes an art as well. Appreciation is the miracle Cécile experiences as she learns to perpetuate the best forms Canadian life can sustain. Summarizing Cather's themes in this book, we infer that any culture or community includes oppositions as surely as French folk plays once traced the pulls between God and the Devil. What a community also includes, by existing at all, is a continuity that is itself a kind of miracle. Quebec is described at the beginning as "the goal of so many fantastic dreams," and by the end as a living miracle. As for miracle, "From being a shapeless longing, it becomes a beautiful image; a dumb rapture becomes a melody that can be remembered and repeated; and the experience of a moment, which might have been a lost ecstasy, is made an actual possession and can be bequeathed to another" (*SR*, 137).

Cather once said, "Those who make good unattractive do more harm than those who strive to make evil attractive."[30] Through the troubling beauty of *Shadows on the Rock,* she herself strives to make good as attractive in twentieth-century fiction as it once seemed in the age of saints and miracles. The goodness embodied in Cécile, the real goodness in question here, is the continuing life of the French tribe hanging precariously to a fortified rock in the Canadian wilderness. That goodness is assaulted by hunger, cold, dark, and prolonged deprivation. It is also attacked by wayward human impulses, physical frailty, mental anguish, and religious doubt. Present in the colony, in fact, are all the recognizable forms of bad faith. A great deal happens to the village during this year in the life of good young Cécile. But by the end of its cycle, Cather's story of communal miracle moves grandly to earned affirmations.

CHAPTER NINE

Death in C Major:
Lucy Gayheart

*Of all romances that of an artist's life is usually
the most cheap, the most tawdry, the most vulgar.
. . . An artist's life, aside from his work, is much
like a machinist's shop after the engine he built
has gone out; there is nothing but broken tools,
the tanks of black water where hot metal was
cooled, and gray ashes in the furnace. We want
heart rather than temperament in a novel, and the
two seldom go together. I am not sure but that
what we call temperament, the sort of temperament that is utilized professionally, only develops
when the heart is dying, like some showy fungus
that is born of decay. At best it is only a gaslight
imitation of the sun, as cold as the calcium moonlight.*

—————— WILLA CATHER, *The World and the Parish* ——————
from the *Leader,* March 11, 1898.

Though David Stouck considers *Lucy Gayheart* Cather's "most
complex novel philosophically" and James Woodress describes it
as "an extremely interesting novel without being a superior piece
of fiction," it has not been a wide favorite. Bernice Slote remarks
that the novel may well be Cather's most perilous voyage of all,
and Susan Rosowski speaks for a great many when she com-

ments, "As did Cather, I grow tired of the slight [title] character."[1] In fact, of all the works Cather wrote, this one is most likely to be ignored, dismissed, or pilloried. For some it is "mawkishly sentimental" and for others it evidences "its author's darkening vision ... [while it remains] the work of an aging novelist who began her seventh decade of life during its composition." Descriptions of it have ranged from "her final and most daring attempt to endow fiction with the levitating power of music" to "a Gothic story of abandonment" and a "dime store romance."[2]

When we start by assuming that Cather was always deliberate, never sloppy or impulsive, and that she was always inclined to try one or more new challenges in every work, our task becomes to explain why in 1935, beyond a desire to make money, this most careful of writers allowed *Lucy Gayheart* to appear in print. What made the novel interesting to its creator? What concerns, in fact, so energized the effort to write it, that Cather was afraid to trust the manuscript to the mails?[3] What kept Cather's hand flying as she hit the last section of her story, though pain in her hands severely impeded her work soon after *Lucy* was completed?

We know enough of Cather's situation when writing *Lucy Gayheart* to make some educated guesses about her mood. We know, for example, that at age sixty she seemed "an old woman" who said life was a biological failure.[4] We know that for years she had been growing steadily more inaccessible to the public, whom she clearly distrusted, and that she had joked for years about writing a satiric novel she punningly called *Blue Eyes on the Platte*.[5] Thus, a hostility to public reading taste, and probably an impulse toward retaliation for public obtuseness, had certainly been brewing. We know that at this time she was deeply concerned about the economic plight of her friends among the Nebraska farmers, and that she serialized this book at least partially to help pay for their farm mortgages, which were being foreclosed during the depression. We know that she kept saying that she was "tired" or "deadly tired."[6] We know that, partially because of her absorption with the Menuhin children, she had begun to respond more enthusiastically to instrumental music than to vocal (and hence might present such a singer as Clement Sebastian equivocally).[7] Last, we know that when she finally got to the third part of her novel—having killed off the hero in part one and the heroine in part two[8]—she was writing with exhilaration, as fast as pencil would fly.[9] Add the facts together and we can plausibly surmise that she may quite self-consciously have been exploring here something more than a Kate Greenaway child-woman, such a heroine's "vapid relationship with a middle-aged singer,"[10] or even such a heroine's relationship with a vapid middle-aged singer. In fact, the release Cather felt by the time she came to part three suggests at the least that the novel gave her, by the time it ended, a positive resolution to a long-standing problem.

Remembering Cather's inclination to pair novels, fashioning first one story and then its opposite, we find the first clue to Cather's intentions in *Lucy Gayheart* when asking which stories it reverses. Two novels seem crucial to the shaping, by contrast, of this book. The first, as countless readers know already, of course, is *Song of the Lark*.[11] Thea Kronborg and Lucy Gayheart start from the same kind of impecunious family background set in the same kind of culturally impoverished midwestern small-town place. They both then go to Chicago for the same reason: to gain musical training. Thea wants a career, and Lucy wants "a natural form of pleasure" and a "means of earning money" (*LG*, 6). Thereafter, Thea falls in love but survives the stumble to become a diva at the Met; Lucy allows her heart to break and soon drowns. What the parallel courses and different outcomes imply suggests several themes consistent with Cather's lifelong preoccupations: for example, the crucial importance of *desire* as an index of future accomplishment; the repercussions of that choice one makes about what to desire; or the fact that if one is among those to whom bad luck happens, then there's nothing much to be done about it.

While almost any Cather reader can add to this list of parallel details in the two novels about professional musicians, thus intensifying the sense of Lucy's inferiority to Thea, it is more important for the purposes of this book to contrast *Lucy Gayheart* with the preceding novel, *Shadows on the Rock*. In *Shadows* Cather depicts that good girl on whom cultures depend for their continuity. Cécile Auclair keeps the home fires burning, the food on the table, the men healthy and happy, and the church in that order that the presence of the devout can provide; in doing so she becomes a part of an enduring culture, the survival of which is a kind of miracle. Such relatively unqualified affirmation could not hold Willa Cather forever; the reaction sets the tone of this next book.

One can read *Lucy* as a slyly satiric presentation of a "girly-girly" (*LG,* 15) lass who lives on the Platte. In an early review of a now-forgotten actress, Cather expressed her aversion to the type:

> Her perpetual "girlishness" bores me to extinction. ... There is something very cheap about her startled-fawn glances and her affectations of shyness. ... Her winning ways do not compensate for her lack of imagination. ... And as for temperament, [she] has no more than a sucking dove, but offers in place of it a presumptuous artlessness. Girlishness and greatness are alliterative, but that is the only thing they have in common. The graces which charm in the drawing room are seldom effective either in the study or the portrayal of human problems and passions.[12]

The passage, written thirty-five years before this novel, serves uncannily as a hostile gloss on the character Cather names Lucy Gayheart.

Spotting a subversive subtext in this novel, Blanche Gelfant describes *Lucy Gayheart* as "a slyly comic book—as though Cather were playing a joke at the end of her serious career."[13] Yet if the book is a joke, it is a rough one. It can also be read as a symbolic assassination. In that light, the novel's purpose is to murder the shallow shadow self its author fears and loathes because that shadow fails miserably from lack of willpower, force of character, or simply focused attention. Lucy's charms duplicate Cather's cardinal sins. The rage that energizes Cather's long-developing impulse to satirize the "pining heroines of true romance"[14] must also be recognized and explored.

Cather may also be gunning here for the small-town or provincial cultures she managed only temporarily to embrace heartily in *Shadows*. Harry Gordon thinks at the end of the book, "What was a man's 'home town' anyway, but the place where he had had disappointments and had learned to bear them" (*LG,* 231). At the very least, Cather is as negative about small-town life in her early criticism as she had been about too-insistent girlishness. And the terms in which she first described it in 1901 still echo in the text of *Lucy Gayheart:* "The small town lets its social arrears go and go until people are buried beneath an ashamed sense of their own remissness, and then they try to make it all up at funerals. When anyone dies whom they haven't broken bread with or called on for years, his fellow townsmen put on their black clothes and go to see him. . . . It's a futile and inexpensive sort of remorse and it's a dishonest way of paying social obligations."[15] Further, whatever else we may say in contrasting *Shadows on the Rock* to its successor, we find in *Lucy Gayheart* a world devoid of significant miracles.

Our first task is to establish the critical edge to Cather's portrait of Lucy. The treacle-sweet name the title emphasizes is so blatant as to suggest parody. It seems thoroughly plausible, in fact, that Cather began this novel intending a parody of nineteenth-century Gothic or dime-store romances. Harry Gordon remembers, for example, that when he first glimpsed Lucy, she was skating in the local rink to "Hearts and Flowers" (*LG,* 20); the song she moves to epitomizes the meretricious accompaniments of exaggerated silent-movie melodramas. But parody is not a mode in which Cather was ever comfortable. She preferred to end on the upbeat, and she always displayed a proclivity for finding paradox within the genuinely real. Hers was a mind that constantly played among the opposite possibilities implied by any given fact. We see that mind at play as she builds into her structured characterization the different implications of her heroine's name.

Lucy, of course, became the favorite name for a romantic heroine (especially after the publication of Wordsworth's Lucy poems) because the name derives from *luce,* or light. Such heroines often function as inspirations, or lights. But *light* also suggests both "insubstantial or frivolous" and "morally lax." Luce-y can also be heard as Loose-y. All these connotations and reverberations operate in deliberately patterned ways within this novel.

The neutral narrator of this novel, speaking as the voice of the town's collective consciousness reshaped by memory,[16] states in the first sentence that "In Haverford on the Platte the townspeople still talk of Lucy Gayheart." They remember her as a symbol of youth and "spring." As such, she inspires all the men with whom she is close—her father, Harry Gordon, and Clement Sebastian. She "has a kind of delicacy" (*LG,* 80), does not "make ugly sounds" (*LG,* 36), and seems "gathered up and sustained by something that never let her drop into the common world" (*LG,* 215). For Harry as for others, "her eyes lighted up with the present moment" (*LG,* 215). As a presence who wholeheartedly enjoyed as well as lightened and lighted up a present moment, Lucy remains important, even in memory. Without her, "there was actually no present" (*LG,* 220).

But Lucy's power is confined to fleeting, present moments. She is associated with the wind, the ephemeral, throughout the novel and from its first page. She leaves light footprints in a seldom-used sidewalk that is preserved only for one caretaker's lifetime. And the footprints are clearly those of a young girl whose lifted heels are running away. Lucy is "a mercurial, vacillating person" (*LG,* 18) whose memory will die with those who knew her personally. She is from the beginning a lass who prefers skating to packing for any calculated movement toward a future she is planning to control.

Skating, in fact, becomes an interesting symbol in this novel. It obviously suggests a capacity to derive pleasure from the iciest weather. It also recalls Emerson's heavily ironic statement, "We live amid surfaces, and the true art of life is to skate well on them."[17] Cather paraphrases Emerson when she writes of Lucy, "life seemed to lie very near the surface in her" (*LG,* 6), and then adds, "There had been good skating all through Christmas week, and she had made the most of it" (*LG,* 7). Emerson pervades this novel, though often ironically. For example, the second sentence ends, "we live in the present," reminding us of Emerson's repeated advice about how to live, in such lines as "He cannot be happy and strong until he too lives with nature in the present, above time."[18]

While skating on surfaces, Lucy lives as one who, in the old phrase, is no better than she should be. She is not above skating with all the guys until Harry Gordon comes to claim her, and then sailing away to nip whiskey with him in a sheltered nook. In fact, in one of Cather's most vivid tableaux, Harry and Lucy enter "the end of the island forked like a fish's tail" and sit while "interlacing twigs threw off red light," in "a stream of blinding light" that "burned on their skates and on the flask and the metal cup" (*LG*, 10). The visual effects of the momentary scene suggest hell and damnation, though Lucy laughs and enjoys it while the proper ladies of Haverford—her sister Pauline, for example—take the more sedate pleasures of afternoon tea. Though she is already half in love with Clement Sebastian of Chicago, Lucy still enjoys flirting and snuggling down beside substantial Harry, under his warm sleigh blankets on the Platte. When she visits Clement's apartment for the first time, she inspects his bedroom, with its well-made bed, and imagines the emaculate order of his bureau drawers. She lives in Chicago, as she lives symbolically everywhere, between bakery and glove factory—between the sweets and the protective disguises.

Thus, Cather explains the significance of Lucy's silly boast to Harry that with Clement Sebastian, she has gone "all the way" (*LG*, 111). It is not that she has actually committed any major infractions of moral law. It is rather that she has accurately conveyed to Harry the reality, like an Impressionist painting, "meant to express a kind of feeling merely, and then accuracy doesn't matter" (*LG*, 101). For realist Harry, of course, "anatomy is a fact ... and facts are at the bottom of everything" (*LG*, 101). Harry must live a quarter-century longer before he can begin to grasp the power of vivid moments infused with feeling. He speaks more truly than he knows, however, when he tells her, "the day of counting costs comes along in the end, Lucy mio" (*LG*, 106).

The real charge Cather levels against Lucy in this novel is her lack of high seriousness, her lack of ambition. Cather the writer, throughout her career, has made a god of success and a fearful threat of failure. And by Cather's lifelong standards, as opposed to Mrs. Ramsay's small-town commonsense wisdom, Lucy is doomed from the beginning to be a failure. Her "predestined" fate, set up carefully by her creator, assuredly suggests the "old morality plays" David Stouck perceptively associates with this novel's "dance of death,"[19] rather than the miracle play undergirding life in *Shadows on the Rock*.

Lucy's destiny is clear when, at the end of the first scene, she joyously salutes the first star and then finds that "The flash of understanding lasted but a moment. Then everything was confused again." Any reader of Cather should know that Lucy will come to no good end when she decides that the star "was too bright and too sharp. It hurt, and made one feel small and lost" (*LG*, 12). Again here, we hear echoes of Emerson: "If a man would be alone, let him look at the stars."[20] The more substantial Harry looks at stars again, twenty-five years after Lucy's death, and feels, "These things he had been remembering mattered very little when one looked up there at eternity" (*LG*, 220).

Lucy's lack of ambition is a fact not only stated explicitly in the text, but also judged negatively: "She was not ambitious—that ... was her greatest fault" (*LG*, 34). Further, Cather seems to associate this fault with gutlessness: "she could never play for him. She hadn't it in her. ... She would decline the risk" (*LG*, 14). Under the pressure of her audition as Sebastian's accompanist, Lucy misses notes not only because she is frightened but also because she assumes she "shouldn't compete" (*LG*, 61). When recovering from Sebastian's death, she feels, "Everything they wanted her to do seemed out of her reach" (*LG*, 120). And when she finally summons enough self-propelling energy to write and retrieve her old job in Chicago as piano teacher for younger pupils, she fears, "Perhaps by March she would have lost her courage and sunk in apathy again" (*LG*, 186).

Just as her ambitionlessness is emphasized in the text, so Lucy's primary hope is defined explicitly: "to please Sebastian" (*LG*, 34).

Her standards for measuring the quality of her life are also clear: "Nothing else mattered, when all was going well with Sebastian" (*LG*, 114). Lucy's joy is "to choose one's master and serve him in one's own way" (*LG*, 86). Her need to serve is so self-abasing that "In her companionship there was never a shadow of a claim" (*LG*, 81); at one point Lucy even envies Sebastian's valet (*LG*, 44). It is no wonder that Cather grew tired of such a heroine, who made no claim even to her own life. One effort the first part apparently required was an effort to suppress Catherian contempt. Certainly Lucy pays for what she cost her creator in her terrible death. But then, as the subject of a morality play, she exists to deserve her fate. The primary moral she conveys is the crucial importance of a woman's self-consciously and energetically choosing the direction of her own life and then willing to make her chosen life happen.

Most critics have remarked on the images of motion that pervade this novel, and more than one has observed the irony that Lucy's motion is best symbolized by running footprints left in concrete. The rush or movement that characterizes Lucy is self-evident; the point to make about it, however, is that it is movement that goes nowhere. It remains the movement of a small-town girl who is fashioned to enjoy, as Professor Auerbach tells her, "A nice house and garden in a little town, with money enough not to worry, a family—that's the best life" (*LG*, 134).

An equally pervasive pattern of images and associations in this novel connects Lucy with lethargy or stasis. Willa Cather throughout her career uses gesture as symbol; and Lucy's gestures—or immobility—also define her. For example, she repeatedly feels tired and stops to rest. She is tired after her first skate with Harry, after her visit to the art gallery with Harry, and "dreadfully tired" after spending a week with Harry (*LG*, 108). After Harry abandons her in their Chicago restaurant, she must ask her cabdriver to climb to her room to get his fare: "I'm too tired to bring it down" (*LG*, 113).

Were Harry the only person who depletes Lucy's energies, we would know about her ambivalences toward him, but little more. Such, however, is not the case. Lucy lies down before going to

Sebastian's first concert (*LG,* 28), feels suddenly tired after first practicing with him (*LG,* 45), must lie down after lunch on the day she first accompanies him (*LG,* 51), and slumps against him before he leaves Chicago, after hearing him say, "You are worn out. . . . Shut your eyes and rest" (*LG,* 124). Left with the privilege of using Sebastian's apartment in his summertime absence, Lucy spends her summer evenings lying on the sofa (*LG,* 134). After her emotional upset when Sebastian teases her about being in love, in fact, Lucy "lay down and slept for nearly two hours" (*LG,* 72).

Obviously Cather's depiction of Lucy is built on a paradoxical blend of pointless motion and will-less rest. The blend should make it easier to understand another imagery pattern in this novel. For one literary challenge Cather obviously undertook here was to prove to the American literary world, which was gleefully allowing more and more sexual explicitness in its books, that one did not need anatomical facts to capture passionate feelings. She undertakes here to write a hot story coldly. The most obvious images in the novel are concerned with ice.

Lucy's first frolic in the opening chapter takes place as she skates on ice. Her last moments occur when she breaks through the thin ice she skates on. She remembers running to one of Sebastian's concerts through "glacial cold" (*LG,* 37) in a light wrap, because she enjoys feeling "one's blood coursing unchilled in an air where roses froze instantly" (*LG,* 37). What Sebastian sings in that concert is *Die Winterreise.* In her happy days, "the weather was miraculous, for January" because it maintains "very little ice" (*LG,* 47). In that happy period, "ice cakes ground upon each other in the Lake" (*LG,* 93) and in March, the time of Lucy's birthday, "the ice on the Platte had . . . gone rotten" (*LG,* 92). Harry's defeated eyes are "cold as icicles" (*LG,* 149), but Lucy, too, experiences defeat in terms of ice: "To have one's heart frozen and one's world destroyed in a moment" (*LG,* 156) is her metaphor for disaster. Even as she recuperates in autumn, "she would come out here among the apple trees, cold and frightened and unsteady" (*LG,* 158), for she finds that only singing Sebastian's songs "melted the cold about her heart" (*LG,* 157). At one point Lucy even stretches her arms out to a snowstorm, in order to make some emotional contact with the dead Sebastian (*LG*, 185). Embracing her own reviving sexuality[21] on Christmas Eve, "She opened the window softly and knelt down beside it to breathe the cold air. She felt snowflakes melt in her hair, on her hot cheeks" (*LG*, 184). Soon thereafter, her life ends on a day in which the weather seems "almost too cold to skate" (*LG*, 196). The end of January, as the end of Lucy's life, is "bitter cold" (*LG*, 190).

Beyond the technical virtuosity required to set a love story on ice, Cather also conveys through her frigid imagery some clear facts abut the emotional condition of the man cast here as Lucy's lover—or beloved. While Lucy's feelings are caught by the reds in which she dresses or which she perceives surrounding Sebastian (red scarf [*LG*, 8]; red jersey [*LG*, 20]; red feather [*LG*, 50]; red-orange light on the steps of the Art Museum [*LG*, 24]; red velvet chair [*LG*, 58]), Clement's feelings are summarized in one word: emptiness (*LG*, 77). His life replicates the artist's life as empty machinist's shop—the image Cather developed in 1898. Summarized, his life seems tawdry and his artistry a matter of temperament instead of heart: "At best it is only a gaslight imitation of the sun, as cold as the calcium moonlight." Of course, Lucy fails to be an adequate protagonist by lacking what Sebastian relies on—an artist's temperament. So both characters, in their no-win predicaments, are fashioned by Cather's design to drown and die. It is nevertheless important to recognize that at the least, Cather's text sets empty Clement Sebastian in as ambivalent a light as it sets Lucy.

The most obvious fact about Sebastian, repeatedly stressed in this novel, is that he smokes (*LG*, 25, 52, 69, 79). Like Lucy's fantasies about going "all the way," Clement's smoking is not an uncommon or serious peccadillo. Nevertheless, the fact remains that singers who take themselves seriously do not do it. It wrecks the vocal cords. But this particular singer is all smoke and no fire. Nothing else about Clement Sebastian establishes him as a tragic figure of great moral stature either. His first song is "more rite than prayer" (*LG*, 29), that is, more a form than a devotion. He chooses songs that are melancholy, and is most impressive when singing such complaints as *Die Winterreise*. As Edith Lewis has reminded us, Cather "had a very sure intuition of the qualities of music—both its aesthetic and, so to speak, its moral qualities; its sincerity, or the lack of it, its elevation or vulgarity. She was quickly aware of the composer's intention, and the character of his style."[22] In this sardonic novel, one cannot assume that Cather believes *Die Winterreise* is great music just because Schubert wrote it, especially when she is in a listening phase that favors instrumental over vocal music. In fact, *Die Winterreise,* when heard unsympathetically, is a work of prolonged self-pity.

While Clement Sebastian is "easy and kindly" (*LG,* 34), indeed full of "amiability" (*LG,* 49), his major problem is that he is bored (*LG,* 58). His generally "gentle and soothing" manner with women (*LG,* 51) allows him to become "a man who has an easy, if somewhat tolerant, enjoyment of life" (*LG,* 52). Thus, in spite of his knowledge that "It was dangerous to go for sympathy to a young girl who was in love with one," he allows himself his safe flirtation with an accompanist who makes no demands on him, because he easily decides, "Lucy was different" (*LG,* 80). Clement believes that "youth, love, hope [are] all the things that pass" (*LG,* 69); he concedes their passage because it costs him nothing, in his renunciations, to attest "he had unclouded faith in the old and lovely dreams of man" (*LG,* 87). As a passing penance for his toying with Lucy, he sings, "It is enough. . . . I am not better than my fathers" (*LG,* 48). Though Clement knows several moments of black despair, he concedes that his chief reaction to the death of his friends is, "I am sorry for myself" (*LG,* 83). By no accident does Fairy Blair misname him "Mr. Saint Sebastian" (*LG,* 176), that saint full of the arrows of outrageous fortune. In fact, "Le Martyre de St. Sebastian" is one of Debussy's compositions, and Clement Sebastian twice refers to the composer (*LG,* 42, 52), whom he knows personally. In his last living moments in this novel, what Sebastian wants is *escape* from everything he is and his name implies. "In what stretched out before him there was nothing that he wanted very much, (*LG,* 126), including Lucy.

In one of his first remarks to Lucy, Sebastian has let her know that "he was attached to James Mockford," whom he considers "one of the few friends who have lasted through time and change" (*LG,* 52). Then in no time, we find Sebastian planning to rid himself of Mockford. He plots not only to fire his accompanist but also his agent. Previously, he has also sent his protégé Marius from his home and has left his wife behind in Europe, with funds she considers inadequate. We catch an oblique glimpse of a possible intimacy that touches him through the flowers "worth their weight in gold" (*LG,* 70) that a rich lover passing through town has sent him on the way to the train. Later, he pockets a letter that he seems to associate with old friends who revive his heart because they are "still interested" (*LG,* 121–22). But when directly asked about being in love, Clement denies ever getting any pleasure from it, then maliciously bruises Lucy's feelings by asking if she gets any. At the very least, Sebastian seems a narcissistic man of weak attachments.

At the most, he is careless of others and a sexual tease. The exact nature of his relationship to the untrustworthy, overfamiliar, detestable James Mockford is profoundly ambiguous—one of the peculiar minor strains in this composition. While Sebastian "seemed very careful never to come too close to people" (*LG,* 53), they still leave him feeling "disappointed in something—or in everything" (*LG,* 53). Sebastian seems willing to use others "to divert him here" (*LG,* 58), but Mockford is unwilling to be so used. He refuses to be played with and discarded. One of the songs in Clement's concert that most moves Lucy is "Die Doppelgänger." Like a doppelgänger, Mockford attaches himself to Clement Sebastian, and in the end both drown.

When we look at this text as carefully as Cather's works always demand, then, we see why she might dispose of both her hero and her heroine as expeditiously as possible. They are not the kinds of people Willa Cather admires or finds interesting for long. Having acknowledged the fact, we are ready to ask why the writer suddenly caught fire, once she had dispatched these tepid lovers. We are also ready to understand why she cautioned Carrie Miner that the story made no sense until after one had absorbed the third part.[23] Cather's identification here, the emotional energy she invests in this story, does not derive from either of the lovers but from Harry Gordon. It is Harry Gordon's predicament that justifies the effort of writing—or reading—the book. It is Harry's viewpoint that is "rooted deep in her experience."[24]

At first Harry and Lucy articulate antagonistic ways of looking at life, which viewpoints become mutually challenging themes in this work. For Harry, "anatomy is a fact ... and facts are at the bottom of everything" (*LG,* 101). For Lucy, such factual objects as paintings are sometimes "meant to express a kind of feeling merely, and then accuracy doesn't matter" (*LG,* 101). In this plot, Harry loses Lucy because he suffers from a kind of "mental near-sightedness" (*LG,* 98) about her feelings; and Lucy loses her life because she is inattentive to facts. Thus, both are slightly right and mostly wrong. There is no right way presented in this novel, and neither facts nor feelings triumph. But at least, at the end, Harry is left alive and in possession of the most complete facts and vivid memories of Lucy that remain in Haverford. If "Lucy was the best thing he had to remember" (*LG,* 223), she still represents "all the fine things of youth, which do not change" (*LG,* 224). Those fine things, in Cather's work, include youth, delight, and desire. Like Eden Bower or Jim Burden's hired girls or Marian Forrester, Lucy represents the eternal theme—that sexual energy or life-force without which there is neither poetry nor meaningful present life. Harry alone in this novel grasps the positive and negative implications of that theme.

Initially, Cather seems to punish Harry as much as she clearly punishes Lucy or Clement Sebastian. Harry has a Scotch heart, is often stingy, is conceited, and is coldly calculating about the egocentric advantages of marrying and possessing Lucy. He is superficially clothes conscious (*LG,* 98) and materialistic (*LG,* 100), and walks "somewhat pompously by" (*LG,* 166). But Harry is also a good fellow, not arrogant or overbearing, and public spirited (*LG,* 9). In any case he ends by punishing himself far worse than the others are punished: his marriage is "a life sentence" (*LG,* 221).

Because Lucy hurt Harry deeply, his reflex was to punish her, and *punish* is certainly a word Cather repeatedly stresses: "He knew that if he were alone with her for a moment and she held out her hands to him with that look, he couldn't punish her any more—and she deserved to be punished" (*LG,* 216). Rushing the years, Cather adds, "And yet, underneath his resentment and his determination to punish, there was a contrary conviction lying very deep, so deep that he held no communication with it. After they had both been punished enough, something would happen" (*LG,* 217). Having punished Lucy enough, Harry Gordon can concede that she "was the best thing he had to remember" (*LG,* 223). And having forgiven Lucy, he can accept himself: "He is not a man haunted by remorse; all that he went through with long ago. He enjoys his prosperity and his good health. Lucy Gayheart is no longer a despairing little creature standing in the icy wind and lifting beseeching eyes to him. She is no longer near, beside his sleigh. She has receded to the far horizon line, along with all the fine things of youth, which do not change" (*LG,* 224).

Here, I'm suggesting, is the most important and sustaining reason behind Cather's writing this novel: to come to terms with the lifetime of pain that survivors—such as she was—can suffer from their betrayals by those beloveds (no matter how immature or silly) who like Isabelle McClung prefer such unworthy love objects as bored musicians to the "tried and seasoned strength" (*LG,* 208) she herself offered. Having punished all principals enough, she accepts her prospects and salutes "all the fine things of youth, which do not change."

I also think Cather wrote this novel to qualify that thoroughly positive view of small hamlets and villages that she had presented in *Shadows on the Rock*. In *Lucy Gayheart* she affirms her *escape* from Red Cloud. While in Chicago Lucy thinks,

> She loved her own little town, but it was a heart-breaking love, like loving the dead who cannot answer back.
>
> Now the world seemed wide and free, like the lake out yonder. She was not always struggling against something, she was going with something much stronger than herself. (*LG,* 136)

Later, at the end of the book, the narrator echoes Lucy from Harry's point of view:

> In little towns, lives roll along so close to one an-
> other; loves and hates beat about, their wings al-
> most touching. On the sidewalks along which
> everybody comes and goes, you must, if you walk
> abroad at all, at some time pass within a few inches
> of the man who cheated and betrayed you, or the
> woman you desire more than anything else in the
> world. You say good-morning, and go on. It is a
> close shave. Out in the world the escapes are not so
> narrow. (*LG,* 167)

Though she made a left-handed job of it, Willa Cather created in *Lucy Gayheart* a novel of forgiveness, after her fashion. In it she confronted those things that had wounded or offended her most, and having retaliated or punished, accepted them. She forgave the love of her youth for being what that beloved figure was: immature, male-identified, male-dominated, and afraid. In doing so, Cather conceded that she, like Harry Gordon, was selfish, possessive, domineering, egotistical. But after writing this novel Willa Cather was able, for perhaps the first time in her life, to lay aside her own egocentric concerns and to selflessly dedicate most of the following year of 1935 to assisting and nurturing the dying Isabelle McClung Hambourg.[25]

Having completed so many essential tasks, she was finally ready for the last gesture, which *Sapphira and the Slave Girl* displays. In her last novel, she took a long and steady look at her own blood. At last she was ready straightforwardly to confront herself.

CHAPTER TEN

The Return of The Native:
Sapphira and the Slave Girl

*My own grandmother was one of those unprofes-
sional nurses who served without recompense,
from the mere love of it. She had a host of little
children and cares enough of her own, poor
woman, but when a child was burned, when
some overworked woman was in her death agony,
when a man had been crushed under the falling
timber, or when a boy had cut his leg by a slip of
the knife in the sumach field, the man who went
to town for the doctor always stopped for her on
the way. . . . She was always an excellent woman,
that nurse of the olden time, with her hair
combed down over her ears and her big breastpin
with a family portrait on it, but she used to make
sad blunders. She and the old doctor would go on
starving diphtheria patients and keeping ice and
water from fever cases, sometimes killing more
people than the disease, and all the while supported by an unwavering conviction that they
were benefiting their kind.*

——— WILLA CATHER, *The World and the Parish* ———
from the *Home Monthly,* May 1897.

165

"My end is my beginning," Willa Cather joked to Alexander Woollcott about *Sapphira and the Slave Girl.*"[1] At that moment she could not have known how apt a pun she had just gotten off. She was referring, of course, to the novel's remarkable Epilogue in which she steps into the narrative's final episode as her child self who witnessed the dramatic end to a real family drama. That Epilogue acknowledges in the author a bloodline associated with temperamental qualities the preceding novel also explored. *Sapphira* was not Cather's first ironic admission about her family, however, for she had published an ambivalent portrait of her grandmother Rachel Boak at the beginning of her editorial career. What caused her to want to repeat that family story is almost as tantalizing a question as what caused her to feel her world broke in two.

In a number of ways to be discussed in this chapter, the joke to Woollcott can be read metaphorically. Certainly the novel set in the place where she was born was her last. Cather actually started another novel that Edith Lewis destroyed when her friend's death left it incomplete. But in several other ways her life, in *Sapphira and the Slave Girl*, seems to have come full circle, as it ends in her beginning. That circle enclosed her characteristic ways of seeing "double," as she focused her last book on her maternal family line and therefore on herself.

Between the publication of *Lucy Gayheart* in 1935 and *Sapphira and the Slave Girl* in 1940, a number of significant and often deeply disturbing events affected Cather's life and obliquely impinged on the last novel she would complete. By spring of 1936 she was working on the collected edition of her works that Houghton Mifflin was to bring out in twelve volumes, to which *Sapphira* was eventually added as a thirteenth. The handsome set began appearing late in 1937 and must have given Willa Cather a clear sense of a deliberate rounding out of her productive life. The summarizing edition itself may have contributed to her decision to return to early childhood scenes for her next story and setting.

The twists and turns the story was to take as Cather creatively shaped it, however, were certainly affected by the hostile criticism directed against Cather in the 1930s. Such criticism must have rankled, and *Sapphira and the Slave Girl* can be read as an answer to it. For example, after Granville Hicks accused her in 1933 of falling into a "supine romanticism,"[2] she produced a book associated with the most supinely romantic genre—the Southern romance; in the maneuver, she not only disproved the label as an accurate measure of herself (one clue to her decision to name herself in the Epilogue), but also proved that the Southern romance itself was anything but supine. The basically unpleasant atmosphere of this novel, ostensibly emanating from its treacheries, attempted entrapments, and betrayals, may also emerge from Cather's determinedly menacing (as opposed to supine) posture here.

Somewhat later, in the *Nation,* Louis Kronenberger charged the collection of essays *Not under Forty* (1936) with "smugness springing from uncertainty, of an odd feeling of guilt, of a deep feeling of regret for the past and a self-righteous loyalty in going to the past's defense" and of a willingness to run "out on the present to hide in the past," which led her to reject "such portions of the past as had the poor judgment to be unsavory or ungovernable."[3] As the reading that follows will show, Cather took on these accusations in order to disprove them, while she wrote *Sapphira* with less joy than "resoluteness, a sort of fixed determination."[4] One can question how much loyalty to the past the novel displays, or how much willingness to defend it. One can certainly see no evasion of facts about moral iniquity. The question of guilt, however, is more troubled. We may have to classify the novel as a guilt-without-sin fiction, for the malevolence is real enough, but it achieves nothing. In fact, ex-Southerner Cather seems guiltlessly to reject the slave system and the economy it supports, while also guiltlessly loving the land that developed both. *Because* she constructs no brief for that system, she can guiltlessly recognize the natural beauties of a setting in which slaves were owned. Yet the loss of this historical past is in no way regretted while it is recalled. What is regretted is the progress that denudes the mountain roads of their beauty. While we will have more to say about this matter, I believe as far as Kronenberger's accusations in the *Nation* go, in *Sapphira* she systematically disproved them all.

There is certainly "fixed determination" and her own resilient will behind Cather's production of *Sapphira and the Slave Girl*. In the interval between her last two novels she lived through a series of devastations. After a pleasant trip back to Virginia to refresh her memories in April of 1938, the accident she had in some sense feared all her life occurred: someone accidentally smashed her hand when she was in a store. Then her brother Douglass died of a heart attack in June of 1938, and her friend Isabelle McClung Hambourg died in Sorrento in October. In November a hurricane devastated the country around the Jaffrey Inn in New Hampshire, where she habitually retreated in autumn. She reported that by this point she had lost the power to feel anything. Worst of all, of course, the world was clearly moving toward another world war, and she, as all others, watched horrified and helpless as a teetering world prepared to tumble and smash—again. though she had started the new novel two years earlier, she was unable to continue it until summer of 1939. The book itself depicts lives lived in a time when a way of life begins to crumble.

In one sense, then, this novel witnesses to Cather's performance under truly maximal pressure. The first point to make is that she continued, in her sixties, to perform. But the effort does not appear to have been a mellow one. We can also see her settling grudges, for the novel is a baited trap for critics and readers. Indeed, her comments about contemporary readers made in *Not under Forty* offended many of a younger generation:

> The title of this book is meant to be "arresting" only in the literal sense, like the signs put up for motorists: "*ROAD UNDER REPAIR*," etc. It means that the book will have little interest for people under forty years of age. The world broke in two in 1922 or thereabouts, and the persons and prejudices recalled in these sketches slid back into yesterday's seven thousand years. Thomas Mann, to be sure, belongs immensely to the forward-goers, and they are concerned only with his forwardness. But

he also goes back a long way, and his backwardness
is more gratifying to the backward. It is for the
backward, and by one of their number, that these
sketches were written.[5]

For her au courant judges, in particular, Cather can be imagined
laying traps in the work to come. She claimed that not very much
of the book was actually fiction,[6] but fiction or family fact, it is
all a Catherian construction and all planned as meticulously as
usual for her complex, varied, and subtle effects.

First of all, *Sapphira and the Slave Girl* is a Southern plantation
story—a genre popular since before the Civil War and familiar
to most Americans in the wake of *Gone With the Wind* (1936).
Second, it's a plantation story that deliberately subverts reader
expectations. While the traditional setting is quickly recognized,
subsequent details do not correspond to the expected picture of
Southern life. That picture exists because of a set of literary conventions about Southern life that had been developing for a century by the time Cather began her narrative. And Cather knew
the conventions well. John Esten Cooke, one of the florid Old
South plantation writers, was such a favorite in the Cather house-
hold that Willa's younger brother Jack was actually named John
Esten Cather after him. Cather herself, in fact, used "John Esten"
as an early pseudonym.[7] Our first task here is to review briefly
the cultural expectations and reflexive associations she could
count on among her unwary readers and critics.

By the end of the nineteenth century a fully developed set of
literary conventions about Southern life was familiar to American
readers in all parts of this country. In particular, Americans knew
a great number of Southern stereotypes: the planter aristocrat and
his variously admirable or hot-blooded family;[8] the cracker or
farmer living through his colorful rural events; the mountaineer
and his always courageous daughter, mainly occupied in protecting an ever-flowing family still; the Creole with his quaintly
self-destructive old-world outlook, transferred and preserved
intact around deadly and alluring New Orleans; the loyal and
happy, if occasionally promiscuous, Southern slave; and the low-

life rapscallion who spoke a bawdy language, played practical or sadistic jokes, and generated hilarious repartee.[9] This Southern world had been presented in hundreds of stories by the turn of the century, some of which Cather herself had read and loved.

In this often-depicted Southern world, stereotyped characters acted within predictable boundaries; and Southern plots—after individually inventive vagaries—usually took a predictable turn. The world evoked was predictable, once the class structure, social situation, and population were understood to be Southern. In fact, such twentieth-century Southern literary giants as Faulkner, Porter, Welty, O'Connor, and Percy created their extraordinary literary tensions by playing upon, or pulling against, the conventional expectations that the previous century created. In reversing, they revitalized the norms. Thus at the end of the twentieth century, we still know what Southern belles, hillbillies, or poor white trash are supposed to look like, talk like, think like, and do. And younger self-consciously Southern writers such as Lee Smith, Charles Portis, or Olive Ann Burns still create characters to delight their readers within the bounds established by these literary expectations.

Cather's work preceded much of today's most admired Southern writing, and in *Sapphira and the Slave Girl*, Willa Cather also invokes such stereotypes and induces reflexive expectations among her readers. But when she invokes such types only to portray them in radically uncharacteristic attitudes and acts, she thoroughly disorients and puzzles her readers. And once we assume that her choices in *Sapphira*, as in all the rest of her fiction, are highly deliberate, the novel assumes an interest that makes it an intriguing finish to a brilliant career.

Before we analyze Cather's purposes or strategy in *Sapphira*, we must review the stereotyped elements to which she alludes. Their inclusion raises initial expectations that her novel will prove "merely," "yet another," "typical" Southern novel, lolling in its "supine romanticism," because its author has truly decided to "hide in the past," while failing to tolerate the unsavory or the ungovernable. A reader who comes to *Sapphira* for proof of such iniquities, and who reads with intelligent attention, must eat such words and choke on such accusations. This time, she shows him good.

The novel centers around the conflict between a privileged aristocratic lady and her personal slave. Whatever critics of the *New Republic* and the *Nation* chose to see or not to see about Cather's writing, she is already exceptional as a Southern-born woman writing in the late 1930s, when she creates an in-depth exploration of the peculiar institution. The guilts and consequences of slavery may well have obsessed many Southern male writers; but delving into slavery's economic complexities is not characteristic of the best Southern female fiction writers. Initially, *Sapphira* stands alone in dramatizing from a clearly Southern woman's point of view the evils of slavery. It describes a harrowing slave escape across a threatening river (pointedly reminiscent, at first glance, of Harriet Beecher Stowe's earlier version); emphasizes the slave girl's vulnerability to sexual abuse by white males; concedes the ability of clever slaves to manipulate the system to their own advantage; acknowledges the existence of widespread miscegenation and the problems it creates; describes "good slave" internalization of the white social code; reminds us that some slaves accepted their freedom only with reluctance; includes a variety of social types from a mountaineer family through a schoolteacher and postmistress to a hardworking, self-sufficient miller; mentions Rachel Blake's husband and son who die while enjoying a luxury vacation in New Orleans; mentions low-life promiscuity among unrestrained mountain girls; and finally stresses "typically Southern" obsessions with family backgrounds and geographic loyalties. All these are thoroughly standard nineteenth-century elements to be predicted and expected in "typical" Southern fiction.

Given these standard clues to Southern plots, it is no wonder that readers since 1940 have been brought up short by *Sapphira*. The slave girl's flight to freedom is terrifying enough to leave her hysterical; yet she is not pursued, while her escape proceeds smoothly with the help of the white mistress's daughter, who arranges a carefully planned journey. Further, here the black female sexual object does not get raped. Furthermore, her fond master does not seduce her. In fact, miscegenation arouses some disgust, but not in the person of black Till, a participant. And when beleaguered Nancy finally marries, she chooses a half-Scot, half-Indian Canadian. The Southern plantation here is ruled by an iron hand, but the hand is attached to an invalid mistress, not to her husband. Any rigid class structure based on inherited and fertile land has broken down before the novel begins, when the mistress Sapphira removed herself to the uncultivated backwoods—to Back Creek. The novel's haphazardly educated male worker is often troubled and confused about issues like slavery that he can neither understand nor resolve; but he, in fact, consistently sticks to his articulated and strongly felt, if contradictory, principles. The strong-willed individual who orders others around does *not* control events or actions in the story at all. And most importantly, arrogance and sinful pride are not much punished.

With predictable irony, the story ends happily after peace and social order have been restored. But unpredictably, the greatest financial success in the novel is associated with ex-slave Nancy, who returns dressed far more opulently than her former owner's family could imagine themselves. Since Nancy is employed as a rich family's housekeeper in Canada, however, her superior wardrobe mostly indicates the present low income of one good Southern white family.

Here, then, is a book in which Cather deliberately aroused a variety of expectations, and then deliberately disappointed them. If asked why she chose to do so, she might have replied that things were not always as others had described them, at least not back in Ole Virginie. And she may have added that only contemporary readers sunk in supine romanticism would have expected or demanded hackneyed characters and plots. Or she may have suggested that if cutting-edge critics would ever inspect the past she invoked here, they might learn a bit about the unsavory and ungovernable elements she recognized. But Cather has never seemed ideologically correct for long, if only because she clearly sees the dark side of every positive fact, as well as vice versa.

Besides the obvious and unconventional twists of plot, Cather also used a large number of unconventional details—that is, facts or assertions that fly in the face of reader expectations about the Old South. For example, her first two paragraphs establish the different but familiar social types that Sapphira and Henry represent: Sapphira is a lady, and Henry is a plain-folk representative. Our first indication that formulas are not to be followed here is our discovery that Sapphira and Henry, exemplars of classes traditionally described as distinctly separate, are married. The first two paragraphs stress the hard physical work that this male head of the "best" family requires of himself. Further, we learn, the family has not so much inherited its position as built it up, house and rank, by hard labor, albeit on inherited but undeveloped land.

The second small shock, foretaste of things to come, registers when we realize that in this community moral leadership is not supplied by the aristocratic lady Sapphira, for Southern women in plantation fiction have ordinarily been ceded the role of moral guardian. The major moral consciousness in this community belongs to the lady's husband, the miller. Henry, a "solid, powerful figure of a man," is known for his fair dealing. Cather compares Henry's face to "an old port" wine,[10] an accolade suggesting sweetness and seasoned maturity. Yet in this isolated provincial community the respected miller still talks little (a suspicious characteristic in nineteenth-century Southern fiction) and seems rather foreign to his neighbors.[11]

Yet it is the middle-status miller and not his aristocratic wife who cares most about blacks. His wife, born a Dodderidge (doddering, dodderer?), ungenteelly plots against servants, makes tasteless remarks about breeding blacks (*SS*, 9), and appreciates the off-color jokes of a crude sense of humor (*SS*, 220). Sapphira has never felt any inconvenient obligation to others, white or black (*SS*, 27). Her imagination duplicates that of her lewd cook (*SS*, 61). Though she is restrained by her own code of behavior, she still thoroughly understands the cannibalistic inventions of old Jezebel (*SS*, 89).

This family, headed by "a lady," is clearly descending the social ladder: the "stalwart" daughter, Rachel, wears a sunbonnet and a calico dress, enters by the back door, has never owned servants, and attends the Baptist church. But the family's decline is *not* due to the aristocrat's unconventionally poor head for business; Sapphira, besides being a woman, has also managed her farm as capably as she once managed her father's business affairs. The decline is directly linked to the quality and location of the land on which they have chosen to settle, and to try to farm—a realistic fact never acknowledged in plantation fiction.

A particularly interesting detail in the novel is the association of Sapphira's behavior with her Episcopal upbringing, especially since in 1922 Cather and her parents left the Baptists to join the Episcopal church. By contrast with the Episcopalians, the Baptists here—collectively the most denigrated Protestant denomination in Southern fiction—are much the more liberal group regarding race. The novel's Baptists include blacks in their church services, though as "rednecks" or physical laborers the Baptists were conventionally supposed to lack the noblesse oblige of the less weather-beaten and richer Episcopalians. For the Cather cognoscenti, this detail alone should be a tip-off that an undertow is running in this book. The novel will not whitewash or sentimentalize those people, groups, or institutions Cather identifies herself with. If anything, they will be judged more coldly. The coldness of the judgments, in fact, helps create the atmosphere that separates this from the majority of Cather's other works.

Given the subtle ripples, however, one of the novel's central ironies is that the slaves love best their arbitrary and autocratic Ole Miss Sapphira, not her Baptist daughter, Rachel (*SS*, 137). Rachel believes that slavery is wrong, whether slaves like it or not. To her, the fact is irrelevant that none of the loosely supervised Dodderidge slaves has ever run off without eventually returning. But Rachel's principles are not unequivocally supported even by sacred scriptures, for nowhere in the Bible can one "find a clear condemnation of slavery" (*SS*, 110). The assertion reflects Willa Cather's strong impatience with dogmatists who require absolutes of any kind.[12] Sapphira's world is based on much simpler principles of self-interest. Yet Sapphira (not unlike her creator) loves a lover, a good meal, and spunk. So she inexplicably tolerates the useless Tansy Dave, or the lazy Bluebell, or the insolent Jezebel. To her servants she appears more generous and merciful than the juster Rachel or Henry.

The fact that most roles—social, sexual, or otherwise—are reversed in this novel is explicitly announced when Henry remarks to his wife, "You're the master here, and I'm the miller. And that's how I like it to be" (*SS*, 50). After their long and faithful marriage, Henry is absent from his own house partially because Sapphira makes him feel out of place there. He appears as a guest, summoned from his mill room, yet does not always stay "at home" when invited: "Thank you for having me up, Sapphy. It's done me good. . . . You might send for me a little oftener"(*SS*, 53).

Again reversing clichés, Cather depicts several blacks as the plantation's best workers. Both Samson and Till, even the cook Lizzie, operate proudly and effectively without supervision. All function as self-reliant and independent opposites to Nancy, who is dependent, uncertain, and scared. Were Nancy the only black character developed here, the novel might be more vulnerable to charges of racism than it actually is. However, Till, Nancy's mother, speaks English about as correctly as Sapphira's daughter, Rachel; both alternate between "accepted" English and dialect, and both sound most proper when speaking to Sapphira. Unlike Rachel's, Till's "genuine cordiality" is "restrained by correctness" (*SS*, 152). But Till is very ambitious, very concerned to be "respectable and well-placed" (*SS*, 72), and rather a snob, as aristocrats were sometimes said to be. Democratic Rachel, conversely, is a good friend of the impoverished and "trashy" Mrs. Ringer. Unlike her mistress, Sapphira, Till is not cheerful, happy, and gay— as slaves were stereotyped. But she is dependable, charitable, and kind—again, stereotypic qualities of the Southern aristocracy— as well as rather dour and withdrawn (*SS*, 70). After Till has taken over the management of the house, it is she from whom her mistress hides her questionable correspondence inviting a profligate nephew to visit, since Till can read. Through all these details, Cather hammers away at the Southern plantation's literary formulae.

If Mistress Sapphira is alternately arbitrary and implacable, quixotic and ruthless, an ineffective plotter but a harsh judge of others, she is anything but a conventional Southern lady, except in her outward manners and in the forms she insists on observing. The portrait of her that emerges in this novel is, in fact, one of the most daring of Cather's experiments. Cather dramatizes in this woman—modeled on her own great-grandmother—a remarkably complex human mixture. For Sapphira is capable of infamous villainy, but also of extraordinary generosity—an audacious mix.

Sapphira concludes correctly that Rachel has helped Nancy escape to freedom. In partially leaving her readers to infer how Sapphira guesses so unerringly, Cather forces us to confront what her deduction implies: that Nancy lacks the nerve or the knowledge to escape alone; that only Rachel, in the whole community, would dare to defy and thwart Sapphira; and that every movement in the neighborhood is faithfully reported to its most powerful, if immobilized, presence. (Rachel's house is closed for the first two days of Nancy's absence.) Then, having swiftly identified her daughter's treachery and asked her never to visit the Mill House again, Sapphira graciously rebuilds the bridges she herself has burned. She forgives Rachel for what she believes is unforgiveable; she tries valiantly by all means in her power to save her diphtheria-ridden grandchildren; she insists that the contagious granddaughter (the one who saves herself through willful disobedience, as Sapphira would have done) convalesce at the big house. Then Sapphira, displaying the strength of her own ego, labels her own act as selfishness and plays her final trump by forcing Rachel to acknowledge her mother's physical weakness. Sapphira further accepts, without denigrating it, her husband's pride in her and reliance on her. "She never lowered her flag" (SS, 268).

In her last novel, then, Willa Cather creates one of her most startling characters. She is physically and morally grotesque and perverse, as well as composed, uncomplaining, and unbreakable. Cather never asks us to qualify our disgust at Sapphira's villainies. We never succumb to her charm, as we (or as I) usually do to Godfrey St. Peter's. She never asks us to "forgive" Sapphira for her human frailties, as we and she forgave Archbishops Latour and Vaillant. Nor does her memory summon up a whole lost golden age, as Marian Forrester's does; nothing in the culture this book describes seems worth saving but the blossoms along the Double S in spring. We are never tempted, or even allowed, to identify with Sapphira, as was imaginable with Myra Henshawe or Lucy Gayheart. At all points, we keep a reserved distance from her because she is clearly dangerous from the first scene.

Instead, Cather creates a far more difficult task for her readers here. For she forces us to realize that Sapphira's sins and her virtues spring from the same self-confident dependence on herself, from her arrogant willfulness, and from her unfaltering courage and self-love. Though debilitated and even deformed by her illness, "She would make her death easy for everyone, because she would meet it with that composure which ... [Henry] had sometimes called heartlessness, but which now seemed to him strength" (*SS*, 268). Sapphira never complains, gives in, buckles under, or even grows testy (*SS*, 292, 293). She dies in her place—in her candlelit parlor, upright in her wheelchair, looking out over the grounds she has planted, pruned, and made beautiful. She dies smiling. What Cather forces us to accept, against all our contrary inclinations, is that Sapphira deserves her beautiful death. Cather insists that we see Sapphira as a woman whose selfishness most enviably preserves and sustains her. The novel is thus as ideologically unconventional as its heroine. The main character is "typically" Southern in her willfulness and freedom from the restraints of conventional decencies. But the main character is also a widely respected and deeply loved woman. No wonder that the novel continues to make us deeply uncomfortable. One surmises that that was its purpose.

In *Sapphira*, as elsewhere, Cather's most inventive experiments are with structure. Perhaps the most useful strategy in this novel is Cather's use of set pieces or episodes that appear self-contained, like parables, and that seem to interrupt the narrative flow without contributing substantially to the main action of the plot. When something looks peculiar in Cather's purposeful work, it needs asking about. The apparently unrelated parables or set pieces in *Sapphira and the Slave Girl* implicitly comment on major incidents.

The seemingly incidental figures of Casper Flight and Mrs. Ringer prove the point. Casper is an earnest and ambitious mountain boy who aspires to better himself, in spite of his family's literally using him as a plow horse (*SS,* 80). In considering Casper's apparent entrapment by family inheritance, environment, and economic circumstance, Rachel comments sadly, "A man's got to be stronger'n a bull to get out of the place he was born in (*SS,* 130). Yet Nancy, born black, slave, and female, still gets out. The simple statement about Casper becomes a comment on Nancy as well, reminding us with brilliant economy that Nancy has been not only an hysterical fugitive but also extraordinarily resourceful in creating her successful life. And the Keysers' sadistic abuse of Casper contrasts to Sapphira's subtler but equally sadistic abuse of Nancy. These interrelated analogies remind us that blacks are not the only "enchained" victims, nor are slave owners worse than nonslaveholders in their capacity for arranging abuse. That all classes do it does not excuse abuse at any point.

Long before she wrote *Sapphira* Cather had developed juxtaposition as a conscious technique. The rich effects her careful placements create are especially evident in this novel. For example, Rachel and Mrs. Ringer are declaring, "There is a kinda-a justice in this world after all" (*SS,* 126), and are talking about a "classic example of belated justice"—a murder solved after twenty years—when news arrives of Casper's imminent beating by the Keysers. The women then rescue Casper, a just act, as women rescue Nancy. We are prepared, however, for the final example of belated justice with which the novel ends. Nancy returns in glory after twenty-five years in Canada. Justice, after all, can provide triumph as well as salvation or retribution.

Mandy Ringer also figures in a thematic juxtaposition. Mrs. Ringer is something of a community pariah, because she has reared not only a crippled son but also two daughters who have been "fooled." One illegitimate pregnancy in a family is shocking enough, but two suggest unconscionable moral laxity. The sexual predicaments of the two white sisters, of course, contrast with

Nancy's superior slave morality. The Ringer excuse—that the girls had no man "to stand up fur 'em" (*SS,* 122)—applies equally to Nancy. But the Ringer sisters, having been seduced and abandoned, retreat in shame or hide; Nancy, who fled from threatened seduction or rape, humiliation, and disgrace, comes home triumphant.

Mandy Ringer is an interesting moral touchstone in the novel, meant to be juxtaposed as a character to Sapphira herself. Because Mrs. Ringer "was born interested" (*SS,* 119), because she can find even the weather entertaining, "misfortune and drudgery had never broken her spirit" (*SS,* 118–19). Her boast is, "If the Lord'll jist let me stay alive . . . I kin bear anything" (*SS,* 120). But if we admire these qualities in Mrs. Ringer, we must also admire them in Sapphira. For Sapphira, no less than Mandy Ringer, is characterized by her lively interest in, her sharp eye for the details of, the isolated world in which she lives. Neither spirit is broken by the adversities of final days.

The looping backward and forward between good and bad, advance and retreat, positive and negative, in all such analogies reminds us of the splendid visual image that comes to symbolize the core of this novel, and perhaps of Cather's entire oeuvre as well. The beautiful double S in the road to Timber Ridge—the lovely spot surrounded by dogwood, laurel, and wild honeysuckle in which the road seems to continue without getting anywhere—symbolizes the pace of this story (the action proper hardly begins until the halfway mark, with the arrival of Martin Colbert), the contrary directions in which the story seems to run, the confusions of debates over slavery, and the twists in each human character depicted here. Thus, Henry Colbert, the community's moral pillar, still fails to act decisively when his beloved Nancy is threatened in a way he most abhors. Merry Tap, who rides heroically to fetch Dr. Clavenger for the morally ill grandchildren, is still hung by a "Yankee jury" for murder (*SS,* 290). Would-be rapist Martin Colbert still dies gloriously as a Confederate captain for whom a local monument is erected. The double S is one of Cather's most effective central symbols. It is first described immediately after Henry Colbert remembers the hymn "God moves in a mysterious way / His wonders to perform" (*SS,* 111).[13] Importantly, the spot is associated with ravishing beauty as well as Martin's hopes to ravish Nancy. It comes to symbolize all human life. And such looping back and forth is required not only for conundrums Cather poses through Sapphira and Henry or Nancy and Till. It also includes the good neighbor and nurse Rachel Blake, whose ignorance of medical fact is so dense that it condemns to death her own daughter. As Cather comments, "The four loops are now denuded and ugly, but motorists, however unwillingly, must swing around them if they go on that road at all" (*SS,* 171). By implication, a reader must be willing to swing around such loops if she travels this road to Cather country at all, and to the place Cather fiction originates.

Finally, however, the most daring and revealing experiment Cather incorporates in *Sapphira and the Slave Girl* involves narrative point of view. The author intrudes directly into this novel *as author,* from the beginning: "How these two came to be living at the Mill Farm is a long story—too long for a breakfast table story" (*SS,* 5). In so doing she deliberately refuses to maintain the formalist boundaries between writer, narrative persona, and characters. She also, by changing the names of her great-grandparents Jacob and Ruhamah Seibert to Sapphira and Henry Colbert, refused to maintain the distinctions between fact and fiction. She occasionally makes her own value judgments, instead of allowing characters or incidents to make them for her. For example, as Sapphira and Martin Colbert share their first tea, "She told herself that Martin's visit would be very refreshing. She almost believed she had urged him to come solely because she liked to have young people about (*SS,* 154). Or she comments directly to the reader, most directly of all in the book's last italicized paragraph. In that curious final word, she acknowledges her childish delight in such funny names as Mr. Pertleball and ends, "to this day, I don't know how to spell it." I have wondered whether this final comment is a way of saying, "I still don't have all the answers to enigmas that puzzled me as a child."

As *narrator* and West Virginia native, Cather occasionally lapses into local idioms or dialect: for example, "Mandy Ringer had lived a hard life, goodness knew" (*SS,* 118); she "got out her blue chiney cups" (*SS,* 121); or "he no longer tried to make hisself smell sweet" (*SS,* 206). Of course, in reminding us by her colloquialisms that she is repeating her own familiar story, and that the scenes she describes were those she actually observed, Cather authenticates all the surprising details she incorporates here. Further, she pointedly reminds us that the book is a *story* that exists because she enjoys telling it, as well as because she once enjoyed hearing it. She reminds the reader to remember the personality doing the telling, beyond the mere sequence of the events. In fact, she explains the large gaps in the narrative by making the book a childhood story, subject to lapses of memory and therefore lacking all merely decorative fact. The book becomes the kind of remembered tale in which one can expect to have many scrubby or background details omitted.[14]

But ultimately, it seems to me, Willa Cather stepped out of her last years' grief and bad health and into her book because this novel makes a summarizing statement for its creator: life is not neatly predictable or ideologically consistent, and neither are people. Real-life characters and events are always more complex than fictional formulas. Living villains can also be heroes, as well as vice versa. And sometimes malicious, isolated, and dying old women can command respect when they have the courage to love what they have made of themselves and the stamina to remain faithful to the lives they have willed into existence. At her end, Cather acknowledges the nature of her own blood, judges it coldly, and then accepts it. Her foremothers are self-centered as well as unselfish. But, she seems to say, that bloodline and those progenitresses produced her and shaped her beginning. Looking back at the end of the book and the life, she finds herself smiling.

CHAPTER ELEVEN

Something More Beyond:
A Summarizing Conclusion

Willa Cather's art . . . has been called elusive,
subtle, complex. There has always been something
more beyond the pages, something we could not
quite put our fingers on, or define. There still is,
for that matter.

——————— BERNICE SLOTE, *The Kingdom of Art.* ———————

The most exciting fact about Willa Cather's fiction is that it is inexhaustible. The second most exciting fact is that scholars have begun to give it the attention it deserves. Many readings of the best-known novels are now available, most of them interesting and in some way illuminating. This study has added another reading for several best-known books, and has also dealt in the light of recent scholarly biographies with several lesser-known novels. Among those least-known books are the novels with which this study begins and ends.

The Willa Cather who has emerged here is a different woman and writer from the "Auntie Willa" described in the past. She is a great deal more human, less saintly, less comfortable, and less comforting. She is ferociously competitive, not only with others but also with herself and her past accomplishments. My Cather was capable of nursing lifelong grudges, but deeply distrusted the critics who caught her at it as well as those who missed her points.

She was thin-skinned. Subject to intense jealousy as well as prolonged anxiety, she often suffered from ills that look psychosomatic. But she had one characteristic that arrests attention: she ruthlessly judged art and artists, and especially judged herself. She cast a cold eye on life and death, but she also loved and valued things of clear quality. She wanted the quintessential best of the truly important things—and therefore remained wary and suspicious of any distractions or imitations.

Cather's willingness to judge coldly and negatively as well as her drive to experience the best of human life and effort allowed her to choose subjects from an exceptional range of human types. Particularly wide was her development of female characters. This study has emphasized, however, the intense drive to know herself, as well as her creations. To do so she seemed willing to pry into every cranny of her psyche—even the most unpleasant or unconventional. She often created male as well as female alter egos or autobiographical protagonists, and she never hesitated to judge any of them as harshly as they deserved. If anything, however, she judged such female surrogates as Myra Henshawe or Sapphira Colbert even more coldly than she did her male mouthpieces— Jim Burden, Niel Herbert, Godfrey St. Peter. We may at least suspect that she was finally more tolerant of male than of female imperfections.

This book has explored the close connections between what Willa Cather was apparently thinking or feeling, so far as we are able to guess, and what she was writing in the years that followed 1922. Such a commonsense practice has in her case been delayed partially by the absence, until relatively recent months, of comprehensively reliable biographical information and partially by the fact that Cather formulated her ideas through oppositions. Moreover, in constructing her novels she habitually went from one (always complex) subject to some opposite (and equally complex) one. Thus, the continuities between her works sometimes seemed hard to grasp.

In 1922, in any case, Cather did what one might predict a person would do whose reflexive thinking patterns emerged from the tense pull of opposites: she felt that the world had broken in two. No exact or single cause of her sensation is possible to identify even now, and perhaps one is not necessary. In any case, the year became Cather's personal symbol for a time of disruption, discontinuity, fragmentation, and loss. We suspect, in fact, that the causes for the feeling were many, but whether many or few, she thereafter viewed the world and her life from the other side of the divide. This book has asked what Cather did after the break.

For one thing, she commenced a period of frenzied activity, travel, and brilliant writing in which masterpieces seemed to bloom from her amaryllis pen at almost regular yearly intervals. Because her mind as well as her body seemed hyperactive, she poured her speculations and anguish into her work. Thus, we can trace her debates with herself and the questions with which she wrestled through her stunning fictions.

One of Ours, the novel that was published in 1922 after four years of prolonged struggle, was actually structured to show graphically the world breaking in two (even before she acknowledged that she had decided it had done so). Everything that happens in the novel is understood in terms of, and classified as occurring before or after, cataclysmic world war. The novel was explicitly based on the life of Cather's cousin, Lieutenant G. P. Cather, with whom she strongly identified. But it had artistic agendas to accomplish as well. For one thing, the work was intended to display Cather's ability to write a "manly battle yarn," since that was the proof Cather had once demanded for excellence in women writers. When critics derided her attempts and patronized her story, the Pulitzer prize did not compensate for their affronts. Thereafter, Cather began her steady withdrawal from public sight. She also began to develop an accelerating hostility toward critics that finally culminated in the deliberate "critic-trap" of *Sapphira and the Slave Girl.*

In 1922, however, Cather was beginning a slide toward despair that seemed to accelerate as she wrote to stop her plunge. From the safe distance at which we view her life today, she suggests Poe's terrified narrator, caught in the vortex of the maelstrom.

Like that narrator, when all else failed she reasoned out an effective strategy for survival.

Yet 1922 was, as far as production goes, a wonderful year. After the prolonged struggles with the intractable Claude Wheeler and the United States Army in *One of Ours, A Lost Lady* seemed almost to write itself in a flash, in the spring of the banner year. The exhilaration of speedy composition led her to pen and publish her most important essay—"The Novel Démeublé"—which laid down her esthetic principles succinctly. It was used as a stick with which to chastize her for *One of Ours* when that novel appeared in the fall. Meanwhile, however, since Cather always chose in one sense or another an opposite subject for her next effort once one book or novel was done, she turned from Marian Forrester, the aging and eventually besmirched but steadily charming protagonist of *A Lost Lady,* to a tale about a fresh and uncompromised young male who died young: "Tom Outland's Story." Outland's story, even more "démeublé" than Marian Forrester's, was apparently completed in the intensifying work phase of 1922, just before the negative autumn reviews jaundiced the tone of the following novel—*The Professor's House.*

Professor Godfrey St. Peter is the immensely complex and tired male autobiographical figure whose story engulfs Tom Outland's. He seems very obviously to represent an increasingly distressed Cather, or at least to ask Cather's distressed questions and to illustrate her knotted concerns. His creation did not lift her spirits or alleviate her anguish, however, for she finished his portrait ahead of schedule, only immediately to dive deeper into a spiritual morass. At that point, then, she contrived for 1926 her most rigidly controlled, symmetrically structured, and opaque story of dying romance and a dying lady—*My Mortal Enemy.* Then, with nothing left to hope for or reach toward, Cather reversed herself in a manner that nobody could plausibly account for who had not looked steadily at her record and at the pattern of reversals her novels themselves illustrate. She followed the desperate measure to save her life that her character Myra Henshawe had feverishly perfected and futilely attempted in the previous book; she embraced affirmation and tried a leap of faith. Her literary as well as philosophical guide was Pascal. The published result in 1927 was *Death Comes for the Archbishop,* a serene masterpiece and, I believe, a great religious book. The exhilaration of this accomplishment lasted only six months, until her next set of traumas overtook it. But while it lasted, she said it felt like a gorgeous party.

Unfortunately several devastations then occurred in rapid order. First, Cather and Edith Lewis, her nearly lifelong companion, were forced to leave their Bank Street home, which was slated for demolition. The displacement felt like terrible anarchy. Then her father died, and her mother had a stroke. Thus, in the intensest distress of her life so far, she began to work on a book that would suggest stability, continuity, safety from a surrounding wilderness. *Shadows on the Rock* was both an unanticipated response to Cather's first glimpse of Quebec—the city seeming to her an anachronistic model of that Norman French medieval culture she had all her adult life wished she could belong to—and also an imaginative retreat to a place like Brigadoon that had escaped time's changes. She built with the Quebec setting her last masterpiece, constructed on an analogy to a medieval miracle play. It asserted the possibility of everyday safety and wonderful transformations. The book was published the month her mother died in 1931.

A four-year interval followed before the appearance in 1936 of the next novel, *Lucy Gayheart,* written in the depths of the depression. *Lucy Gayheart* seems to me Cather's most sardonic work, a judgmental story of artistic shallowness, professional timidity, and emotional bad faith. The composing eye seems to see cynically, and the view of life seems colored by disgust. It also seems a hostile gesture toward a public whose taste filled Cather with apparent contempt. After such a gesture was predictably misunderstood, Cather baited a trap for critics and sprang it in 1940 with *Sapphira and the Slave Girl.* She was working on a novel set near the papal palace in Avignon when she died. Obviously at the end she had turned again to questions of justice and religion, and this time seemed ready to reverse her previous stance and to associate torture with her once-beloved medieval period.

The Willa Cather whose portrait emerges from this arrangement of her facts is complex and brilliant. She is neurotically controlling and self-conscious about her work, but she knows at all points what she is doing. Above all else, she is self-conscious. She herself is the manipulator of her texts and subtexts. I have assumed in this study that there are no accidents, excrescences, or unrelated details in Cather's fiction. I believe that everything she left there served her conscious purposes and led to her final effects, as her mentor Poe had taught her it should. Most important, out of her arrogance and pain, she fashioned fictions of such intricacy and resonating depth that all of them—even the meanest—are still astonishing to read and explore today. I hope the reader who has explored them with me has completed this study with a new sense of their value.

NOTES

INDEX

Notes

─────────────── CHAPTER ONE ───────────────

1 • Sharon O'Brien, *Willa Cather: The Emerging Voice* (New York: Oxford University Press, 1987), 288. Hereafter cited as O'Brien, *Emerging Voice.*

2 • James Woodress, *Willa Cather: A Literary Life* (Lincoln: University of Nebraska Press, 1987), 205. Hereafter cited as Woodress, *Literary Life.*

3 • H. L. Mencken quoted in "Willa Sibert Cather: To Our Notion the Foremost American Novelist," by Henry Blackmun Sell, *Chicago Daily News,* March 12, 1919; reprinted in *Willa Cather in Person: Interviews, Speeches, and Letters,* ed. L. Brent Bohlke (Lincoln: University of Nebraska Press, 1986), 17. Hereafter cited as *In Person.*

4 • Woodress, *Literary Life,* 300.

5 • James Woodress, *Willa Cather: Her Life and Art* (Lincoln: University of Nebraska Press, 1970), 190. Hereafter cited as Woodress, *Life and Art.*

6 • Woodress, *Literary Life,* 309.

7 • Flora Merrill, "A Short Story Course Can Only Delay, It Cannot Kill an Artist, Says Willa Cather," *New York World,* April 19, 1925, sec. 3, pp. 1, 6, cols. 1–5, 4–5, in *In Person,* 77.

8 • For example, her British publisher, Heinemann, had turned down *Song of the Lark* because he objected to Cather's trying to tell "everything about everybody." He advised her to return to her former and sparer style. (Willa Cather, "My First Novels [There Were Two]," in *Willa Cather on Writing: Critical Studies on Writing as an Art,* Foreword by Stephen Tennant [1949; Lincoln: University of Nebraska Press, 1988], 96. Hereafter cited as *Cather on Writing.*

   Similarly, Nebraskans objected strongly to "A Wagner Matinee" because of its bleak presentation of farm life in the state.

9 • Edith Lewis, *Willa Cather Living: A Personal Record* (New York: Alfred A. Knopf, 1953), 117. Hereafter cited as Lewis, *Cather Living.*

10 • Woodress, *Literary Life,* 303.

11 • Ibid., 319.

12 • Ibid., 319, 320.

13 • Ibid., 323.

14 • Ibid., 305.

15 • Elizabeth Shepley Sergeant actually thought otherwise: "she liked this prize and never ceased to say, in print and out of print, that Claude was

her favorite of all her heroes." *Willa Cather: A Memoir* (Lincoln: University of Nebraska Press, 1953), 182. Hereafter cited as Sergeant, *Cather Memoir.*

16 • *In Person,* 58.

17 • Willa Cather, Prefatory Note to *Not under Forty* (1936; New York: Alfred A. Knopf, 1988).

18 • Woodress, *Life and Art,* 190.

19 • O'Brien, *Emerging Voice,* 225.

20 • Ibid., 227.

21 • Ibid., 384.

22 • Woodress, *Literary Life,* 301.

23 • Ibid., 479.

24 • Willa Cather, *One of Ours* (1922; New York: Vintage Books, 1950), 10, 25. Page references for quotations from this edition will hereafter be cited in the text with the abbreviation *oo.*

25 • Josephine Humphries begins her recent novel *Rich in Love* (New York: Penguin, 1988) with this definition of a story worth telling.

──────── CHAPTER TWO ────────

1 • Willa Cather, *The Professor's House* (1925; New York: Vintage, 1973), 32. Page references for quotations from this edition will hereafter be cited in the text with the abbreviation *PH.*

2 • Willa Cather, "On the Art of Fiction," in *Cather on Writing,* 102.

3 • Willa Cather, "The Novel Démeublé," in *Not under Forty,* 44.

4 • Willa Cather, *O Pioneers!* (1913; Boston: Houghton Mifflin, 1962), 119.

5 • Willa Cather, "Miss Jewett," in *Not under Forty,* 44.

6 • An extended exploration of this technique can be found in David G. Massey's Ph.D. dissertation entitled "Simplicity with Suggestiveness in Willa Cather's Revised and Republished Fiction" (Drew University, 1979).

7 • Willa Cather, *My Ántonia* (1918; Boston: Houghton Mifflin, 1954), 43. Page references for quotations from this edition will hereafter be cited in the text with the abbreviation *MA.*

8 • Willa Cather, *Alexander's Bridge,* Introduction by Bernice Slote (1912; Lincoln: University of Nebraska Press, 1977), 136. Page references for quotations from this edition will hereafter be cited in the text with the abbreviation *AB.*

9 • Willa Cather, *A Lost Lady* (1923; New York: Vintage, 1972), 119. Page references for quotations from this edition will hereafter be cited in the text with the abbreviation *LL.*

10 • Willa Cather, *Lucy Gayheart* (1935; New York: Vintage, 1976), 101. Page references for quotations from this edition will hereafter be cited in the text with the abbreviation *LG*.

11 • Willa Cather, *Shadows on the Rock* (1931; New York: Vintage, 1971), 137. Page references for quotations from this edition will hereafter be cited in the text with the abbreviation *SR*.

12 • Willa Cather, *Death Comes for the Archbishop* (1927; New York: Vintage, 1971), 51. Page references for quotations from this edition will hereafter be cited in the text with the abbreviation *DA*.

──────────────── CHAPTER THREE ────────────────

1 • Merrill, "A Short Story Course Can Only Delay," in *In Person*, 77.

2 • Cather, "My First Novels," in *Cather on Writing*, 96–97.

3 • The heavy use of detail here leads John J. Murphy to argue that this novel is Cather's experimentation with realism or naturalism: "*One of Ours* as American Naturalism," *Great Plains Quarterly* 2 (Fall 1982): 232–38.

4 • Sergeant, *Cather Memoir*, 163.

5 • As Susan Rosowski puts it, "In *One of Ours*, Cather further explored the relation of American consciousness to its Old World heritage, this time in terms of discontinuities threatened by World War I." *The Voyage Perilous: Willa Cather's Romanticism* (Lincoln: University of Nebraska Press, 1986), 95. Hereafter cited as Rosowski, *Voyage Perilous*.

6 • Eva Mahoney, "How Willa Cather Found Herself: After Ten Years of Practice at Following Henry James' Style, She Finally Wrote Her Own Nebraska in Her Own Way," *Omaha World-Herald*, November 27, 1921, in *In Person*, 39.

7 • In reviewing this material, Mr. Woodress has written, "I have always thought she meant that she did not create pictures when she slips into Claude's mind and is reproducing his stream of consciousness.... It seems to me that in the instances [discussed later in the chapter] it is the omniscient third-person narrator who is doing the describing for the reader and it's not Claude seeing the scene. An exception [occurs when] Cather does have Claude seeing the what fields and the corn-planters. A good example of what I think is Cather avoiding having Claude visualize a scene occurs when he visits St. Ouen in Rouen. The only thing that catches his eye is the rose window which he sees from the choir. This church is a magnificent example of Gothic architecture, and it strikes me as significant that Cather at that point has Claude *hear* the bell tolling

the hour; and immediately he sits down and begins silently practicing his French" (personal correspondence, February 1989).

8 • Sergeant, *Cather Memoir,* 163–64.

9 • Mahoney, "How Willa Cather Found Herself," in *In Person,* 39.

10 • Susan Rosowski develops this argument further in *Voyage Perilous,* 110.

11 • Mark Harris, ed., *The Selected Poems of Vachel Lindsay* (New York: Macmillan, 1963), 118–19.

─────────────── CHAPTER FOUR ───────────────

1 • Merrill, "A Short Story Course," in *In Person,* 77.

2 • Ibid.; Woodress, *Literary Life,* 340.

3 • Woodress, *Literary Life,* 341.

4 • Ibid., 342.

5 • Sergeant, *Cather Memoir,* 185–86.

6 • Ibid., 130–40.

7 • Rosowski, *Voyage Perilous,* 123–24.

8 • Merrill, "A Short Story Course," in *In Person,* 77.

9 • Woodress, *Literary Life,* 352.

10 • Cather, "The Novel Démeublé," in *Not under Forty,* 50.

11 • He is also, at one point, somewhat gratuitously compared to Grover Cleveland (*LL,* 48). Since no such references are extraneous, especially in this "unfurnished novel," we may speculate about several implied resemblances: to Cleveland's physical bulk; to his democratic loyalties; to his acknowledged passion for financial straight dealing or reform; to his rather simplistic ethical outlook on challenges to social order; even, perhaps, to a sexual past that did not disturb his middle-aged rectitude. In the 1884 campaign, Republicans taunted Cleveland for an illegitimate child by chanting, "Maw, maw, where's my paw? Gone to the White House, haw, haw, haw."

12 • Woodress, *Literary Life,* 341.

13 • Merrill, "A Short Story Course," in *In Person,* 77.

14 • Kathleen L. Nichols, "The Celibate Male in *A Lost Lady:* The Unreliable Center of Consciousness," in *Critical Essays on Willa Cather,* ed. John J. Murphy (Boston: G. K. Hall, 1984), 195; Sharon O'Brien, "Mothers, Daughters, and the 'Art Necessity': Willa Cather and the Creative Process," in *American Novelists Revisited: Essays in Feminist Criticism,* ed. Fritz Fleischmann (Boston: G. K. Hall, 1982), 288.

15 • David Stouck, *Willa Cather's Imagination* (Lincoln: University of Nebraska Press, 1975), 59. Hereafter cited as Stouck, *Imagination.*

16 • The interpretation in this paragraph was suggested to me by Professor Larry Berkove of the University of Michigan at Dearborn.

17 • Cather does seem to suggest that Ivy is little more than a rawly phallic form of natural energy. He "stood stiffly upright" (*LL,* 21), we are told, and his face "was red, and the flesh looked hard, as if it were swollen" (*LL,* 21).

——————————— CHAPTER FIVE ———————————

1 • Woodress, *Literary Life,* 367.

2 • Evelyn Thomas Helmick published a good start to the scholarly investigation of Cather's medieval theme in August of 1975. Her essay, "The Broken World: Medievalism in *A Lost Lady,*" later reprinted in John J. Murphy's collection of critical essays, explains, "Her previous 'medieval' novel, *One of Ours,* is an epic or *chanson de geste* in which war is the subject; *A Lost Lady* is an Arthurian romance in which courtly love is the subject. If the first reflects the crude power of romanesque art, the second reflects the complexity and refinement of later Gothic art. The romance was an ideal, and traditional, vehicle for the expression of certain attitudes towards society. The original romance literature ... was nourished on the awareness of the crisis in the conscience and instincts of twelfth-century man. Cather's use of the genre of courtly romance seems almost inevitable in view of her own time" (in Murphy, ed., *Critical Essays on Willa Cather,* 181).

I believe that Helmick's points apply equally to Cather's frame of mind as she wrote *The Professor's House.* In fact, I think this medieval theme in Cather's fiction needs to be the focus of an entire book. As I will point out later in this chapter and elsewhere, however, the strain can certainly be heard quite audibly in both *The Professor's House* and *Shadows on the Rock.* David Stouck hears the same echoes in *Lucy Gayheart* (Stouck, *Cather's Imagination,* 219), which would suggest a second "trio" of novels containing medieval resonances in *Archbishop, Shadows,* and *Gayheart.* Further, we know that Cather was in the middle of her most overtly medieval novel when she died. Eventually, the medieval may come to seem one of her most central and integral themes.

3 • Whether the theme of religion will come in time to seem as central to Cather's fiction as her medieval theme is for me a very open and active question. John Murphy has helpfully pointed out to me that the theme is also important in the great short stories of the *Neighbor Rosicky* collection, as well as in *Sapphira and the Slave Girl.*

4 • We know, in fact, that at the end of her life Willa Cather once again returned to both themes. At the time of her death she was working on a novel set in "France of the Middle Ages, the period of the Babylonian captivity when the Church of Rome was ruled from Avignon. Cather

had been moved by her first visit to the city in 1902, and the Papal Palace built in the fourteenth century by Benedict XII 'stirred her as no building in the world ever had done'" (Woodress, *Literary Life,* 492–93).

5 • In a speech at Bowdoin College delivered in May of 1925 (after *The Professor's House* was finished and just before it was published), Cather is quoted as saying, "I suppose plot is a part of technique. There are two kinds of novel writing. One affects the plot a lot, the other not at all. . . . It is manifestly wrong to consider plot as an essential part of the novel, when the writer has obviously not considered it." "Menace to Culture in Cinema and Radio Seen by Miss Cather," *Christian Science Monitor,* May 14, 1925, in *In Person,* 155–56.

6 • For example, as book three resumes St. Peter's story, it begins, "All the most important things in his life, St. Peter sometimes reflected, had been determined by chance. His education in France had been an accident. His married life had been happy largely through a circumstance with which neither he nor his wife had anything to do" (*PH,* 257).

7 • Judith Fryer, quoting Nina Baym and Ellen Moers, "reads" the landscape very helpfully and convincingly, in *Felicitous Space: The Imaginative Structures of Edith Wharton and Willa Cather* (Chapel Hill: University of North Carolina Press, 1986), 245–46. Hereafter cited as Fryer, *Space.*

8 • I take the name *Hamilton* to be an obvious reference to Alexander Hamilton, the first secretary of the treasury, who placed the nation on a firm financial footing, devised the nation's monetary and banking systems, and encouraged sound credit practices, investment, commerce, and trade.

9 • The Professor's design for his histories unfolded as he lay in a boat and looked up at mountain ranges: "And the design was sound. He had accepted it as inevitable, had never meddled with it, and it had seen him through" (*PH,* 106).

10 • Inconsistently, Godfrey critically judges Professor Crane's laboratory workspace where Crane "was working by the glare of an unshaded electric bulb of high power—the man seemed to have no feeling for comfort of any kind" (*PH,* 144). When St. Peter clings to similar habits, his wife declares him "perverse" (*PH,* 97).

11 • When St. Peter eventually *does* reconnect with his most youthful and primitive past self, the experience convinces him that he is about to die, that he will not even live to teach his fall classes.

12 • Since Cather knew Pascal well, as we will see when we discuss *Death Comes for the Archbishop,* she may actually have had in mind at this point Pascal's Pensée no. 7 (of the Brunschvicg edition, which she would have used [see note 10 to chapter 7, below]): "The greater intellect one has, the more originality one finds in persons. Ordinary people find no difference in persons." St. Peter seeks maliciously at this point to demon-

strate the ordinariness of his rival Langtry by suggesting Langtry acknowledge he finds no originality in their students.

13 • Cather, *Courier,* September 14, 1895; quoted in *The Kingdom of Art: Willa Cather's First Principles and Critical Statements, 1893–96,* ed. Bernice Slote (Lincoln: University of Nebraska Press, 1966), 280. Hereafter cited as *Kingdom of Art.* In reviewing the performance of a particular Mephisto, Cather continues, "The only fault that I have to find with John Griffith's Mephisto is that it lacks dignity, awfulness. I should not be afraid of that kind of a devil. His Mephisto is a thoroughly jolly fellow with occasional bursts of very bad temper. He is so jolly that he is humorous even when he is angry. I do not object to the comedy which Mr. Griffith introduces, but to the kind of comedy. It's too good natured, too undignified, the kind of fun one hears among good fellows who are cynical but bear no malice. It should be, I think, a deeper comedy than that, a humor that would make one's blood run cold" (*Courier,* 8). It may be relevant that St. Peter is one of Cather's few characters distinguished by ironic wit and a sense of humor.

14 • Cather, "On the Art of Fiction," *Cather on Writing,* 102–3.

15 • Margaret Doane, "In Defense of Lillian St. Peter: Men's Perceptions of Women in *The Professor's House,*" *Western American Literature* 18 (1984): 299–302. See also Jean Schwind, "'Tom Outland's Story,' and *The Professor's House:* The Frame Up of Eve in Cather's Framed Narrative," Ph.D. dissertation, University of Minnesota, Minneapolis, 1983.

16 • "Miss Jewett," *Not under Forty,* 77–78. Cather writes in this crucial passage, "The design is, indeed, so happy, so right, that it seems inevitable; the design is the story and the story is the design."

17 • "Four Letters: 4. On *The Professor's House,*" in *Cather on Writing,* 31–32.

18 • The "forms" in the attic "were the subject of much banter" (*PH,* 17) between Godfrey and Augusta. "Augusta enjoyed the Professor when he was *risqué,* since she was sure of his ultimate delicacy" (*PH,* 18). She narrowly averts a giggle when the Professor insinuates a sexual incident for her priest (*PH,* 24).

19 • Robert Alan McGill, "Heartbreak: Western Enchantment and Western Facts in Willa Cather's *The Professor's House,*" *South Dakota Review* 16 (1978): 56–79.

20 • Woodress, *Literary Life,* 339.

──────────── CHAPTER SIX ────────────

1 • Woodress, *Literary Life,* 380.

2 • Willa Cather, *My Mortal Enemy* (1926; New York: Vintage, 1954), 85.

Page references for quotations from this edition will hereafter be cited in the text with the abbreviation *ME*.

3 • Sergeant, *Cather Memoir,* 140.

4 • Woodress notes the similarity between the comments on Edna Pontellier and Myra's life, in *Literary Life,* 386.

5 • Cather in *Leader,* July 8, 1899, p. 6, reprinted in *The World and the Parish: Willa Cather's Articles and Reviews, 1893–1902,* ed. William M. Curtin, 2 vols. (Lincoln: University of Nebraska Press, 1970), 2:698–99. Hereafter cited as *World and Parish.*

6 • For example, in both chapters one, Nellie arrives to encounter Myra and registers vivid impressions of Myra's "old self"; in both chapters two, we receive the background facts of Myra's present situation; in both chapters three, we meet the Henshawe friends and share some poetry; both chapters four explore secret arrangements; both chapters five record definitions of Myra; both chapters six describe cataclysmic ruptures in relationships.

7 • In a newly published study, Jo Ann Middleton argues with great skill that the style of Cather's "démeublé fiction," based on excision, demonstrates her incorporation and redefinition of modernist aesthetics. Middleton introduces the biological term *vacuole* as a metaphor to explain Cather's method. *Willa Cather's Modernism: A Study of Style and Technique* (Rutherford, N.J.: Fairleigh Dickinson Press, 1990).

8 • *Kingdom of Art,* 312. Susan Rosowski's whole book, *The Voyage Perilous: Willa Cather's Romanticism,* is based on the recognition of Cather's clearly and frequently expressed opinions on this subject. A further point is that Cather hated the *excess* of too much detail and too little suggestiveness, not any particular subject identified with "real life" or dark human potential.

9 • *World and Parish,* 2:712.

10 • *World and Parish,* 1:458.

11 • For example, "Ah! There is something in Romanticism, after all, and the drama has only been the poorer since it left us" (*World and Parish,* 1:460–61).

12 • Bernice Slote explains of the "moon-myth":

> One of the most deeply affective and complex symbols in Willa Cather's writing, the moon is the goddess Diana, the desire of Endymion, the queen of witches, the cat-goddess, or the pagan goddess of all motion. Like any writer who uses myth organically, Willa Cather had some habitual emotional values for particular stories or figures, and by the invocation of a name could gather in the whole body of associations. The moon is generally seen as some high, illimitable beauty; the sign of yearning and

desire; the radiant or mysterious illumination of darkness; and the sign also of the voyage perilous (anyone can dream *Endymion* but only the artist can create it). In the 1893–96 writing, however, she refers often enough to three literary sources of moon symbolism to suggest that their individual qualities might be important. We assume the moon of romance in *Romeo and Juliet;* in addition there were Keats's *Endymion,* Heine's *The Gods in Exile,* and Flaubert's *Salammbo.* From the overt and plainly marked allusions in the early years, we can see how the elements blend and are absorbed into the whole texture of the work. (*Kingdom of Art,* 97–98)

13 • Slote has written:

> Like the goddess of triple sight, three-fold Diana who rules three realms—... the artist is not only himself but also man and god. As we see it in Willa Cather's pages, the kingdom of art is poised, with intricate balance and mingling, between two other worlds. The artist may look to the kingdom of heaven, and sometimes the gods come down: but on earth he is caught in time, living at once in two worlds and with two selves, a duality even the gods would find hard to divide. Of all the dilemmas which appear in Willa Cather's frank statements during these first years, none is stronger or with more permanent implications than this one of artist and person. It is one form of the duality of self which was to appear in many guises through her yet unwritten pages. (*Kingdom of Art,* 66)

Slote's comment is helpful in explaining the association of a triune goddess with insistent dualities, especially the conflicting demands of life and art.

14 • Rosowski, *Voyage Perilous,* 153.

15 • *Kingdom of Art,* 240.

16 • As translated in the (anonymous) 1968 libretto of the London Records release of Bellini's *Norma* (side 5, p. 17, col. 2), the song begins,

> "See, Norma, see at your knees
> these dear children.
> Oh, be moved by pity for them
> if you have no pity for yourself."

17 • Cather's important fascination with Brontë's character was first mentioned in my presence by Bruce Baker at the Northeast Modern Language Association, Philadelphia, 1984.

18 • Stouck, *Imagination,* 124.

19 • For an expanded treatment of the implications here, see Marilyn Berg

Callander, *Willa Cather and the Fairy Tale* (Ann Arbor: U.M.I. Research Press, 1989), 29–45. Hereafter cited as Callander, *Fairy Tale.*

20 • See ibid., 45–60, for a subtle tracing of the extremely complex possibilities suggested here.

21 • Cather wrote, "In New York I went to see Modjeska in *Mary Stuart.* I had not seen her for six years and I was almost afraid to go—afraid that she might have changed too greatly. She has changed, but only as a flower from which the rains have washed the brilliance of its color, as an antique marble which time has ravaged but never lost its high significance" (*Courier,* March 5, 1898, pp. 2–3, in *World and Parish,* 1:459).

22 • Professor Larry Berkove, of the University of Michigan at Dearborn, has called my attention to the fact that Bacon writes, "Cosmus, Duke of Florence, had a desperate saying against perfidious or neglecting friends, as if those wrongs were unpardonable. 'You shall read,' saith he, 'that we are commanded to forgive our enemies, but you never read that we are commanded to forgive our friends.'" In the same essay we also find this relevant passage: "Public revenges are for the most part fortunate; as that for the death of Caesar ... and many more. But in private revenges it is not so; nay, rather vindictive persons live the lives of witches, who, as they are mischievous, so end they unfortunate" (*Bacon's Essays with Whateley's Annotations (Student's Edition) and Notes and a Glossarial Index,* ed. Franklin Fiske Heard [Boston: Lee and Shepard, 1873], 53.

23 • Professor Edwina Lawler of the Drew University German Department has generously translated these poems by Heine as follows:
"Am Kreuzweg wird begraben" from *Lyrisches Intermesso* (1822–23)

> Whoever committed suicide
> Is buried at the crossroads;
> A blue flower grows there,
> The flower for a poor sinner.
>
> I stood and sighed at the crossroads;
> The night was cold and silent.
> The flower for one condemned to die
> Moved slowly in the moonlight.

"Was will die einsame Träne?" from *Die Heimkehr* (1823–24)

> What does the solitary tear mean?
> Indeed it blurs my sight.
> It remained behind in my eye
> From olden times.
>
> It had many bright sisters
> Who have all dissolved;

Dissolved into night and wind
With my pains and joys.

The blue little stars
That smiled those joys and pains
Into my heart
Have also dissolved like clouds.

Ah, my love itself
Dissolved like a futile breeze
Dissolve now too
You old solitary tear!

24 • Walt Whitman, "Song of Myself," *Leaves of Grass* (Comprehensive Reader's Edition), ed. Harold W. Blodgett and Sculley Bradley (1965; New York: Norton, 1968), ll. 633–38, pp. 57–58.

25 • Walter B. Gibson and Litzka R. Gibson, "Fortune Telling with the Fifty-two Card Pack," *The Complete Illustrated Book of Divination and Prophesy* (Garden City, N.Y.: Doubleday, 1973), 246.

26 • Barbara G. Walker, *The Secrets of the Tarot: Origins, History, and Symbolism* (New York: Harper and Row, 1984).

27 • The last subtle detail suggesting a disingenuous narrator is perhaps this matter of Nellie's possibly *deliberate* search for the Henshawes in the West. She tells us without "holding the note," that "I had known that the Henshawes had come on evil days, and were wandering about among the cities of the Pacific coast. But Myra had stopped writing to Aunt Lydia, beyond a word of greeting at Christmas and on her birthday" (*ME*, 60). Paraphrased, this information tells us that twice a year, Myra had been in touch with Lydia and that Nellie's family had been able to infer the Henshawes were "wandering about" because of the succession of return addresses. Nellie had probably known their address when she moved into their hotel.

28 • Amethysts are symbols of sobriety and, by extension, coldheartedness. These amethysts, however, may trace specifically to a description of the heartless Mademoiselle Nioche in Henry James's *The American:* "I will warrant that she has not a grain more of sentiment or heart than if she were scooped out of a big amethyst. You can't scratch her even with a diamond" (1877; Boston: Houghton Mifflin / Riverside, 1962), 204.

───────── CHAPTER SEVEN ─────────

1 • Fray Baltazar illustrates the fact that both food and gardens can be prized excessively and can be agents of damnation. Latour "often quoted

to his students that passage from their fellow Auvergnat Pascal: that Man was lost and saved in a garden" (*DA,* 267). Nevertheless Vaillant cooks and Latour gardens, and both these activities, in spite of Baltazar, are valued very highly.

2 • Jean Steinmann, *Pascal,* (1962; New York: Harcourt, 1966), 107.

3 • Ibid., 108, 153.

4 • Martin Turnell, Foreword to Steinmann, *Pascal,* v.

5 • Steinmann, *Pascal,* 27.

6 • J. H. Brome, *Pascal* (New York: Barnes & Noble, 1965), 48.

7 • Steinmann, *Pascal,* 74.

8 • Ibid., 27.

9 • Blaise Pascal, *Pensées / The Provincial Letters* (New York: Modern Library, 1941), 7.

10 • Many recent editions in English are based on the Lafuma editions and the Lafuma ordering of the *Pensées.* In those newer (and perhaps better) editions, the number at the beginning of the passage is the Lafuma order, and the number in brackets at the end is the number of the older Brunschvicg edition, which Cather would have used. Since Lafuma editions appeared in 1952, 1962, and 1963, their order is not relevant to this chapter. The authoritative Meynard tricentenary edition is also not relevant here, for the same reasons.

11 • *Pensées,* Modern Library edition, 3–5.

12 • Steinmann, *Pascal,* 182.

13 • Clinton Keeler, "Narrative without Accent: Cather and Puvis de Chavannes," *American Quarterly* 17 (1965): 119–26. Interestingly, Pascal is actually buried in the church of St. Etienne-du-Mont, located just across the street from the Pantheon, in which church Ste. Geneviève is especially venerated.

14 • Robert L. Gale, "Cather's *Death Comes for the Archbishop,*" *Explicator* 21 (1963): 75.

15 • Mahoney, "How Willa Cather Found Herself," 39.

16 • "My book was a conjunction of the general and the particular, like most works of the imagination. I had all my life wanted to do something in the style of legend, which is absolutely the reverse of dramatic treatment. Since I first saw the Puvis de Chavannes frescoes of the life of Saint Geneviève in my student days, I have wished that I could try something without accent, with none of the artificial elements of composition. In the Golden Legend the martyrdoms of the saints are no more dwelt upon than are the trivial incidents of their lives; it is as though all human experiences, measured against one supreme spiritual experience, were of about the same importance. The essence of such writing is not to hold the note, not to use an incident for all there is in it—but to touch and pass on. I felt that such writing would be a kind of discipline in these

days when the 'situation' is made to count for so much in writing, when the general tendency is to force things up. In this kind of writing the mood is the thing—all the little figures and stories are mere improvisations that come out of it" ("On *Death Comes for the Archbishop,*" in *Cather on Writing,* 9–10).

17 • Steinmann, *Pascal,* 289.

18 • Quoted ibid., 175.

19 • *Pascal's Pensées,* translated and with an Introduction by Martin Turnell (New York: Harper & Brothers, 1962), 399 [no. 904]; *Pascal Pensées,* translated and with an Introduction by A. J. Krailsheimer (Baltimore: Penguin Books, 1966), 281–82 [no. 830.2].

20 • Krailsheimer, ed., *Pensées,* 297 [no. 872].

21 • "While *Death Comes for the Archbishop* was running in *Forum,* Cather was happily reading proof for Knopf's edition of her book. It was like having a gorgeous party all over again, she said, but the pleasure of this moment could not last. By summer she had to give up the apartment she had lived in for fifteen years. It was a wrenching blow" (Woodress, *Literary Life,* 412).

CHAPTER EIGHT

1 • Cather, "Old Books and New [September 1897]," *Home Monthly,* 14, in *World and Parish,* 1:355.

2 • The word *trope,* now a commonplace of literary criticism, was first used to describe poems or passages interpolated in medieval times into the liturgy, but which were, in terms of the liturgy, not strictly essential. Out of such beginnings emerged early liturgical drama. See Grace Frank, *The Medieval French Drama* (1954; Oxford: Clarendon Press, 1960), 19–23.

3 • Slote, *Kingdom of Art,* 90.

4 • In her 1931 letter to Governor Wilbur Cross of Connecticut, reprinted in the *Saturday Review of Literature* on October 17, 1931, Cather states, "You seem to have seen what a different kind of method I tried to use from that which I used in the *Archbishop*" (in *Cather on Writing,* 14–15). We will return to this letter later.

5 • Phyllis C. Robinson, *Willa: The Life of Willa Cather* (Garden City, N.Y.: Doubleday & Company, 1983), 258.

6 • Lewis, *Cather Living,* 119.

7 • Woodress, *Literary Life,* 412.

8 • Ibid., 413.

9 • Mildred Bennett, *The World of Willa Cather* (1951; Lincoln: University of Nebraska Press, 1961), 28–29.

10 • Woodress, *Literary Life,* 414.

11 • Ibid.

12 • Lewis, *Cather Living,* 153, 153–54.

13 • Ibid., 156.

14 • Cather to Governor Cross in *Cather on Writing,* 15.

15 • V. A. Kolve, *The Play Called Corpus Christi* (Stanford, Calif.: Stanford University Press, 1966), 7.

16 • Woodress, *Literary Life,* 433.

17 • Callander, *Fairy Tale,* 66; Stouck, *Imagination,* 156; Rosowski, *Voyage Perilous,* 184; Woodress, *Literary Life,* 430; Cather to Governor Cross in *Cather on Writing,* 15.

18 • Benjamin Hunningher, "The Primitive Phase," from *The Origin of the Theatre* (Querido, Amsterdam, 1961), reprinted in *Perspectives on Drama,* ed. James L. Calderwood and Harold E. Toliver (New York: Oxford University Press, 1968), 53–54.

19 • "Actually, changing social and historical conditions have made the plays differ little in spirit from their sources, predecessors, and successors: the same naive reverence and faith in heaven's omnipotence occurs in the thirteenth-century miracles of Gautier de Coincy and Rutebeuf, in the sixteenth-century miracles of Jean Louvet" (Frank, *The Medieval French Drama,* 119).

20 • "Interest centres in the Virgin's intercession, her aid to sinners, however wicked, who have repented. This moral may be tucked away in various exciting tales intended to keep a restive medieval audience entertained, yet it is always there. Modern taste may be offended by the way in which the worst of criminals have only to offer opportune prayers to be forgiven. But the spectators who first witnessed these miracles performed were concerned in paying homage to their tutelary saint, and the greater the crime the greater the power of the Mother of God" (ibid.).

21 • Ibid., 166.

22 • R. George Thomas, *Ten Miracle Plays* (Evanston, Ill.: Northwestern University Press, 1966), 12.

23 • Arnold Williams, *The Drama of Medieval England* (Lansing: Michigan State University Press, 1961), 105.

24 • Ibid., 23.

25 • Ibid., 31.

26 • John J. Murphy, "The Art of *Shadows on the Rock,*" *Prairie Schooner* 50 (1976): 37.

27 • Frank explains, "The characters of the *Miracles* are for the most part neither hallowed persons nor remote heroes of antiquity but men and women like the spectators, and even when of more elevated station they respond to familiar motives and emotions. Fleshly temptations and guilty

passions, faithless spouses and over-zealous gossips, misunderstandings and false accusations, these are of all times. . . . Universal too is the appeal to emotions of horror, pity, and terror and to the titillation emanating from the sight of the degradation of the powerful. Malefactors about to be burned alive, children who meet violent deaths, women on the point of being raped, nuns and monks yielding to worldly lures, an abbess who becomes pregnant, all are certain to produce fascinated shudders in an audience" (*Medieval French Drama*, 120–21).

28 • For one thing, she called attention to the fact that she had based the incident on a family memory in which her young nephew donated his treasured wooden *cow* to a Nativity scene. Cather chose to change the animal. (Bennett, *World*, 38–39).

29 • Cather to Governor Cross in *Cather on Writing*, 16.

30 • Bennett, *World*, 135.

—————————— CHAPTER NINE ——————————

1 • Stouck, *Imagination*, 214; Woodress, *Literary Life*, 460; Slote, *Kingdom of Art*, 112; Rosowski, *Voyage Perilous*, 231.

2 • John H. Randall III, *The Landscape and the Looking Glass—Willa Cather's Search for Value* (Cambridge, Mass.: Riverside, 1960), 353; Woodress, *Literary Life*, 449; Richard Giannone, *Music in Willa Cather's Fiction* (Lincoln: University of Nebraska Press, 1968), 214 (hereafter cited as Giannone, *Music*); Rosowski, *Voyage Perilous*, 230; Stouck, *Imagination*, 214.

3 • Lewis, *Cather Living*, 174.

4 • Woodress, *Life and Art*, 243.

5 • Lewis, *Cather Living*, 173.

6 • Woodress, *Life and Art*, 246, 248.

7 • Brown and Edel, incorporating information from Edith Lewis, tell us that Cather met the Menuhin family at the Paris home of Isabel and Jan Hambourg in 1930 (E. K. Brown and Leon Edel, *Willa Cather: A Critical Biography* [New York: Alfred A. Knopf, 1953], 297). Music, fleeting youth, lost love, and musicians who steal away one's loveliest image of youth, may therefore have blended in her associations before she began writing Lucy's story—or Harry's.

8 • These homicidal structural choices were the subjects of literary gossip before the book was even published, according to reviewer Dorothea Brande, [Review of *Lucy Gayheart*] *American Review*, 5 (October 1935): 625–29; reprinted in Murphy, ed., *Critical Essays on Willa Cather*) (Boston: G. K. Hall, 1984) 282–83.

9 • Lewis, *Cather Living*, 174.

10 • John J. Murphy, "'Lucy's Case': An Interpretation of *Lucy Gayheart*," *Markham Review* 9 (1980): 26–29.

11 • John Murphy provides one survey of similarities in "'Lucy's Case,'" 26.

12 • From the *Courier*, March 18, 1899, p. 5; reprinted in *World and Parish*, 674.

13 • Blanche Gelfant, *Women Writing in America* (Hanover, N.H.: University Press of New England, 1985), 119.

14 • Ibid., 120.

15 • *Courier*, August 17, 1901, p. 2; reprinted in *World and Parish*, 2:850.

16 • Paul Comeau, "Willa Cather's *Lucy Gayheart*: A Long Perspective," *Prairie Schooner* 55 (1981): 199–209.

17 • "Experience," in *Selections from Ralph Waldo Emerson*, ed. Stephen Whicher (Boston: Houghton Mifflin, 1960), 261.

18 • Emerson, "Self Reliance," in *Selections*, ed. Whicher, 157.

19 • Stouck, *Imagination*, 219.

20 • Emerson, "Nature," in *Selections*, ed. Whicher, 23.

21 • I follow here Rosowski's reading of the scene (*Voyage Perilous*, 227).

22 • Lewis, *Cather Living*, 48.

23 • Phyllis Robinson, *Willa*, 270.

24 • Lewis, *Cather Living*, 173.

25 • Ibid., 178.

CHAPTER TEN

1 • Mentioned in Woodress, *Literary Life*, 481.

2 • Granville Hicks in the *English Journal* (1933), quoted ibid., 469.

3 • Louis Kronenberger, quoted ibid., 473.

4 • Lewis, *Cather Living*, 184.

5 • Prefatory Note to Cather, *Not under Forty*, v.

6 • Woodress, *Literary Life*, 481.

7 • *World and Parish*, 1:307.

8 • In an exceptionally interesting two-part article entitled "Willa Cather's Aristocrats," Patricia Lee Yongue beautifully traces the literary results of Cather's ambivalence toward aristocrats depicted from *Alexander's Bridge* to *A Lost Lady*. Yongue points out, "For some reason which we will try to examine more fully later on in this essay, she was delighted by the grandeur of aristocratic life—as Niel is delighted by the Forrester's grandeur—and desired and even pursued it up to a point; yet she expressed an almost Puritan reluctance to live wholly in the aristocrat's worldly fashion and atmosphere" (*Southern Humanities Review* 14 [1979]: 48). I thoroughly agree with Yongue and admire her discussions, but note sym-

pathetically that she does not include a discussion of *Sapphira and the Slave Girl*. The points I'll make in this chapter will explain, I hope, why Sapphira would never fit such an essay: she is fashioned to undermine the stereotype of the Southern aristocrat.

9 • For an extended treatment of these types, see Merrill M. Skaggs, *The Folk of Southern Fiction* (Athens: University of Georgia Press, 1972).

10 • Willa Cather, *Sapphira and the Slave Girl* (1940; New York: Vintage, 1968), 4. Page references for quotations from this edition will hereafter be cited in the text with the abbreviation *SS*.

11 • Jenny Hale Pulsipher's recent discussion of the "pilgrimage tradition" in *Sapphira* seems to me especially useful for considering Henry, the reader of *Pilgrim's Progress* and the Bible. ("Expatriation and Reconciliation: The Pilgrimage Tradition in *Sapphira and the Slave Girl*," *Literature and Belief* 8, John J. Murphy, guest ed. [1988]: 89–100.)

12 • Compare, for example, Cather's letter to the editor "which followed an exchange between Edmund Wilson and Bernard De Voto, then editor of the *Saturday Review of Literature*. Wilson had asked De Voto what principles he followed in editing the magazine, what theory of the world, what metaphysics, what structure of abstraction. Cather was so pleased with his answer that she sent him a letter of thanks.... De Voto had written that he followed no theories or philosophy in editing the magazine. He profoundly disbelieved in such systems and had come to think that absolutes were a mirage. He opposed people who were out of touch with known facts and common experience, who preferred logical conclusions to the testimony of their senses.... The human tragedy did not seem to him an economic tragedy" (Woodress, *Literary Life*, 477).

13 • Illuminating comments on this and other hymns mentioned in *Sapphira* are found in Giannone, *Music*, 231–37.

14 • Stouck develops a very illuminating and much more extensive discussion of the effects of the child's point of view in *Imagination*, 226–27.

Index